# The Manifest Dream and Its Use in Therapy

# The Manifest Dream and Its Use in Therapy

Roy M. Mendelsohn, M.D.

**JASON ARONSON INC.**
*Northvale, New Jersey*
*London*

10  9  8  7  6  5  4  3  2  1

**Library of Congress Cataloging-in-Publication Data**
Mendelsohn, Roy M.
    The manifest dream and its use in therapy / Roy M. Mendelsohn.
        p.  cm.
    Includes bibliographical references.
    ISBN 0-87668-766-4
    1. Dreams—Therapeutic use.   2. Mentally ill—Psychology.
3. Psychotherapy.   I. Title.
RC489.D74M46   1990
616.89′14—dc20                                                89-18361
                                                              CIP

Manufactured in the United States of America. Jason Aronson Inc. offers books and
cassettes. For information and catalog write to Jason Aronson Inc., 230 Livingston
Street, Northvale, New Jersey 07647.

*To my patients who entrusted me with their dreams*

# Contents

## Part II

### The Manifest Dream
### across the Spectrum of Pathology

**9**   Dreams in the Borderline Personality                        163

**10**  Dreams in the Narcissistically Determined
         Phobic Disorders                                                      190

**11**  Dreams in the Neuroses:
         The Obsessive and the Hysteric                               216

        **References**                                                        253
        **Index**                                                               257

# Preface

The unconscious realm of mental activity is a world of the implied and inferred, only identifiable through its derivatives, with the dream being a remarkably suitable vehicle for representing these unseen forces. Over the years a great deal of attention has been paid to defining the processes at work in the construction of a dream and to the means by which its unconscious meaning can be elicited and translated. At the same time, controversy has been generated as to whether the dream is a unique psychic production, or whether it should be considered equivalent to all other associative material. Nevertheless, every therapist has noticed an intuitive response to the manifest content of a dream, which often plays a role in how the treatment is handled, without necessarily being able to articulate just how it has exerted an influence.

I have outlined the specific attributes of the manifest dream and addressed some heretofore unrecognized aspects that are of particular value in guiding the conduct of a therapeutic relationship. The imprint of developmental experiences has always been known to be an integral feature of a dream, although how such knowledge can be used has not always been clear. This characteristic enables the underlying personality structure that is required to produce a specific dream to be elucidated, and provides direction as to *how* or at times *whether* it should be interpreted. In addition, there are signs to determine the most accessible pathway toward solving the latent dream.

The interrelationship of perception and mental structure formation is especially highlighted by the manifest dream, shedding light on the evolution of a self and delineating the factors incorporated in the construction of a self boundary. Because the dream represents a segment of observed mental content, itself the consequence of an act of observation under another set of conditions, there is an unparalleled opportunity for examining what constitutes the composition and boundaries of these differing selves.

Recent discoveries concerning the manifestations and significance of unconscious perceptions have made it possible to identify the way they appear in a dream, with the day residue emerging as a derivative. This representation of immediate contact with the external world thereby gives a picture of how the treatment is registered, aids in noting and correcting empathic lapses, and facilitates the unfolding of a therapeutic regression. Thus, rather than being important, because it is relatively insignificant and allows censorship to be evaded, the day residue plays a vital role in the construction of a dream and indicates how emotionally important events are unconsciously perceived.

Finally, examples are presented to illustrate the nature and makeup of dreams across a spectrum of psychopathological entities, emphasizing the information they contain along with their prognostic implications at various stages of the treatment. Any given dream contains the potential for revealing all of these varied facets of mental structure and psychic functioning, although what is remembered and reported may highlight only a small portion. Therefore, some of the clinical examples have been selected to illustrate only a single point, while others are repeated to demonstrate a number of key factors.

## Acknowledgment

I would like to express my appreciation to a study group devoted to discussing developmental concepts, consisting of Michael Joy, M.D., Nadia Ramzy, Ph.D., Diane Rankin, M.D., and Marilyn Wechter, M.S.W. Their participation contributed greatly to the ideas presented in this book.

# Part I

# The Significance of the Manifest Dream

# 1

# Dynamic Understanding of the Manifest Dream

This book describes the ways a manifest dream is a unique and helpful part of therapy. It outlines the relationship between perceptual functions, dreaming, the dream, and the self boundary. It delineates the role of the day residue in the construction of a dream, stressing the implications for treatment. It discusses the potential of the manifest content for increasing the accuracy of diagnostic assessments, and demonstrates the configuration of dreams across the broad spectrum of pathological entities. Finally, it points out the particular features in a dream that have prognostic significance at different phases of therapeutic contact. Although the major emphasis is on the manifest content, the importance of the condensations, displacements, symbolic representations, and secondary revision comprising the dream work is interspersed throughout.

Any attempt to elucidate the meaning of dreams, or the process of dreaming, must begin with the groundwork initiated by Freud (1900) and confirmed by a multitude of investigators. Freud's major focus was on a psychology of the id, whereas the role of the ego was primarily limited to description. A psychology of the ego had not yet been explored, and Freud felt enlightenment in this area would eventually come from work with severely narcissistic disorders.

This expectation was subsequently realized, and an intimate interrelationship between mental structure formation and developing ego functions was revealed. Along with these advances in psychoanalytic theory and technique, it was recognized that there was no royal road into the unconscious without resistance. For a time, the central position of the dream in treatment was replaced by the analysis of the transference and of defense.

Prompted by the impact of the structural hypothesis and psychophysiological studies on dreaming, a new look is being taken at the composition of the manifest dream. It gives a revealing picture of the perception of the self in relation to objects and of changes taking place in a treatment relationship, although it can never be taken in isolation. It is particularly suited for the inferential task of illuminating unconscious processes, which can never be expressed directly. Greater attention has been directed to the importance of the day residue, and to a recognition that it represents much more than an insignificant event. There has been no description of its structural role in dream formation, but it does appear to be an essential component for a dream to be retained within consciousness. Experimental investigations of sleep and dreaming have raised many questions about the role of the dream in mental life, indicating that it goes beyond the preservation of sleep, but the information gained from these investigations has not yet specified for sure what may be multidetermined functions.

## Freud's Conception of the Dream

Freud continually stressed that the source of a dream resided solely in a stimulus disturbing to sleep, that the dream was a reaction designed to preserve the sleeping state. The stimuli could come from external sensory perceptions, internal sensory excitations, internal somatic processes, or, in fact, have psychical origins. Memories in both modified and unmodified forms were utilized in the construction of dreams. These included events that were registered and not recalled, childhood experiences under repression, and insignificant mental impressions.

Freud addressed the reasons dreams were forgotten, outlining the importance of repression and the different ideational material present in the altered state of consciousness during sleep that is untranslatable in waking life. In this respect the role of secondary revision was delineated and connected to the latent dream thoughts. The psychological characteristics of a dream primarily encompassed imagery, a disregard of contradictions, and detachment from the external world. Affects appeared to be the closest link to the actual dream experience, and the wish fulfilling aspects of a dream were noted, with special emphasis placed upon their infantile sexual character.

The dream work was deemed to be the essential part of dreaming. The more one was able to find a solution to unraveling the encoded meaning, the more one was driven to recognize that most dreams dealt with sexual material and gave expression to erotic wishes. Freud carefully asserted that not all dreams required a sexual interpretation, and gave many examples of simple wish fulfillments, dreams stimulated by somatic needs, and dreams of convenience. Even these dreams, however, were readily libidinized, so it is easy to contend that practically all dreams have an erotic component. The reason seemed to have more to do with the fact that no other instinct was subjected to so much suppression, and no other source had so many powerful unconscious wishes left ready to produce dreams. It might be said that nothing of importance can occur without the excitation of the sexual instinct making some contribution. Recent physiological studies on the presence of erections during dreaming appear to confirm this facet of Freud's work.

Freud was able to discern the wish fulfilling features of seemingly contradictory anxiety dreams through identifying the existence of conflicting wishes and the prohibiting role of dream censorship. He also discovered a point of contact with the experiences of the previous day in every dream; it was related to the manifest content usually around an apparently insignificant event and to the latent content concerning an important event. The repressed unconscious was conceived as meeting with the day residue, using it to satisfy corresponding wishes. The day residue was thereby viewed as the vehicle by which the repressed entered consciousness and evaded censorship. Little effort was directed toward explaining the supposed indifferent nature of the day residue, except as a means of escaping censorship. The idea of it representing the derivative of an unconscious perception was not identified, although the description would fit within that context.

The processes of condensation, displacement, symbolization, and secondary revision required for the dream work were clearly depicted. It was necessary for all sources acting as stimuli to be combined into a single unit, receiving strong reenforcement from memories reaching into infantile life. Ideational material underwent displacement and substitution with affects remaining relatively unaltered. Unconscious instinctual drives utilized relevant percepts for symbolic representation.

The final element in the revision of the dream wish was accomplished by ego functions operating to fill in gaps and make the dream acceptable, underscoring the significance of intellectual activity. When somatic sources are intense enough they can serve as a fixed point for the formation of a dream, acting like a day residue by calling up a wish fulfillment. The dream work highlighted the interrelationship of primary and secondary process thinking, and the existence of varying systems of consciousness. Freud called the unconscious the true psychical reality. He pointed out that its instinctual nature is as much unknown to us as the reality of the external world, and that it is as completely presented by the data of consciousness as is the external world by the communications of our sense organs. Although Freud warned against a reliance only on the manifest content, he remarked upon its potential usefulness in demonstrating the relationship of observable psychic functions to the more hidden forces in the unconscious system.

Later, Freud (1917) distinguished two types of temporal regression in sleep: the libido to primitive narcissism, and the ego to hallucinatory satisfaction of wishes. He made reference to the diagnostic capacity of dreams, since they externalize an internal process. Incipient physical disease is often detected earlier and more clearly than in waking life as a consequence of body sensations assuming gigantic proportions. The regression to narcissism is not complete, due to the lingering presence of day residues, and the reduction in censorship during sleep allows its reenforcement by unconscious wishes. Three steps in dream formation were identified: first, the reenforcement of a preconscious day residue by an unconscious drive, second, the setting up of a dream wish, and third, a topographical regression from a push to motility and discharge to perception. The mechanisms of condensation, displacement, and symbolization shape the manifest content. Words are modeled on recent mental impressions, and the dream work is always ready to replace abstract thoughts by concrete ones connected to it in some way.

The completion of the dreaming process consists of the content worked over into a wishful fantasy, becoming conscious as a sense perception while it undergoes secondary revision. Hidden wishes are brought into consciousness and represented with belief. The belief in reality is bound to perception, and the regressive pathway to unconscious memory traces allows the wishes to be accepted as real. Freud explained the belief in reality during the dream by attempting to base it on a turning away from the external world, thereby eliminating reality testing. He defined reality testing as the function of orienting the individual in the world by distinguishing the internal from the external, a task ascribed to the conscious system alone. The conscious system has motor innervations available, which determine whether a perception can be made to disappear or whether it remains resistant. External perceptions can be made to disappear through motility, whereas internal perceptions persist. This conception of a belief in reality was incomplete, and was not addressed until a psychology of the ego evolved.

Freud (1911, 1923, 1925) elaborated upon the use of dreams in the treatment situation, cautioned against pursuing dream interpretation for its own sake, and stressed the need for it to be handled according to the principles governing the conduct of the treatment as a whole. It is often possible for an experienced analyst to become relatively independent of a patient's associations, but in doing so he departs from the established methods of psychoanalytic treatment. Freud noted several options in interpreting a dream: proceeding chronologically to gain associations to the elements as they appear, starting from the greatest intensity or with spoken words, asking for the events of the previous day, or leaving it to the dreamer to decide.

Regardless of how it is approached, the level of resistance is most important. When resistance is high there is little chance for collaboration, and associations broaden instead of deepen. Freud noted that a dream was merely a thought made possible by the relaxation of censorship and reenforcement by unconscious wishes. A dream is distorted by secondary revision, even though it provided a unique pathway toward understanding the unconscious realm. He felt it was misleading to say that dreams were concerned with the tasks of life or with finding a solution for problems of daily work. In his view, useful work and any intention of conveying information to another person were in the domain of preconscious thought and therefore remote from dreams. The only task of a dream was to guard sleep. When dreams dealt with problems of actual life, they were solved in the manner of an irrational wish and not in reasonable reflection.

The manifest dream is a facade resulting from censorship, explaining why the ego can accept in dream imagery what would otherwise be offensive. Only a portion of a dream can be translated, and even then incompletely, with success depending largely upon the depth of the resistance. When an unconscious wish emerges in the imagery relatively undisguised, it can arouse intense anxiety, which substitutes for the distortion. Freud also referred to the dreamer's ego appearing in the guise of different figures, but felt it was unjustified to consider all figures as a fragment of the patient's own ego.

## Evolution of Ego Psychology
and the Manifest Dream

Prior to the postulation of the structural theory, conflict was assumed to result solely from the antithesis between conscious and unconscious. At that time, dreams having a predominantly distressing affect appeared to contradict their wish fulfilling nature. The concept of id, ego, and superego resolved the apparent contradictions. Conflict between the functions of these different structures gave rise to the unpleasant features in both dreams and symptoms, and it accounted for the phenomena of unconscious resistance.

Resistance to the emergence of unconscious psychic content was itself unconscious, and both instinctual and prohibitive forces and a shifting balance between them were of major importance in determining the configuration of a dream. The id was thought of as the repository of sexual and aggressive drives from all stages of development, which find mental representation as wishes and fantasies and utilize the dream for an outlet. Even in the dream, they meet with the demands of the ego and superego. The perceptual function of the ego is necessary to register a dream. The integrative functions operate to maintain logic and order. Ego mechanisms of defense oppose id derived impulses to modify their expression. The superego introduces punishment in response to a forbidden infantile wish and as an extension of the ego adds to the creation of anxiety.

The structural systems are not totally independent and though they are in opposition, they cooperate to insure survival. The ego, not completely in opposition to the drives, aids in procuring satisfaction, and may also contain elements of superego approval. As Altman (1969) pointed out, a dream not only reflects the outcome of conflict between these various systems, but demonstrates the presence of contending aims within each. A dream expresses the mutual modification of opposing forces and the compromises arrived at between antagonistic strivings. It is a meeting ground for condemnation and approval, love and hate, convenience and necessity, resulting in compromises with contributions from id, ego, and superego.

Transference manifestations were discerned in dreams but were also in the patient's free associations, behavior, and symptoms; the dreams became meaningful only in the context of free associations. It was therefore viewed as a communication similar to all others, which was in sharp contrast to giving it exceptional status. Sharpe (1937) noted this development and was concerned about the shift in emphasis. She acknowledged the positive aspects of the alterations in technique, but was critical of the underevaluation of dreams. In the beginning, psychoanalytic technique was almost synonymous with the technique of dream interpretation; every dream was eagerly exploited as the one and only way into the unconscious mind, and a nondreaming patient presented a great problem. Sharpe felt there was a need to understand the value of dreams, which remained an indispensable means for understanding unconscious psychical conflict. Other investigators confirmed again and again that there was no shortcut to the discovery of the unconscious, that dreams were its royal road, and the manifest dream was unique for a variety of reasons.

Blitzen and colleagues (1950) directed attention to the important lessons learned from a patient's attitude toward a dream once it is reported. It revealed an ego level effectively hidden in all other life situations. Although the general features of character are continuously present and are delineated in associating to a dream, these authors went a step further. They showed how fundamental facets of the ego may be evoked in associating to a dream, how the manifest dream seems to provoke the waking ego to regress to an archaic mode of dealing with the internal and external world, and how profound disturbances are exposed that might otherwise be too subtle and go unrecognized.

Kanzer (1955) thought a dream with its symbols could serve to bridge the present with the past and fantasy elaborations with reality perceptions. Falling asleep was not a simple narcissistic regression, but the consummation of a conflict in which the good parent was reattached to the ego and the bad parent eliminated. The sleeper was thereby not truly alone but "sleeps with" an introjected good object, and in anxiety dreams, this endeavor was unsuccessful. Communication with these introjects is complex, involving the dreaming process itself, and extends into a desire to tell the dream to others.

Hirschberg (1966) explored the effect on a young child of drawing the content of dreams, outlining how the process of looking and seeing aided in defining the limits of reality. Dreams reflect conscious and unconscious conflicts, wishes, powerful affects, and reality. They help the child's efforts to organize and cope with these difficult struggles. The dream, a product of the ego's functioning, can itself place demands upon the ego and thereby stimulate the development of organizing psychic structure.

Grolnick (1978) viewed dreams and dreaming as a dimension of ongoing structural development. During the period in which early self and object representations are forming and not clearly separated, the nonhuman environment, the transitional object environment, and the nighttime in dreaming environment become both identificatory building blocks and catalysts, and thus can have a progressive or regressive influence upon development. He described the role of the dreaming process, dreams, and secondary elaborations in providing nightly transitional phenomena, creating a bridge between the self and object and a means of regaining the comforting presence of the parents. The dream, part dreamer and part introjected parent, is held during the night and then given up until the next evening. It repeats the use of transitional objects as developmental guideposts assisting in the traversal of the difficult course from symbiosis to object constancy. Once object constancy is achieved, the dream allows regression to organize object fusion and gives the opportunity for this refueling to assist in maintaining stable self and object representations.

Modern dream theorists have focused upon the information processing and problem solving aspects of the language of dreams. In contrast to Freud's emphasis on wish fulfillment, drive discharge, disguise, and censorship, the adaptive facets of dreams are placed in the forefront. Greenberg and Pearlman (1975) saw the manifest dream reflecting an individual's attempt to cope with recent emotionally important material, rather than a vehicle for expressing latent dream thoughts. The language of dreams processed experiences, feelings, and knowledge of the past and present in an effort to find new solutions or new viewpoints. It can involve a search for new solutions to emotional conflict as well as intellectual and scientific problems.

French and Fromm (1964) portrayed the dream work to be primarily a struggle to solve a current problem, with the manifest dream shedding light upon the character and intensity of defensive operations. These authors believed that Freud failed to recognize the significance of problem solving in dreams, but was satisfied in discovering the infantile wish, and did not deal with the dreamer's motive. Wishes are the dynamic stimulus activating problems, and wish fulfilling fantasies are the attempt to solve them.

## Dreams, Perception, and Belief in Reality

Perceptual functions and the various defensive operations of the ego, in addition to motility, play a significant role in the complex task of distinguishing between inner and outer and between the distortions created by fantasy and the memory traces reflecting accurate perceptions. The belief in reality is bound to perception, but reality testing is not solely dependent upon motility. The consolidation of part self representations into a whole occurs in harmony with the unification of disparate sensory functions into an integrated entity. Consensual validation is thereby established, and body ego experiences and their object impression counterparts can be registered and represented through all sensory modalities. The stimuli of the external world can then be internalized and their source identified, in the absence of motility. Conversely, although motility is markedly diminished and limited in the sleeping state, it is not entirely unavailable. It is the manner in which perceptual processes function that determines the belief in reality, and perceptual functions are, in turn, profoundly influenced by the mental structures at their foundation.

Therapeutic work with individuals exhibiting profound narcissistic disturbances has shown that the stimuli of the external world have a powerful effect, particularly upon the activity of unconscious perceptions. The impact of external reality can be ascertained even in those whose reality testing is either severely impaired or seemingly nonfunctional. There is always "a grain of truth" to any distortion, no matter how extreme. It is the nature of mental structuralization (and the particular level of psychic organization) that is the decisive factor in determining the belief in what is real.

In order to gain a clear picture of how stimuli are registered, it is essential to delineate the specific mental structures engaged in a given act of perception. The reporting of a dream involves self observation based upon one structural foundation. The content of the dream is registered by an act of perception involving another. The interrelationship between these two discrete sectors of perceptual functioning presents a view of the regressive pathway followed in moving toward sleep and dreaming. The nature of perception at the surface of the personality is reflected in remembering and communicating the dream. The nature of perception in the deeper layers is reflected in the manifest content. The dream is useful in outlining the transition from one to the other. The manifest dream provides a starting point for discerning the role of perception in establishing a self boundary, and with the unraveling of the dream work and latent dream thoughts, the potential is opened for tracing its developmental lines.

The core perceptual experience of dreaming may precede the development of language, although language is essential for describing a dream. The earliest dream experience may not be verbally structured, but since dreams have such intense affective power, they play an integral part in building language. Isakower (1938) described the phenomenon of dropping off to sleep as an approaching enveloping mass associated with a rough, corrugated sensation in the mouth and skin. It seemed to reflect a loss of boundaries, reproducing the earliest experiences of the breast.

Lewin (1953) referred to a similar phenomenon, which he labeled the dream screen. He thought it represented the hallucinatory fulfillment of one or more of a triad of oral wishes: to eat, to be eaten, and to sleep. Lewin initially considered a dream to be a picture projected onto the screen, assuming it persisted, was only rarely attended to, and symbolized sleep at the breast. Later he recognized that it was not solely a screen but an integral wish fulfilling element. The Isakower phenomenon, the dream screen, and blank dreams appear to be memory traces in the perceptual system deep in the unconscious. Focusing the mental "eye" on the screen during and after waking assisted in reinstating the regime of waking reality, and in this phase the superego asserts itself with exaggerated vigor, often resulting in emphatic, condemning comments on the entire dream. Lewin (1955) also felt there was a relationship between the processes involved in dreaming and those in a psychoanalytic situation. The narcissism of sleep coincided with the narcissism of a therapeutic regression. Blank dreams were the equivalent of falling asleep on the couch, and both expressed a profound oral regression. (Blank dreams are those with no psychic content and reflect the memory traces of prerepresentational life.)

Observations such as these called attention to the correlation between perceptual functioning in a dream and during a therapeutic regression. They contrasted with the similar perceptual functions at work in discerning mental productions prior to the onset of a regression and in reporting a dream. The two perceptual agencies were sufficiently different to function separately, yet were linked to each other on a continuum. The manifest dream then presents a unique opportunity for delineating the interrelationship of perception and mental structure formation, and the role of perception in establishing a self boundary.

Kohut (1977) described two types of dreams with some overlapping. One expressed verbalizable latent contents, and the other attempted to bind the nonverbal tensions of traumatic states with verbalizable dream imagery. The first type lends itself to following free associations into the depths of the psyche until its unconscious meaning is uncovered and gives expression to elements of structural conflict. In the second type, free associations do not lead to unconscious meaning but to further imagery on the same level. Kohut called this second type a "self state" dream, since it portrayed aspects of an archaic self that had emerged. The act of dreaming represents an effort to deal with danger by covering frightening, nameless processes with nameable visual imagery.

## The Role of the Day Residue in the Manifest Dream

For many years there was very little added to Freud's original formulation of the role of the day residue in dream formation. It was taken for granted that it existed solely as a means of escaping censorship, and consequently the idea of it centering around a relatively insignificant event was readily accepted. This was quite striking, for the relationship between the external and internal world is expressed through the day residue. Psychoanalysts began to notice that the treatment relationship was a prime source of material for the day residue, often, though not exclusively, in some direct form. When the concept of transference is broadened to include unconscious perceptions, it calls attention to the need to search for derivatives, and the day residue emanating from the therapeutic relationship fits the criteria exactly. The developmental line of unconscious perceptions is linked to the representations of good self experience structured at the foundations of the personality, which makes them particularly useful in serving as a nidus for the construction of a dream. Their derivatives are the only contents in the preconscious system possessing the stability necessary for enabling the dream to be retained with the attributes of a memory.

When a therapist's image appeared in a dream in undisguised form, it evoked interest in a deeper exploration of its significance, leading to a variety of explanations. Steiner (1937) observed the frequency with which the psychoanalytic situation was an instigator and source of dream material, and felt it was not accorded a due measure of consideration. He postulated its occurrence as the result of a patient's need to defend a narcissistic position. In the course of a session, the patient's functioning seemed cooperative in nature, yet the process attacked an underlying narcissistic attitude. In Steiner's opinion this explained the constant reflection in dream symbolism of the analyst as an attacker.

Gitelson (1952) considered the early emergence of the analyst in the manifest dream as indicative of a poor prognosis, whereas its later emergence was due to a countertransference problem. He thought it reflected an actual resemblance in behavior or appearance to an important figure in the patient's past, making the transference too real, or that it showed that the analyst was using the patient as a transference object. Rosenbaum (1965) presented evidence to refute Gitelson's ideas, and showed that the direct portrayal of the therapist had no prognostic value. These dreams were associated with a longing for the good mother and good breast. Harris (1963) suggested that manifest dreams about the analyst represented a very early ego defense against anxiety by fusing with the mother. He noted the relationship between these dreams and orality, and that they gave an opportunity to gain information as to how a new libidinal object finds its way into the perceptual system, memory traces, and identifications.

Sharpe (1937) illustrated how the day residue, which was a stimulus for the dream, was often the meaning of the dream. Including the day residue in an interpretation brought a sense of life and cogency to the associative material. Kanzer (1955), in placing emphasis upon the urge to communicate arising out of the dream, noted that the day residue could be seen as a continuation of the tendency to establish contact with reality. Arlow (1969) showed how the day residue entered into the structure of a dream precisely because it was characterized by a high degree of consonance with unconscious fantasy activity. He did not specifically refer to the day residue as a derivative of an unconscious perception, but his description was congruent with this idea.

Langs (1971) was concerned with the day residue because it was derived from reality experience and was a significant part of an ongoing interaction between the psyche and reality. Day residues and dreams, in their manifest and latent aspects, form an interwoven totality of a genetically significant past (those memory traces that are resonant with a current emotionally important experience) blended with the present, and of conscious and unconscious fantasy. Any part of this totality may represent instinctual drives, superego expressions, and ego functions including defense and adaptation. He observed how day residues were an important reference point in the analysis of dreams because of their strategic position in the interplay between reality and the psyche, past and present. The day residue is sought out by the total personality; the ego utilizes such reality experiences as vehicles for defensive operations, gratification, or resolution of conflict on both reality and fantasy levels. Important experiences and fantasies from the past are a constant unconscious factor in the selection of the particular day residue. Langs noticed how reality events of sufficient psychical meaning, when imposed upon the personality, generated anxieties and connected with unconscious fantasies that must be dealt with and mastered by the ego. The formation of a dream, with both its manifest and latent content, was a part of these attempts at mastery. He emphasized the place of

interventions and experiences within the psychoanalytic situati
being among the most crucial sources of the reality factors conti
ing to the day residue. The day residues, and the dreams to w ...ch
they relate, are a totality modeled upon the relationship between the
organism and the environment. External reality can initiate a reaction, or intrapsychic strivings and conflicts may seek out reality for
resolution, gratification, or defense.

Pontalis (1974) made the point that something significant is lost
between the dream existing in images and the dream put into words.
Interpreting the meaning of a dream was ineffective when the
experience of it was unavailable. He noted that the patient's resistance
was not to uncovering meaning but to recovering the experience. He
conceived of the dream as an object, and had the impression that the
dreamer attached the self to the dream in order to be anchored, and
when deprived of it, fell into loneliness. This suggested that the
dream screen not only was a surface for projection, but necessary for
protection.

Khan (1962) defined a "good dream" as one that incorporates an
unconscious wish through successful dream work enabling sleep to be
sustained. Then it can be available upon awakening for a psychic
experience to the ego. He felt Freud had intuitively recreated a
physical and psychic ambience in the psychoanalytic setting, corresponding significantly to the intrapsychic state in the dreamer conducive to a "good dream." It implied a relationship between the
holding functions of an unconsciously empathic environment and the
holding power of unconscious perceptions in enabling a dream to be
retained with the characteristics of a memory.

Klauber (1967) tried to explain why dreams are reported on some
occasions and not on others, attributing it to their special communicative properties. He offered many examples of dreams reported in
response to an unconscious perception of the analyst's interest in
dreams. In addition, the dream generally contained some element
significantly related to a fragment of the therapeutic interaction, and
although it was usually possible to explain on the basis of resistance,
it often meant that there was a new problem of communication
coming to the surface. It implied that the ego was effecting an
acceptable attitude to the underlying conflict, which could not be in
accord with the reality principle, leading to the communication of a
mixture of primary and secondary processes in achieving an act of
integration. The representation of latent dream thoughts in the
manifest dream requires an integration of id derivatives into a form
compatible with the demands of external reality and the superego. In

this way, the ego was searching to obtain assistance in communicating more directly.

Fisher (1954) addressed the vital interrelationship between dreams and perception and was able to demonstrate the enormous amount of visual material selected and registered peripherally in brief time intervals by preconscious visual perception. He demonstrated how these visual perceptions were treated as thought elements or concrete objects and could be fragmented, torn apart, and mutilated. Word percepts and visual images were treated similarly, and new visual patterns or new speech constructions were not created. Fisher gave conclusive evidence that Freud's discussion of day residues did not give an adequate idea of the degree to which the structure of a dream may be anchored in the visual percepts of the day before. Freud had focused primarily on memory pictures of the past, in the transformation of dream thoughts into perceptual forms, and did not take into sufficient account the visual images of the manifest content incorporated in the current day residues.

The chief function of the day residue is to provide perceptual material out of which visual and auditory images of the manifest content are composed; these cover memory pictures from the past as well. Fisher presented convincing illustrations of how these recent impressions are the only psychic content possessing this capacity. This was the first discrete exposition of the role of day residues, in both serving as a nidus around which a dream is constructed, and in possessing the necessary anchoring capacity for it to be retained within the preconscious system. Later, Fisher (1957) described perception as a process extended in time, which could be broken down into three phases: first, the registration of the percept, second, the content of the percept with preexisting memory schema, and third, the emergence into consciousness of the percept. The first two phases take place outside of consciousness.

## The Function of Dreams

The benefit of dreaming has been ascribed to a variety of functions, both physiological and psychological. Fisher (1966) investigated the rapid eye movement (REM) state of dreaming during sleep, which verified the irresistible force of the sexual drive. Most structured remembered dreaming takes place in the REM state, when all body systems are in a condition of alert activity and all organ systems are attuned to rapid responsivity except for motor activity and external perceptual awareness. In REM periods there is an attunement to internal mental events, and the body is intensely physiologically responsive.

Dowling (1982) referred to the primary process activity characteristic of the REM state, which has achieved a special and lasting importance in dreams. Although it is derived from an early period of mental organization, it is clearly not the earliest. A still earlier sensory motor mental organization is touched upon in the unformed mental impressions embodied in night terrors. They consist of amorphous, static, or absent representations. He felt it was similar to the Isakower phenomenon and different from the usual dream experience. There is a lack of distinction of sensory modalities, none of the sharp visual imagery of a dream, and affects are less differentiated. Lewin and Isakower had attributed these features to a regression of perceptual processes to a level at which they were intimately associated with the body ego.

Isakower (1954) described the function of speech in meeting the human need for orientation. Auditory input from the outer world through incorporation includes not only the verbal components, but also the correct combination of verbal images and the development of grammar, logic, and order. Speech is of fundamental importance for the functions of the superego, and serves to orient the individual in the external and internal world. The auditory sphere modified for the capacity of language is the nucleus of the superego, just as the nucleus of the ego is a body ego. In Isakower's opinion speech elements seemed to be a direct contribution of the superego to the manifest dream, and though often reported as unintelligible jargon words, they frequently have a threatening or criticizing superego tinge.

Hartmann (1970) emphasized that dreaming sleep has a function quite independent of what one recalls about dreaming. Dreams appear to have a multiplicity of overlapping functions, and dream deprivation studies suggest it is as likely that an essential function of sleep is to enable the process of dreaming as it is for the function of dreams to preserve sleep.

Bergmann (1966) questioned Freud's belief that repression was solely responsible for forgetting dreams, since the fraction of dreams recalled indicates that other factors are involved. He postulated that forgotten dreams were successful in disguising latent content fulfilling a dream wish. Those dreams failing in the attempt at disguise, or in which id wishes and superego demands are particularly strong, cannot be forgotten. Segments of latent content break into the dream work, or the dream work succeeds in eliminating censored content, but cannot prevent disturbing affects. He also thought some dreams

were remembered and communicated because the telling of the
dream completed a discharge function, some because they portrayed
a conflict that could not be expressed in any other way, and others
because they contained a hidden communication of encoded intrapsychic conflict.

Khan (1976) stressed the importance of distinguishing the dreaming experience from the meaning of the remembered dream text.
The dreaming experience is an entity that actualizes the self in an
unknowable way. The dream text gets hold of some of its aspects and
works it into the conflictual data from the remembered or repressed
to make a narrative capable of being communicated, shared, and
interpreted. Dreaming itself exists, influences behavior even though it
cannot be brought into representational form, is actualized through
the primary process, and is beyond interpretation. Dream space is an
area where new experiences are initiated; they can be either affirmed
or negated. There are psychic states that further self experience
through primary process functioning, and the dream text can be a
negation of dreaming.

Rycroft (1979) believed dreams were an integrative experience,
observing this effect when they are retained and speculating about a
similar influence when they are not. Dreaming is an imaginative
activity in which the contents are metaphorically understood, while
the function may be engaged with psychophysiological arrangements.
Dreams have a logic of their own, bringing together various bits of
experience disparate in time, space, and quality, due to similarities in
common, making them relevant to specific aspects of one another and
to a particular idea, problem, or desire preoccupying the dreamer in
the present. In this concept, day residues include unassimilated
thoughts, sensations, and memories remaining as sources of tension
until they can be integrated into some meaningful whole by which
they can be explained. A dream can then provide the setting for
discharge of these tensions.

De Monchaux (1978) thought there were special features of dream
telling, presenting a great advantage to the ego in its task of
recognizing and reconciling the two sides intrinsic to any argument in
the unconscious. This is most clearly seen in the use of symbols and in
the telling of a dream as a medium of communication among internal
objects, self, and others. It expresses a conflict between acknowledged
and disclaimed intentions, leads to the detection of what a person
wants in life, and reveals the capacities existent at a given point in
time. Dreams help structure internal and external experience, and
communicating dreams aids in attaining mastery.

Foulkes (1969) underscored the implications for dream theory of electrophysiological studies of sleep, and especially of dream formation. These studies have shown a variety of mentation in all stages of sleep, failing to confirm Freud's belief that mental activity suddenly attracts consciousness at the dream's onset. The nature of predream mentation, however, supports Freud's concept of day residues. There is also evidence supporting the idea of the dream work distorting day residues into sometimes barely recognizable components of bizarre dream episodes. Those who insist upon a continuity of waking and sleeping thought find support in the nature and extent of nondreaming mentation in sleep. Emotional complexes may take advantage of the dreaming state, but they seem neither to precipitate it nor to determine its initial ideational content. Efforts to refute dream theory on the basis of physiological findings in REM sleep have been abundant.

Wasserman (1984) reviewed the activation synthesis hypothesis of dreaming, which tries to show that the instigation and form of dreams are physiologically determined by a brain stem neuronal mechanism. These hypotheses have suggested that a major revision in psychoanalytic dream theory is necessary, and Wasserman was able to demonstrate the inconsistency of the neurophysiological data, illustrating their lack of coherence with the hypotheses offered. Physiological findings are central to understanding the neurophysiology of REM sleep, but they do not alter the meaning and interpretation of dreams gleaned through psychoanalytic study.

## The Special Position of the Manifest Dream

Although there may be considerable disagreement concerning the adaptive, problem solving function of dreams, it is certainly evident that the manifest dream is unique in resting between external reality and internal psychic structuralization. It leads via associations to latent dream thoughts, gives expression to id, ego, and superego, and bridges the pathway from the day residue representing a perception of the external world to the infantile wishes emanating from the unconscious system. The manifest dream amalgamates the meaning of reality with unconscious determinants, the past and present, and a totality of the structural organization of the dreamer's personality. In conjunction with the associations it evokes, the dream may be used extensively as a guidepost in determining interpretive interventions.

Kramer (1969) considered Freud's focus upon the latent dream thoughts to have hindered the study of manifest dream content. Dream physiology has raised questions concerning the large number of dreams taking place at night and the paucity reported the following day. REM technique has revealed the gap between the dream report and dream experience and underscored the elusiveness of the dream experience. The dream transpires in one state and is reported in another. The relationship between them is open to question, and all that can be studied is the manifest dream. Jones (1970) felt that any psychology of dreams must rest on a study of the manifest dream images.

Babcock (1966), in reporting on a panel discussion of the manifest dream content, saw a renewed interest in its significance. The panel made frequent references to those features that had circumvented the dream work, including the spoken word, the day residue, the dream within a dream, and infantile memories. Attention was called to how the manifest dream serves as a window into preverbal life, since somatic responses are the only memory traces guiding an exploration into this realm of psychic functioning. When these somatic responses, of which the Isakower phenomenon is an example, are registered, they give a vision of the earliest developmental experiences. It was also noted that the manifest dream is a source of information about the body through the abundant use of symbols, although they are often less recognized and accepted. It is frequently possible from the symbolism alone to reach conclusions about the nature of a given conflict, but the potential for misuse by considering it entirely from an adaptational perspective must always be kept in mind. Freud warned against the clinical use of the manifest dream, although he did so himself, probably because of a concern about arbitrary interpretations. That the manifest dream brings the excitations of the unconscious under preconscious control, has been corroborated by dream deprivation studies. With the growth of the structural hypothesis, and especially ego psychology, interest in the style and form of the dream has grown.

Renik (1984), reporting on the clinical use of the manifest dream, defined the prevalent conflicting attitudes. On the one hand it was called the royal road to the unconscious because it contained symbols directly revealing unconscious meaning, but on the other hand meaning could not be determined without the dreamer's associations. The dream form was originally seen as distorted by the primary process, whereas now the contribution of the secondary process is well documented and recognized. It is a compromise of id, ego, and superego, and reflects the level of regression in these various mental organizations. The manifest dream thus occupies a favored position in clinical work. Rather than being different it might best be described as a concentrated mental production, and the principles applied in dealing with dreams do not differ from any other experience in a therapeutic relationship.

Silber (1983) paid special attention to the dream within a dream, emphasizing its linkage to memories latently charged with affect. The dream work, and especially secondary revision, allows the affect to emerge in other segments of the dream, so that the dream within a dream is manifestly devoid of feelings. The censorship, guided by the defensive function of the ego, is designed to ward off the dreamer's knowledge of the dream's meaning. It is a compromise formation, is thus indicative that an unconscious impulse is given expression in disguised form, absorbs and obscures affect, and prevents progression to an anxiety dream. Secondary revision preserves the intactness of the dream, and simultaneously attracts attention and tries to negate it. Silber considered it to be a signal, indicating that what was hidden merited making the effort to expose and understand it.

Greenson (1970) felt the manifest dream had special importance, and noted how psychophysiologic research made this emphatically clear. The dream is a unique form of mental functioning produced during a REM phase of sleep, which is unlike any other of the sleep cycle. Dream deprivation can cause severe emotional and mental disorders, suggesting sleep is necessary to safeguard the need to dream. A dream is produced by bursts of psychic activity seeking sensory relief. The dream state allows reduction and regression of conscious ego activity and the censorship of the superego. The perceiving function of the ego when deprived of the external world turns energy to internal psychic activity.

A dream usually appears as a picture, is recorded by an indefinite "psychic eye," and along with affects and body language, sinks closer to the almost unreachable depths plumbed in psychoanalytic work. The dream reveals aspects of the id, the repressed, unconscious ego and superego, and certain conscious ego functions, particularly observing capacities, with unusual clarity. The dream experience itself, often without interpretation, leads more directly and intensely to the affects and drives than any other clinical material. Primitive mentation takes place in fantasies or impressions, and is closer to unconscious processes than verbal representations. Greenson was convinced that some psychoanalysts denied the exceptional position of the dream because of difficulties in learning the technique of dream interpretation. Others denigrated its importance in order to enhance theoretical convictions or to attack or defend the beliefs of an honored teacher. Greenson thought the tendency to disparage the special place of the manifest dream was a reflection of defensiveness within the analyst.

The manifest dream cannot give undisguised expression to unconscious mental activity. It is clearly no substitute for the arduous work of revealing unconsciously derived impulses. Nevertheless, many investigators have pointed out the special features of mental functioning that it represents. De Saussure (1982) focused upon the particular importance of dreams following a trauma. They include fantasies that were a part of the original situation and give clues as to why and in what way a given situation was traumatic. The fantasies developed in response to the trauma at times constitute a trauma in themselves. A dream plays a significant role in the development of neurotic symptoms and behavior, and may be remembered while the trauma is forgotten. This does not mean that dreams serve as screen memories, but this may be an indication of their functioning as new traumatic experiences based on the same fantasies encompassed by the trauma. The fantasies crystallize in the dream in a dramatic way, which integrates them into relatively stable neurotic patterns.

Knapp (1956) observed the way in which sensory impressions were included in the manifest dream. Color, sound, kinesthetic sensations, smell, and taste seemed linked to areas of affective life and specific instinctual drives. The sensory qualities in most dreams are not apparent, giving the impression of colorless, soundless, motionless, and tasteless mental impressions. An overall helplessness is implied, consonant with the protective nature of the dream work in forming a barrier against the vividness of sensations charged with affect and promoting wakefulness. It suggests that the dreamer is closer to wakefulness and that the censorship is diminished when sensory impressions are present. There appears to be a hierarchical organization of sensory experience. Color and sound are associated with more advanced psychic structures, whereas kinesthetic sensations, smell and taste, are linked to more primitive, archaic structures.

Saul (1967) paid particular attention to the sensation of falling, which seems to be a universal symbol representing the impulse to regress, give up, or fall away from responsibility. The sensation of falling is on a continuum with other dreams of descent, reflecting the degree of regulation that is functional. Hendrick (1958) saw the manifest dream as a mental production different from others, which was indicated by the nature of the resistance it aroused in associating to its content. He likened this resistance to the mental activity of the schizophrenic, who tends to engage in prolific fantasy and symbolic behavior in order to deflect hostility. The dreamer also becomes occupied with fantasies to deflect attention away from the dream elements. In the schizophrenic it is secondary to a fundamental defect, rather than the result of repression or a libidinal regression.

## Structural Theory

Other psychoanalysts objected to the idea of placing the manifest dream in a special position within the chain of associative material. This attitude was most exemplified by Brenner (1976), who believed the structural theory required a revision in the theory of dream psychology. The dream was seen as a compromise formation, not explained by postulating its beginning in the unconscious, and only subsequently subjected to the secondary process by the preconscious system. In this view, a dream is a compromise formation from the start, and the sense of reality in the dream results from the suspension of reality testing during sleep. It explains punishment dreams and dreams in which a sense of reality is not maintained. It also makes explicit that the unintelligibility of dreams is a consequence of defense, and does not result from the dream thoughts being translated into the primary process.

The manifest content is never the dream itself, but only what is reported. Brenner felt it was a great advantage that the report of the dream was actually a statement of the first spontaneous association to it. In his opinion, the manifest content was valuable precisely because it was not just a memory of a conscious experience during sleep, but was in itself an association. He criticized the frequent references to the dream's communicative properties, since every experience has this attribute. It exists along with the opposite wish of not wanting to communicate. The communicative function of the dream can be assumed to be of no special importance, although it is omnipresent, unless the telling is highlighted. He thought it was as unwise to unduly emphasize something of minor dynamic importance as it was to neglect something of major importance.

## The Manifest Dream
## and the Treatment Situation

An ego-psychological approach to mental functioning led to an increased understanding of the significance of the manifest dream, which is subject to id, ego, and superego influences, and placed it within the overall context of the transference relationship.

Altman (1969) believed that the difficulty with dream interpretation grew out of the extraordinary degree to which latent dream thoughts were distorted in the manifest dream. They were distorted by the nature of the dream work through condensation and displacement, added to the symbolization and the limitations imposed by largely visual representation of ideas and feelings, and further exaggerated by the conflicting needs of id, ego, and superego. Every manifest dream owed its content to both the past and the present. Infantile memories as well as drives seeking satisfaction come from the remote past, since there can be no dream without the impetus of a wish representing an instinctual drive. Although they are of infantile origin, they continue to seek gratification throughout life, and are accompanied by infantile prohibitions just as primitive in character.

The portion of a dream that owes its derivation to impulses, feelings, and ideas of early life is often referred to as "the dream from below." Current experiences, whether conscious or unconscious, also make a contribution to the dream and are referred to as "the dream from above." Dreams owe part of their content to a recent mental event, although this day residue is insufficient by itself to produce them. A dream is born when a current impression makes contact with an infantile wish. When a contemporary experience is exceptionally powerful, it may be evocative for an otherwise dormant infantile wish. Conversely, a remote event by virtue of its persisting importance may invest a recent experience with a significance it would not have had in its own right.

Altman pointed out the three distinct entities to a dream: the manifest dream, the latent dream thoughts, and the dream work. The manifest dream is a cryptic message requiring deciphering. Underlying it are ideas and feelings from the present and past, both preconscious and unconscious, giving rise to the dream. The transformation into recallable imagery is the dream work. All the elaborate measures employed to disguise latent dream thoughts are at the behest of the dreamer's never totally dormant ego. The visual means of representation demanded by a dream result in a distortion of latent content by the use of images to express ideas. Affects may be displaced, replaced by their opposites, or omitted altogether, but they are not changed. While the ego, spurred by superego requirements, supplies the motive for dream distortion, it may not be satisfied with the result. An impulse occasionally comes through relatively undisguised. The ego and superego react with a last ditch effort at rendering it acceptable, thereby adding another distorting factor. Secondary revision utilizing advanced ego functions attempts to supply consistency and coherence, filling in gaps to create order and molding the dream into an intelligible whole. Whenever there is continuity and logic in the manifest dream, secondary revision is responsible.

Sloane (1979) described the vast amount of information about the individual's character, habitual patterns of behavior and defense, and relationship with others that can be determined from a dream. The compromise between id, ego, and superego shows the strength or weakness within each of these psychic agencies, and although the manifest dream is not a replica of the actual dream, it nevertheless reflects the dreamer's defensive operations. The day residue provides a framework of recent experience around which unconscious thoughts can arrange themselves, serves as a connecting link with unconscious infantile drives, and may range from something seemingly trivial to a crucial problem occupying the preconscious mind. Sloane criticized those who considered the solution of contemporary problems to be the sole aim of a dream, feeling it overlooked the extensive distortions and the need to translate unconscious meaning through an associative process. Maintaining a focus upon the sense of the manifest dream, however, was frequently a pathway leading to further insights, since affect seems to be on a direct line toward the latent dream thoughts.

Blum (1976) regarded the "analyzable" dream as a remarkable communication, a different psychic product with special access to the unconscious mind, which explained its importance. He believed it belonged alongside all psychoanalytic data, with the analyst maintaining a consistent attitude toward the entire psychic field. The dream as a stimulus for analytic attention is likely to provide a focus for directed association, and can enhance the therapeutic properties of the treatment relationship. The dream may also further resistance to free association, while at the same time require associations for its elucidation and interpretation. The clinical use of the dream requires adequate ego and superego functions and some degree of ego autonomy. Although the capacity to recall and report dreams is in itself an ego achievement, the mere reporting is insufficient. Blum felt the fascination of some patients with the manifest dream was matched by the renewed theoretical interest in its content, but to interpret the manifest content alone was arbitrary, simplistic, speculative, and unjustified.

Ego psychology affirmed the limitations of a dream's relevance for clues to unconscious conflict and compromise formation. Although a reduction in manifest disguise may occur, there is always a question of what is concealed. The ultimate interpretation of any dream depends upon its fit with all other material. No dream can be completely analyzed. Exhaustive interpretation would disturb the analytic process, and not every dream can or should be analyzed. The dream may serve as a guide to the transference, as a valuable source of information about the nature of resistance and regression, and present a graphic picture of the relationship to objects, of developmental phase, and of central conflicts. The dream may also facilitate memory and give access to infantile experience unobtainable from any other data. Ego psychology provides a new opportunity to use dreams to study ego and superego functions, in addition to drive derivatives. Defensive and integrative functions, character trends, and indications of developmental transformations can be observed in a dream, but the creative, constructive clinical use of dreams is made possible by the controlled regression and shared analytic work in the treatment situation.

A dream may be employed in self analysis and in creative imagination, but such use depends upon ego resources. It may be converted to creative enrichment by using unconscious processes for the goals of the ego, and it can be utilized to widen self understanding. This is an ego adaptation, however, and not an intrinsic function of the dream. It may promote awareness of what is unknowable and unthinkable, and hence be understood as an intrapsychic communication. Without appropriate interpretation of the latent content, a dream by itself is not a mode of mastery or ego expansion. Dreaming is an archaic process not suited to considerations of logic or reality. It does not have a primary function of information processing, problem solving, or adaptation. The announcement or appearance of discovery through the manifest dream is a particular ego choice and a probable disguise for an underlying conflict. The creative process makes use of unconscious activity, which may be related to dream work, but it also uses preconscious and conscious refinements. All of these may be incorporated into a dream through the day residue, facilitating creative inspiration under conditions of diminished censorship.

The manifest dream is thus a multifaceted, complex, mental production, characterized by its symbolic qualities. Symbolism is a universal, primal language representing an association between ideas with something in common. The association is made by an infantile mode of thinking wherein the concrete automatically takes precedence over the abstract. Symbolic language employs an elementary means of conceptual identification that is a remnant of infantile ways of thinking. A failure to recognize the connection between the symbol and what it stands for stems from having forgotten or not having available these primitive means of expression. The application of symbolism to dream interpretation is often regarded as arbitrary and generates a great deal of suspicion.

The manifest content of a dream may sometimes be immediately translatable from its symbolism on the basis of typical universal symbolic images. The referents for symbols are surprisingly limited in number, corresponding to the basic universal preoccupations of children: birth, death, the body and its functions, sexual organs, and important people. On the other hand, there is a wide discrepancy between the plethora of symbols and the ideas being symbolized. Each dreamer employs a preferred set of symbols, chosen from the vast number available, and thus a translation of symbols without an intimate knowledge of the dreamer may lead one astray. At the same time, the universality and meaning of certain symbols may be useful in beginning the translation of the language of a dream.

# 2

# The Manifest Dream as the Symbolic Language of the Internal World

Unconscious forces can only be determined from the derivatives evoked in consciousness. Even though primitive ego functions may be operative within the boundaries of the unconscious, they do not include the function of perception. Therefore it is a world of the implied and inferred.

When there has been sufficient structuring in the personality to establish continuity of experience, the id of the dynamic unconscious is organized with primitive psychic mechanisms that are predominant and that contain those aspects of instinctual activity incapable of being consciously retained. This sector of the personality is then delineated by a nonperceptual boundary formed during the oedipal period. Biophysiological demand exerts an impact through the wall of primary repression. The effect is registered within the id of the dynamic unconscious initiating the process of instinctual integration. These unconscious impulses are transferred across the barrier of repression proper. They activate contents in the preconscious, selecting those that are resonant with the particular impulse seeking expression. A given internal stimulus echoes throughout the entire personality, and its unconscious meaning is determined by the pattern and sequencing of derivatives reflecting its nature. The movement toward expression depends upon the developmental events shaping the composition of the personality, the conflicts encountered from opposing trends, and the alignment of defensive regulation. The stimuli of the external world are internalized, resonate throughout the entire personality, traverse a pathway eliciting the derivatives of unconscious perceptions, and depending upon their quality, heighten the need for defense or facilitate the process of integration.

## Limitations on Reading the Unconscious Significance of a Patient's Productions

It requires the special conditions of a psychoanalytically derived treatment modality to create the benign regression essential for unfolding a pattern of derivatives, which, with the aid of interpretive interventions, exposes their unconscious meaning. The mechanisms of condensation, displacement of affect, and symbolization enable this transfer of unconscious impulses onto preconscious psychic content. They are then subjected to processes of secondary revision that give order, logic, form, and defensive regulation to what otherwise might emerge as incomprehensible or disruptive.

In the primitively organized personality, splitting mechanisms predominate, continuity of experience is not structured, unconscious mental activity is potentially traumatic and must be more vigorously defended against, the formation of derivatives is limited and less discriminating, and the unconscious meaning of a given psychic production is more difficult to ascertain. Gaps in an associative chain are consistently present, and action discharge modes of expression tend to be dominant.

All mental events rest upon a foundation of self and object representations, reflecting the underlying psychic organization of the personality. The determination of its specific components is extremely difficult because most psychic contents have been exposed to a variety of integrative and defensive forces rendering their origins obscure. The multiplicity of ego functions involved in creating internal thought and language, and the accompanying depersonification of self and object imagoes, makes a delineation of their developmental underpinnings highly inferential and often inaccurate. A clear picture of this developmental line is of inestimable value in outlining the associative pathway establishing continuity with the unconscious realm of mental activity.

A therapist's listening attitude is devoted to receiving and internalizing encoded, unconscious messages, unraveling the defensive and regulatory responses in which they are covered and disguised, and translating their meaning into a form that can be articulated so as to further the patient's self knowledge and awareness. Embedded in these unconscious communications are the patient's perceptions of the qualities needed in a relationship to facilitate constructive growth, which can then serve as a guideline for the management of the overall therapeutic framework. An accurate appraisal of the particular manner in which a patient's personality is structured is imperative for a therapist to be effective. The means a patient has available for adaptive and integrative functioning is highlighted by the expressions of unconscious forces, and an important dimension of the therapeutic interaction revolves around a therapist's understanding of how to facilitate their use.

## The Intrapsychic Role of Symbol Formation

The process of symbolization operates as a bridge between unconscious drives pushing for expression and the evolution of internal thought and language. This is necessary to develop the capacity for internal and interpersonal communication. In a progressive direction symbolization leads to the increasing depersonification of self and object images required for thought and language to be functional. In a regressive direction symbol formation enables the expression of unconscious experience.

Symbols must contain the properties of the body ego experiences and object impressions they are meant to represent. Those least exposed to advanced psychic functions are most revealing of the infantile experiences at their foundation. In order to have meaning a psychological event must be based upon a body ego experience, an object impression counterpart, and a fantasy linkage between them. The absence of this constellation is indicative that meaning has either been destroyed or disrupted, usually from the distortions created by an inordinate need for defense. In the primitively organized personality, splitting mechanisms are the major ego defense. They interrupt the elaboration of meaning, and a free associative mode of communication can be extremely confusing to follow.

The construction of a manifest dream relies heavily on the use of symbols, which contain the components encompassed in the production of meaning. A dream by its very nature is therefore of inestimable value in gaining a penetrating view of how the personality is organized and can aid in comprehending what otherwise appears as a scattered flow of associations. The visual representation of unconscious affects and ideas also sheds light upon the process of symbolization itself. Symbols must have resonance with and parallel the infantile experiences they represent, and embody id, ego, and superego elements. This multidimensional task is accomplished by utilizing the specific, concrete attributes of an unconscious drive to evoke similar percepts in the preconscious. Much information can thereby be gleaned from the manifest content, even though it has undergone considerable alteration in being remembered and reported, and may only be dimly related to the actual dream experience. The strengths and weaknesses of the underlying personality are often clearly reflected, offering important guidelines for the conduct of the treatment.

A vast majority of psychic contents are so distant from their infantile origins that it is difficult at best to make an accurate assessment. Although the regression induced by a free associative process fosters the emergence of childhood memories and fantasies, permitting a closer inspection of these developmental roots, identifying the interrelationship of the underlying mental representations is not always feasible. The manifest dream, however, presents a symbolic picture of the mental structures used in its construction, delineates the specific composition of the representational world, and illuminates the infantile experiences responsible for their evolution. The basis of character defenses, the emergence of unconscious id impulses and the conflicts they engender, superego prohibitions, movements toward integration, or structural defects and deficits may all be reflected. The manifest dream is also especially suitable for symbolically representing traumatic and repressed infantile memories.

## Symbolic Representation of the Self in the Manifest Dream

A study of the composition of a manifest dream provides an opportunity for illuminating a workable concept of what constitutes a self. It is especially relevant because a self is represented in the body of a dream, and a self is engaged in the act of reporting it. The dream report is thereby a segment of psychic content that is available. In addition, a self may be represented in two separate positions simultaneously within the context of dreaming, one involved in the imagery of the dream and the other in observing. Material is thereby available for determining the means by which the boundary of a self is established and for explaining the relationship between these differing selves.

When the self is defined on the basis of an interrelationship between perceptual processes and mental structure formation, the manner in which perception functions to establish the expanding boundary of a self becomes explicable. A structural bond is formed, uniting and differentiating the self and object systems of representation, which is coupled with the evolution of two separate but continuous perceptual agencies. They serve as the foundation for the function of self observation, with each containing the wherewithal to define a self boundary.

The eye of consciousness is the predominant perceptual agency functioning at the surface of the personality. It is regulated by the reality principle, and is consonant with the requirements of secondary process thinking. The superego eye is the predominant perceptual agency operating in the deeper layers of the personality. It is regulated by the pleasure principle, and is subject to the conditions of primary process thinking. These two agencies of perception maintain continuity with each other, are monitored by regulatory principles consonant with the predominant mental structures in each locale, and possess the capacity for registering mental impressions consistent with the functions that are available.

The movement from the dream experience to the formation of the manifest dream to reporting what is observed reflects the transition from the more regressive perceptual agency functioning in the deeper layers of the personality toward the more advanced function of self observation available at the surface. The traversal of this perceptual pathway is accompanied by an increasing accessibility of the integrative functions of the ego, and the changes that take place from the dream experience to the remembered manifest dream are largely due to and determined by these different qualities of perception.

The boundary of the self in a waking state encompasses the totality of the personality with the most advanced functions predominant. The regression induced with sleep involves a suspension of these advanced psychic functions. As a consequence, more primitively organized psychic structures become ascendant. Their incorporated perceptual functions then give definition to the boundary of a sleeping and dreaming self. Thus the perceptual agency involved in registering a dream and the one involved in remembering and reporting it, although they exist on a line of continuity with each other, possess different and distinct properties. This is exemplified by the manner in which a self boundary is defined within the context of the dream imagery and the manner in which it is defined during wakefulness. The shift from one to the other takes place in the transition from sleeping to waking, and becomes more discrete as the dream is remembered and reconstructed.

The interconnection between the two perceptual agencies is sometimes reflected in the body of the dream itself, when the dreamer is aware of both dreaming and observing. The dreamer is then carrying advanced but not fully suspended functions into the regression induced by sleep, and they are accessible to the mental structures utilized in constructing the dream. This is also illustrated when the ability to institute defense in the dream experience has reached its limit, and the only avenue available is to evoke a new set of perceptional conditions. The superego eye, registering the dream and defining a dreaming self boundary, does not have the advanced functions associated with the eye of consciousness readily available. When the unconscious drives giving impetus to a dream are beyond the capacity for regulating their intensity, the level of anxiety reaches panic proportions. The integrity of the dreaming self is in jeopardy, a nightmare situation is created, and it becomes necessary to bring the advanced functions suspended during sleep into play.

## Symbolization of Unconscious Perceptions in the Manifest Dream

The intrapsychic process of transference is defined as the transfer of an unconscious impulse across a repressive barrier onto a percept in the preconscious system. This concept of the transference is equally a description of the dream work, as latent dream thoughts are transformed into the symbolic imagery of the manifest dream by utilizing appropriate contents in the preconscious system. The one additional element in the construction of a dream is the inclusion of an immediate life experience. This day residue must echo and resonate with the unconscious drives demanding expression and is a significant feature of the dreaming process.

It is not surprising for the attributes of a therapeutic relationship to enter the manifest dream in some fashion, since the process of transference underlies both. Nevertheless, the consistency with which it occurs does make it imperative to seek a fuller explanation for its presence and of its role in constructing a dream. At times, the day residue clearly depicts an experience directly related to the therapeutic relationship, while at other times the day residue seems, on the surface, to be relatively independent of that relationship. When the concept of transference is broadened, however, to include unconscious perceptions, it becomes apparent that the events selected for inclusion in the dream as the day residue are not insignificant. They not only resonate with unconscious wishes, but also represent the derivative of an unconscious perception of the most forceful emotional experience of the previous day.

In most instances this will refer to the treatment because it is evocative of affect-laden memories and fantasies and powerful infantile feelings. In addition to its other functions the manifest dream emerges as an important mental production portraying the manner in which the therapeutic relationship is unconsciously perceived. Dreams have always been recognized as a means of validating the accuracy of interpretive interventions and the growth-promoting properties of the therapeutic relationship. However, by virtue of identifying the derivative of an unconscious perception in the day residue, a more penetrating view of what either facilitates or impedes therapeutic progress is available.

Some aspect of the external world, having enough emotional importance to be anchored to the stabilizing forces in the personality, must be included in the dream in order to allow the dream work to be accomplished and the resulting dream to be retained in consciousness. The derivative of an unconscious perception possesses this attribute to its fullest extent, since it emanates from the structured representations of good self experience. The derivative is then incorporated in the body of the dream as the day residue, and though it may be elaborated in fantasy or become highly symbolized, it takes on the characteristics of reality, presenting a picture of an unconscious truth the dreamer has perceived.

This hypothesis offers an explanation for the small number of dreams reported when measured against the plethora that occur. It suggests that dreams based on the derivative of an unconscious perception have the necessary stability to possess the attributes of a memory, whereas those utilizing other psychic contents are probably incapable of being retained. The transference relationship in psychoanalytic treatment is concerned with strong infantile emotions and is therefore a powerful stimulus to unconscious perceptions. Although there may be other events in an individual's life periodically having the same effect, it is generally the primary source of remembered dream activity.

The process of dreaming requires a stable memory trace to serve as a focus for constructing the symbolic imagery constituting the manifest content. The resulting dream reflects the structural organization of the personality, depicts the particular intrapsychic difficulties in the forefront, and is a starting place for unraveling the unconscious perceptions and instinctual drives being granted expression.

## The Manifest Dream: A Symbolic Picture of the Structural Organization of the Personality

The psychoanalytic diagnosis of a psychological disturbance is not based on symptoms or behavior, but on the underlying structural organization of the personality and the specific nature of a dynamic interplay of conflicting forces. Unconscious instinctual demands give impetus to a dream. It is symbolically represented by the available mental structures, and thereby illuminates the foundation of a psychic disorder. The specific level of developmental progression accessible at the moment of dreaming, under the regressive conditions associated with sleep, presents a valuable picture in gaining an accurate diagnostic assessment.

In order to determine the structural composition of the personality from the manifest dream, a symbolic portrayal of the self system of representations, the object system of representations, the interconnection between the two, the areas of conflict, and the degree of stability must be exposed to view. In addition, it is important to examine the manifest content for the components symbolizing instinctual activity. It then becomes possible to delineate the particular impulses striving for expression, the intrapsychic conflicts they engender or deficits they uncover, and the defensive alignments mobilized to stand in opposition. Instinctual activity fuels the construction of a dream, is characterized by impulsion, and is symbolically represented by movement.

The makeup of the psychic structures accomplishing the mental functions most in evidence in the dream is reflected in the symbolic imagery, giving a picture of the level of psychosexual development at which the dreamer is primarily operating. This developmental perspective deepens an understanding of the infantile experiences represented in the deeper layers of the personality. An orally derived object possesses nurturant or incorporative qualities; an anal object fosters mastery or exerts sadistic control. A phallic object is approving or humiliating, and a genital object supports independent genital interest or is castrating.

The good qualities of an object depict the composition of the mental structures establishing cohesiveness, whereas the bad qualities of an object show how differentiation is maintained and prohibitive responses function.

The nature of the anxiety present in a dream is also of a diagnostic significance, but it is the quality rather than the intensity that is important. From the point of view of the ego, the primary anxiety in a genitally organized personality is castration, phallically it is humiliation, anally it is a loss of control, and orally it is losing functional capacities. From the point of view of an attachment to an object, the primary anxiety in a genital organization is of superego disapproval; in a phallic organization it is the disapproval of an object. Anally it is the loss of an object's love, and orally it is the loss of the object.

A dream symbolizing the loss of attachment to an object, in addition to its specific unconscious meaning, has diagnostic implications. When the loss represents the attachment at the foundation of the fixation point in the object system, object constancy is threatened, and identity and the dreaming self are in danger of fragmentation. When the loss is of an attachment encompassed in the grandiose self or ego ideal, the dream will be abruptly interrupted, for these structures incorporate the perceptual functions registering the dream experience. Any process engendering an attack upon these linkages places the integrity of the dreaming self in jeopardy, precipitates the need to invoke a different set of perceptual conditions, and the dreamer is awakened in a state of extreme anxiety. When the loss represents an oedipal attachment at the interior of the personality, it is indicative of the primacy of genital strivings and that prohibitive opposition has gained dominance. The loss of an oedipal attachment does not threaten cohesiveness or place the dreaming self in danger, and consequently the dream does not include anxiety of nightmare proportions.

The nature of the defense symbolized in the manifest content can be helpful in delineating whether an impinging stimulus is primarily internal and instinctual or the result of an unempathic external stimulus. Distinguishing between the way instinctual impingements and those of the external world are defended against can be an effective aid in denoting those derivatives emanating from an unconscious perception. The symbolic representation of turning attention away from a threat or of invoking prohibitions is usually the defensive response to the impact of an internal instinctual stimulus, whereas the symbolic representation of fight, flight, or withdrawal is generally the defensive response to an external impingement.

A therapist's interpretive interventions and management of the treatment framework are validated by their effect upon the unseen forces emanating from the unconscious system of mental activity. The functioning of this unconscious realm can only be inferred through the communication of derivatives or from the overall reaction to the therapeutic relationship. A wide variety of responses is taken into consideration and their pattern and sequencing are the most reliable indicators of therapeutic progress. When continuity of experience is well structured within the personality, instinctual derivatives and the derivatives of unconscious perceptions are accessible as a means of expressing the unconscious significance of any intrapsychic event.

The manifest dream is then one of many psychic productions adding to the understanding of the way unconscious forces are incorporated in the total fabric of the personality. Although a dream does occupy a special place, in that its symbolic representations are closer to more obscure and hidden infantile experiences, in the cohesive personality it is not necessarily of decisive importance. With the noncohesive disorders, this situation is entirely different. The effects of splitting within the self or ego, in conjunction with the urgent pressure to attain reenforcement of pathological defenses, makes what is growth-promoting very difficult to ascertain. The manifest dream may then be a crucial ingredient for that determination. In the more primitively structured personality, a dream is often the only psychic production maintaining some degree of continuity with the unconscious and therefore can serve well as a map for highlighting therapeutic progress or identifying existing obstacles.

Self knowledge and self exploration require periods of solitude, in order for the patient to achieve full communion with his internal world. It is a world that represents attachments to objects possessing a variety of differing qualities, self experiences having been rendered defensively inaccessible, and a whole gamut of the derivatives of unconscious wishes and perceptions whose activity and meaning have been difficult to keep in focus. Sleep creates the conditions necessary for solitude by largely eliminating the stimuli of the external world, and the process of dreaming is a means of engaging in that much needed internal communion. Dreams that can be retained express in symbolic language the consequences of that exploration, and in its translation, self knowledge is broadened and self expansion is enhanced.

# 3

# The Manifest Dream as an Aid to Therapeutic Communication

## Therapeutic Dialogue and the Manifest Dream

A 9-year-old encopretic boy began therapeutic contact in the same way that he entered almost all facets of his life, recalcitrant and dragging his feet. He passively resisted every expectation, stubbornly plodded through all the activities of his day, taking endless time to dress, eat, accomplish school tasks, or to move in any direction. He soiled himself, was seemingly oblivious to the reaction of others, who were unable to tolerate his odor, and remained messy until forcibly cleaned. He was never openly defiant, and appeared unaffected by the increasing hostility and exasperation of those close to him. In the therapeutic relationship he was sullenly silent, occasionally responding with monosyllabic answers to questions, and displayed little in the way of initiative or of any open expression of affect. At the end of a session, the therapist commented on his aura of sadness, eliciting a spontaneous expression of surprise that quickly disappeared as he left. At the next session he initiated the discussion for the first time by referring to a very disturbing dream. He explained that after leaving the therapist's office he had found a coin and felt momentarily excited before losing it again in the grass. The dream follows:

> I was looking for the coin in the grass, and just as I found it a car came toward me with its lights on. It was out of control and in control at the same time, like a devil trying to hit me but skidding. Just before the impact I started to shake and woke up.

Upon entering the office he had felt his body shiver, immediately remembered the dream, and in an amazing fashion began to talk about the things it brought to his mind. He had been sleeping with a brother in the same bed and the brother's arm was about to touch him. He must have sensed what was happening as he slept. He was fearful of the contact, began to shake, and it entered his dream. It also made him think of his bowel movements. He can feel them coming, cannot stop them, becomes frozen, begins to shake, and soils himself. He then recalled an oft repeated daydream whenever he rides in a car. He imagines the car door opening, himself falling out, and once again beginning to shake. He reflected on how immobilized he felt while sitting in silence. Nothing came into his mind. He did not know what to say, and when he had the dream it felt like a gift since it gave him something to talk about. The dream served as a center from which other thoughts, feelings, memories, and fantasies emerged, enabling him to feel effective and alleviating a sense of inadequacy that pervaded him in the silence.

Associative connections to the latent dream thoughts are of primary importance in exposing the powerful impact of unconscious forces. When attention is directed exclusively to the unconscious realm, however, the significance of the manifest dream is often overlooked, and the relevance of the dream report may not be fully appreciated. This 9-year-old boy's dream, for example, was his first openly communicative expression and was important in and of itself. It gave him a focus for revealing his thoughts and feelings and operated as a stepping stone towards attaining meaningful therapeutic dialogue.

In addition, the manifest content provided a skeletal framework for understanding the structural foundation of his personality, and a number of mental configurations could be identified. These included symbolic portrayals of the self system of representations, the object system of representations, the manner in which the two were united and differentiated, the movement toward expressing instinctual drives, the defensive opposition mobilized as a response, and the day residue reflecting his unconscious perception of the therapeutic relationship. The context in which the dream was reported, and the associative material it evoked, added links to the latent, implied unconscious impulses giving impetus to the dream.

The unsteadiness and lack of regulation within the self system, the overpowering prohibitions emanating from the impressions of an object, and the archaic aggression embodied in their unifying and differentiating connection were all vividly depicted. The image of the car with its lights on symbolized the danger associated with being understood, with his subsequent thoughts implying that this involved exposing homosexual impulses, repressed anal sadistic drives, and their accompanying primitive superego responses. The impact was of traumatic proportions, shaking his entire being and rousing him from sleep. It was also possible to identify the day residue in his excitement at finding a coin, which appeared to be a derivative of his unconscious perception of the therapist's search for a deeper understanding instigated by the recognition of his underlying sadness. The understanding, like the coin, was lost and then recovered in the dream.

## Symbolization and the Manifest Dream

The dreamer uses mental contents in the preconscious system, which resonate with the most active unconscious forces, as the source of symbolizations in constructing a dream. For this reason it is important to know the uniquely personal significance of the dream elements in order to fully understand their symbolic meaning. At the same time a sketchy grasp can be gained from the properties attributable to a given image. Universal symbols are simultaneously extremely useful, since the number of experiences apt to be symbolized are limited, and an obstacle to understanding because there are such a vast array of symbols. Symbols must contain the properties of the body ego experiences or object impressions they are meant to represent; consequently universal symbols can be a help if associations are unavailable. However, individual meaning overrides any universal attribute, and validation is always necessary.

The process of condensation concentrates a series of ideas, emanating from different sectors of the id of the dynamic unconscious, into a single image. It is one facet of the dream work, and the free associative process sheds light upon these varied strivings. Thus, in the 9-year-old boy's dream, the car with the lights on was united with the anticipation of being touched by his brother and its resonance with unconscious homosexual impulses, with the body ego sensations associated with uncontrollable bowel function, and with the unconscious meaning of the therapist's empathic awareness of the youngster's inner feeling of sadness. The dream work also requires a displacement in order to attain access to representation, and the accompanying affect is relatively unaltered. The affective tone of the dream is thereby the clearest path to the latent dream thoughts.

Symbolization is another aspect of the dream work, granting expression to bodily functions or erotic interests incorporated in an unconscious wish. There is an abundant conglomeration of symbols potentially accessible to portray a limited number of concerns, and these are illuminated through the dreamer's associations. These symbols must be invested with the nature of the experiences being symbolized to lend credence to the universality of certain symbolic productions. A car, for example, can only be molded to a certain extent. Its qualities of independent movement and immutable shape must fit the dimensions of the unconscious forces demanding expression. The final facet of the dream work is its secondary revision, as a multiplicity of ego functions are combined to create logic, order, and some relative comprehensibility.

## The Relationship of the Manifest Dream to the Latent Dream Thoughts

The visual representation of unconscious affects and ideas sheds light upon the process of symbolization and underscores the remarkable position of the manifest dream in revealing the nature of latent dream thoughts. The transformation into dream imagery disguises latent dream thoughts primarily because of the limitations imposed by the nature of symbols and the deficiencies in our ability to translate their individual meaning. Unraveling the dream work to expose latent dream thoughts is usually accomplished by overcoming the opposition of repression through a therapist's interpretive interventions. This is not always the case, because the indications for interpretive help are dictated by the circumstances of the treatment. In the situation described with this boy, for instance, none was called for. The manifest dream was reported in the context of a free associative mode of communication, and it was not necessary or desirable to interrupt the flow.

The structural underpinnings of a dream can be determined from the manifest content, and they elucidate the unconscious forces at work. A dream is not the equivalent of all other mental content, even though it has been subjected to secondary revision, because most psychic productions are so depersonified that it is extremely difficult to identify the underlying mental representations upon which they are based. The emergence of a dream within a sequence of associations, by virtue of lending itself to an exposition of its structural components, highlights the deeper unarticulated meaning of the entire pattern of thought. The manifest dream gives a picture of the mental structures operative in its construction, and thereby shows the particular composition of the representational world in the ascendency at the time.

Every mental production is based upon body ego experiences and their object impression counterparts and reflects the way in which they are interrelated. Nevertheless, most thoughts are so distantly connected to their infantile roots that it is difficult, if not impossible, to unveil their composition with any degree of certainty or precision. The regression induced by a free associative process fosters the emergence of mental contents allowing a closer inspection of these developmental origins, but many thoughts with the potential for revealing much needed information pass unnoticed. In addition, as illustrated by the aforementioned 9-year-old boy, available mental content can be so sparse, carefully protected, and fraught with danger that there is only very limited access to an in-depth view of the personality.

Although the unconscious urges giving impetus to a dream's construction mobilize defensive responses, creating distortions that are then furthered by the effects of secondary revision, the symbols themselves must have resonance with and parallel the infantile experiences represented. The visual representation designed to portray an unconscious affect or idea must surround it, contain its essential nature, and encompass id, ego, and superego components. The process of symbolization accomplishes this multidimensional task by utilizing the specific concrete properties of an unconscious force to evoke resonant percepts in the preconscious system. Thus there is a degree of truth in the idea that universal symbols are either nonexistent or unreliable, but for the same reason they can be useful and relevant.

This function of symbolization was shown in the dream of a 30-year-old man, recalled when he was thinking about ending therapy on the eve of a business trip:

I was driving in a car in my old neighborhood. I stopped, and as I got out I noticed a mist. It surrounded me and was suffocating. I had the thought in the dream that it was my own feelings.

After reporting the dream, his thoughts moved to previous relationships in which there had been a separation and he missed a loved object. Immediately upon saying the word *missed* his face lit up, as the mist in the dream was transformed into the idea of missing the therapist. The feeling of missing therapeutic contact was joined with his infantile experiences where closeness and intimacy were associated with being smothered, and then expressed symbolically in the imagery of a suffocating mist.

The unconscious realm of mental activity is a world of the implied, for it can only be expressed through derivatives. Associations to the content of a dream form a pathway for determining the latent dream thoughts, by virtue of their implied meanings. The manifest dream is composed of psychic content having a direct connection to the unconscious realm, and thus the understanding of all associations must begin with their relationship to this focal point. The unconscious wishes instigating and fueling the dream experience are manifested in derivatives, which are then incorporated within the body of the manifest dream and can be traced more effectively when the significance of the manifest content is fully appreciated.

## Structural Composition of the Personality as Revealed in the Manifest Dream

The representation of body ego experiences, their object impression counterparts, and the interrelationship among them form a foundation for all mental productions. Most psychic contents are so distant from the concrete experiences upon which they are based that it is not possible to distinguish the structures required to produce them. Since a dream is composed of mental contents closest to this dimension of psychic life, it exposes the status of the specific structural unions that are established. In examining the manifest dream, identifying the symbolic representation of the self system, the object system, and the way they are united presents a picture of the underlying structural composition and psychic organization of the personality.

This was demonstrated in the dream of a 38-year-old man who had sought therapeutic help for symptoms of premature ejaculation and periodic impotence. He continually exerted an effort to present himself as a thoughtful, considerate, hard-working patient. The therapeutic relationship began to deepen in importance; and longings for closeness or frustration with inevitable interruptions were pushed aside, and he constantly searched for the slightest nuances of what would be most pleasing to the therapist. He then reported the following dream;

I went to see a girlfriend and her father, and found them brutally murdered. I didn't know how it happened or even if I did it, and I was horrified. The dream shifted and I was driving a bus very high up in the driver's seat. My position was extremely precarious. It felt like the bus would topple if I turned it in any direction. It had to be kept moving extremely straight and even then was unsteady. From the outside of the bus everything was in proportion, but as soon as I stepped inside I was too high up.

The status of the self system was reflected in the symbolic portrayal of the bus. From the outside and at a distance it appeared intact, well contained, and easily controlled. On the inside, however, conditions were quite different, and the dreamer's precarious position immediately made his inability to manage instinctual drives apparent. The status of the object system was depicted in the figures of the girl and her father, reflecting the almost total unavailability of the influences of an object for self-enhancing identifications or for regulatory and defensive functions. The nature of the dreamer's connection to these objects captures the extent to which narcissistic rage and frustration have been embodied in the attachment, and gives some limited expression to the infantile experiences at the foundation of the structural union between the two systems of representation.

The manifest dream may represent the functioning of character defenses, the emergence of unconscious id impulses, superego prohibitions, or movement toward integration. Instinctual activity gives impetus to the construction of a dream, is characterized by impulsion, and is symbolized by movement. The components of the dream representing instinctual experience illuminate the specific impulses striving for expression, the conflicts they engender, and the defensive structures activated to stand in opposition. Self experience originates from registering the functioning of perceptual processes, the self system of representations is symbolized as the initiator of movement, and the manner in which movement transpires is indicative of the degree of freedom in attaining discharge of instinctual demands.

The following dream reported by a 16-year-old boy, after a session in which he had expressed positive feelings toward the therapist, is illustrative. His warm feelings had been accompanied by derivatives expressing concern about the homosexual meaning of his attachment, and the therapist's interpretation of his underlying negative oedipal strivings was reacted to with a silent, pensive attitude.

I was in an auditorium playing tennis and hit the ball up on the stage. I lost when the ball came back to me. I knew I could hit it, but something inside made me miss.

The dream imagery displays the effects of defensive opposition upon his ability to function, suggesting a fear of his sexual impulses and their lack of adequate regulation. It clearly presents the self as the instigator of movement, since the impetus for propelling the tennis ball emanates from the dreamer who is then unable to keep it in motion.

The independence of an external object evokes mental impressions more distant from self experience, and their representation is more susceptible to fantasy distortions. These object impressions can be more easily molded to fit the particular defensive needs in the foreground when constructing a dream because they are not bound to the body ego.

> This was exemplified in the dream of a 35-year-old man. He had been describing efforts to be different from his mother, whom he perceived as controlling and destructive. The therapist commented on his identification with her, which was emphatically denied. That night he had a dream:
>
> > Some men were robbing a bank and I got a chain to help in stopping them. Suddenly I was one of them, and the woman bank teller was a hostage with her hands chained. I realized I was now involved with them and had to get away. I ducked into a pipe system with no way out and tried to get over a fence but it was endless and had barbed wire. I kept looking for a way out and had a strong feeling I would eventually find one.
>
> Initially the dream pictured his avoidance of being associated with the bank robbers. With no transition, he joins the robbers and when he realizes he might be caught, attempts to escape. The readiness with which he was incorporated into the realm of these object impressions gave expression to his identification with them, resonated with the therapist's interpretation, and the remainder of the dream symbolized his attempt to escape discovery. It demonstrates the ease with which the representations of an object can be shaped to fit the circumstances of the moment, although the dreamer was confident that his characteristic defenses would ultimately be successful.

The object system of representations possesses qualities that are impinging, depriving, prohibitive, and overstimulating, or that are caring, restraining, attracting interest, and are needed as a source of supply. The particular manner in which an object is represented encompasses the way relationships are perceived at the time, and gives an implicit picture of how the therapeutic relationship is being received and registered. The manifest dream can then be a valuable adjunct when therapeutic understanding has had to rely heavily upon subjective inference.

> This was the case with a 33-year-old man seeking help for an intense fear of intimacy who was worried about his tendency to withdraw from what he most desired. He had great difficulty in articulating the specific

nature of his internal sensations and felt frustrated in trying to bring clarity to them. He reported a dream:

> I am searching for something hidden . . . like a treasure hunt, but I'm extremely frustrated and anxious. The scene shifts and I'm in my bed at home. My mother comes in to talk to me and climbs on top of me. I struggle to get free. It is an intensely sexual involvement and I'm actively wondering about it. I realize that I'm most frightened, not of the sexuality, but of being trapped.

The manifest dream symbolized his perception of attachments to objects, giving substance to the vagueness that dominated his conscious experience, and by implication pointed to what was activated in the therapeutic relationship.

## The Manifest Dream and Early Trauma

Another unique feature of the manifest dream involves its particular suitability for representing traumatic, repressed infantile memories. The imagery in a dream is based upon infantile body ego experiences and object impressions, and their appearance in symbolic form creates the degree of distance, distortion, and disguise required to enable an attempt at mastery and integration.

> This was shown in the dream of a 14-year-old boy referred for treatment because of extreme difficulties in school despite his vast intellectual potential. He showed a cold, cynical, distrustful attitude toward all of life's events and an increasing tendency to withdraw from relationships. He had been living with an aunt and uncle since the age of 7, when his mother had been brutally murdered and his father confined to a mental institution. The father had been suspected of the murder and was considered unable to stand trial. The boy had been questioned at the time but had no information to give. His lack of emotional response to his mother's death was attributed to its overwhelming nature. During the course of treatment he was gradually able to recover and talk about memories from his earliest years, expressing thinly veiled hostility toward his mother but concern over his father's plight. Periodically he would be flooded with fantasies of a sick or injured man, and these fantasies were accompanied by high levels of anxiety, which would trigger an intense effort to create distractions and suppress any introspective attention, and which mobilized an irritable, defensive attitude. He then reported the following dream:

> A small man was walking down the street with a big dog. A large woman approached walking a small but vicious dog. The man kept trying to pass and keep his dog out of the way, but the little dog

persisted in provoking the big dog until the big dog finally attacked and tore it apart.

The dream immediately brought forth remembrances of numerous parental fights. He perceived his father as weak, helpless, and impotent and his mother as overpowering, demanding, and highly critical. He felt sorry for his father and wished desperately for his mother to leave him alone. Upon uttering these words, an anguished silence, interspersed with deep and painful sobs, followed. He had suddenly been engulfed by the return of previously repressed memories of observing his mother's death. His father had been watching him while his mother was out to a meeting. She returned late and proceeded to attack the father for being lazy. He pleaded with her to back off but she persisted, and the father erupted in a brutal, murderous act. Awakened by the noise, the boy observed the entire scene paralyzed with fright and unable to yell out, convinced himself it was a bad dream, and went back to sleep. From that moment he directed all of his efforts, and based his entire internal posture on maintaining the memory under repression.

The process of symbolization, in conjunction with the diminished censorship embodied in the construction of the manifest dream, was the only vehicle by which this traumatic memory could return. The symbols had to contain characteristics consonant with what was symbolized, and the small, provocative dog carried by the large woman and the large, potentially violent dog carried by the small man captured the essence of what he had perceived in the parental relationship. The destructive ending of the dream was a pathway to the recollection of what had been repressed.

## The Manifest Dream as a Guide
## for Therapeutic Intervention

A dream by its nature is especially valuable for allowing a comprehensive perspective on the manner in which the personality is organized, for determining the level of psychic structuralization that is functional, and so guiding a therapist's management of the treatment relationship.

The 9-year-old encopretic boy mentioned earlier, for example, after presenting his first dream, was periodically fluently communicative, but would frequently retreat into his previous immobilized stance. It looked as though the more he became involved in the relationship, the more he met obstacles to his ability to articulate his internal reactions. At a time when he was anticipating a summer break in treatment he saw a pregnant fish in a tank in the therapist's waiting room, which made him think of his mother's pregnancy. He remembered feeling he would lose her and that it would be all his fault. He stopped abruptly with tears welling up in his eyes. The therapist was silently formulating a transference interpretation concerning the impending separation when the boy reported a dream:

> I was the pilot of an airplane. It ran out of gas and the plane dived. I jumped out to save myself. The parachute didn't open, and just as I was about to hit the ground I shivered and woke up.

The dream was recalled in response to the threat of losing a love object, which he perceived as the consequence of his hidden, unbridled, sadistic aggression. It helped to explain what was occurring when the flow of his thoughts and feelings was broken off, and gave a clearer view of how his defenses thwarted the impetus toward spontaneous movement fueled by instinctual energy. The ensuing regression was reflected in the dream of the plane diving, pointing to the need for immediate interpretive assistance, when he lapsed into silence.

The dream work is accomplished by making use of the mental structures available to represent unconscious forces symbolically, and the manifest dream alludes to what is most relevant for exposing them. A deeper understanding of the structural organization of the personality, as revealed by the manifest dream, is an absolute imperative in determining an effective pathway for eliciting latent dream thoughts.

This was seen in the treatment of a 22-year-old college student suffering acutely from his longing to make heterosexual contact and from the paralyzing anxiety preventing it. While describing his fear he remembered a dream:

> There was a screaming voice that felt like my conscience. I watched it trying to take me over and felt terrified that it was so powerful.

The content of the dream shed light upon the overwhelming prohibitions opposing any expression of instinctual drives. The enveloping presence of the screaming voice reminded him of his father's last years. His father had recently died of a brain tumor, which had caused a profound personality change manifested in furious eruptions with little provocation. This led him to earlier memories of closer contact with his father, eliciting the tears and sadness he had held in abeyance. The dream initiated a process of mourning, and a highly ambivalent relationship with his father gradually emerged. He then had the following dream:

> I was in bed with a sensual blonde girl, and there was a marvelous feeling of making sexual contact. Several people were in the same

bed. There was an older man completely repulsed by what I was doing. Two young homosexual men who appeared exhausted were silently watching. A woman grinning in amusement, as though making fun of me, was also there. The girl I was with was uncomfortable with all those people there and wanted to find a private place. I was able to ignore the people, but said it was okay.

The dream highlighted the obstacles to instinctual attachments. The older man made him think of his father's prohibitive attitudes and of his fear of evoking paternal disapproval. He recalled being overly attached to his mother in his younger years and his father's disgusted reaction to his feelings. The homosexual men brought back memories of his teenage years when he worried about his effeminate characteristics and wondered about his homosexual tendencies. This teenage concern had escalated whenever he felt blocked in his attempts to form heterosexual relationships. The woman grinning in amusement was associated with a feeling of inadequacy and uncertainty about his sexual prowess. The manifest dream gave him a means of exploring areas of uneasiness that were otherwise difficult to bring to the surface.

In the more primitive, narcissistic individual, associative mental content is highly unreliable, since continuity of experience is not structured within the personality. Associations are scattered and disconnected by the effects of splitting, which obscures any discernible pathway to unconscious meaning. The clearest understanding may come specifically from the implied meaning in the dream itself, which represents the only accessible psychic production built upon continuity with unconscious forces. The manifest dream can then serve as a good map to highlight therapeutic progress.

The dream of a 15-year-old boy who had initiated therapeutic contact after experiencing frightening episodes of disorientation while engaged in a disappointing love relationship is illustrative. He felt totally overwhelmed, impelled to cling to the attachment, and was terrified of losing his boundaries. The therapist had directed interpretive interventions toward identifying the infantile experiences aroused by his longing for closeness, but they seemingly had little overt effect. He then reported a dream:

My conscience was arguing with God about whether I really loved my girlfriend or whether I was trying to replace a previous love. They went over a checklist, and the final question was whether I could see her as herself. The answer was yes. I felt myself as separate, and was relieved.

The patient's spontaneous associations during the course of a session were constantly disrupted by splitting mechanisms, defensively guarding him against the longing for intimacy mobilized by the therapeutic relationship. The manifest dream showed that the therapist's interpretations were received constructively. It stood as a guidepost giving validation to this approach and indicated progress was being made.

The manifest dream may also underscore potential or existing barriers to treatment which is of particular importance when the manner in which they are manifested is subtle and can be readily overlooked.

An example was given by a 16-year-old boy referred because of his phobic avoidance of school. His father was a minister, his mother a teacher. Both were involved with doing "good" works and led very busy lives. He was the youngest of four, all other siblings having established independent families of their own. There was a constant demand for him to grow up and be independent, with mounting irritation as his symptom interfered with his parents' activities. All his thoughts were filled with thinly disguised hostility toward parental figures, and instigated a flurry of qualifying statements emphasizing the depth of his love and respect. At the same time he noted an intense feeling of guilt descending upon him whenever he thought of pleasurable pursuits or constructive ventures. He described it as an enemy within working against him. He frantically appealed to the therapist for aid in understanding what was happening to him, and reported the following dream:

> I was trying to see my enemy and face him once and for all. I did see him! He was so monstrous and terrifying I knew it was impossible to confront him and I awoke in fright.

He unconsciously knew he was incapable of integrating the depth and extent of his infantile rage, yet felt duty bound to do so in order to return to school and alleviate the burden upon his parents. The portrayal of an overwhelming threat suggested that if his aggression was interpreted, it might precipitate a flight from treatment. The dream signaled the therapist to his need for help in modulating the archaic nature of his prohibitions before anything else could be addressed.

It may be useful to encourage associations to specific dream content actively, depending upon the circumstances of the treatment and the structuralization of the patient's personality. For some, it activates advanced psychic functions utilized in the service of reenforcing a defensive stance, whereas for others, it enables a fuller exposition of the manifest content, giving a broader picture of the underlying unconscious conflict. Although the manifest dream may be clarified through such encouragement, it does not necessarily foster the emergence of latent dream thoughts or facilitate a free associative process.

# 4

# The Prognostic Significance of a Manifest Dream

Symbolization transforms unconscious forces into the imagery comprising a manifest dream, with the various features giving a picture of the structural organization of the personality. The day residue is included in the body of the dream, in order for it to be retained within consciousness. It consists of the derivative of an unconscious perception, elicited by an emotionally important experience, and is resonant with the unconscious drives pushing for expression. The manifest dream thus has prognostic value, in that it portrays the unconscious meaning of a helping process.

The anticipation of therapeutic contact can be a strong emotional stimulus and serve as the day residue for a dream. The resulting manifest content will likely give some idea of the latent resources or obstacles in readiness to support or work in opposition to a therapeutic regression. The act of reporting the dream suggests at least a reactive awareness of the importance of this form of communication, in deepening and furthering self knowledge, and in indicating a willingness to bring difficult self revelations into the context of a treatment relationship.

Dreams following an initial session are especially noteworthy, since they occur at a time when patient and therapist know least about each other. The conditions of the treatment situation and the therapist's unique style of obtaining information are most visible, and the patient's unconscious perception of these facts will express whether it is likely that growth will be promoted. Similarly, the progress of a therapeutic relationship can be monitored by a sequence of dream reports as the treatment proceeds. Validation of a therapist's unconscious understanding delivered through interpretive interventions and management of the framework, the uncovering of empathic lapses and failures, and guidelines for fostering constructive growth are all furthered with the aid of the manifest dream. In a gradual manner the overall prognosis of a given treatment situation can be extracted from dreams across a span of time.

## Prognostic Implications in the Manifest Dream Prior to Initiating Therapeutic Contact

Frequently a prospective patient will have a dream in anticipation of an impending therapeutic encounter, and the manifest content will contain symbolic images of the intrapsychic events most likely to be activated in the treatment situation. The idea of forming a new and unknown relationship serves as the day residue around which the dream is constructed. Since there is no actual experience for it to be based upon, the preconscious body ego experiences and object impressions associated with seeking help are symbolized in the body of the dream. Latent resources or potential obstacles are elicited, and a great deal of information with prognostic significance can be revealed.

This was exemplified in the dream of a 13-year-old boy who was referred after he became desperately anxious and refused to go for a tetanus shot in preparation for summer camp. He also had a splinter in his finger that had become infected, and he adamantly resisted having it removed. He began his first session by reporting a dream from the night before:

I was going away to camp. I had mosquito bites on the inside of my thigh and was going to the doctor. A lot of other children in the camp had poison ivy and the doctor was giving shots. I was on a conveyor belt with three other children, moving toward the doctor. The doctor said that if the first three children had poison ivy, the fourth one did too. The first three had poison ivy. I didn't want another shot. I started to scream, and my mother came to hold me.

The manifest content depicts the dreamer faced with leaving familiar surroundings, having difficulty with body sensations near his genital area that must be attended to by a doctor giving shots, and the doctor assuming the patient would have the same problem as the other children. An inexorable force outside of direct control, symbolically represented by a conveyor belt, is carrying him to a frightening injection because of a misunderstanding. The reason for the misdiagnosis is attributed to his being the fourth in line.

The patient's father and two younger brothers were already involved in psychoanalytic treatment. He was about to enter a similar situation, and this aspect of his external life was reflected in the expectation of being diagnosed in accordance with the three in front of him. The portrayal of a misdiagnosis with the idea of receiving help also suggests some lack of empathy in scheduling the first appointment. This would not be surprising, for the chances of an accurate understanding during an initial contact are minimal, but the implication is of being dealt with in a routine rather than a personal fashion. Furthermore, the dream imagery of moving toward a supposedly helpful person on a conveyor belt hints that an element of coercion was involved. The arrangements had been made by the father without the child's direct participation, and the content of the dream points to the importance of the therapist addressing its meaning in the course of the first session.

The location of the mosquito bites appears to refer to phallic-genital sensations only slightly displaced that are evoking anxiety and conflict, while the rescuing entry of the mother highlights the defensive regression mobilized as a response. The dreamer is thus approaching a therapeutic relationship expecting unconscious genital instinctual impulses to be aroused, and in spite of the accompanying dangers, the structural foundation of the dream remains intact and there is enough stability for the dream to continue. Regardless of the defensive meaning of this dream segment, it has prognostic importance. It indicates that the dreamer possesses the resources to invoke protection and containment when confronted with inordinately conflicted instinctual activities, and suggests that there is a great capacity for managing a therapeutic regression.

A manifest dream elicited in response to the idea of engaging in an unknown therapeutic relationship may symbolically represent a growth-promoting influence, or, conversely, having to overcome a self-defeating obstacle. The difference is dependent upon the particular life history and structural organization of the dreamer's personality. The content may contain hints concerning specific roadblocks or dangers that need to be addressed relatively early.

A 9-year-old girl had the following dream on the night before beginning therapeutic contact; it was expressive of her search for independence, containment, and growth-promoting experiences, but also revealed her enormous separation anxiety and the regressive dangers she anticipated.

> I am in the house with my parents and brother. A kind old man invited me to come out and play. There were other kids and I went with them to a clubhouse built in a tree. I was very excited and it was fun. Then I realized it was in a swamp. Crocodiles were all around. I couldn't climb down, and I was separated from home and in great danger.

Movement in the dream symbolic of instinctual activity, at first was accompanied by a sense of liberation and excitement. It was instigated with the encouragement of a figure representative of the expected treatment, and reflected her striving to successfully disengage from the implied limiting attachment to parental objects. The dream progressed. The separation from infantile objects placed the dreamer in an increasingly anxiety-arousing position. It ultimately led to her being confronted with overwhelming regressive dangers.

This manifest dream intimated that infantile attachments were preventing instinctual progression, that she looked forward to the impending therapeutic relationship as a means of attaining greater access to instinctual representation, and that the regression this entailed was extremely frightening. Her ability to represent a figure symbolizing safety and containment, even momentarily, and of effecting a separate attachment to an independent object, was indicative of a capacity to establish an effective therapeutic alliance. It signified that this bond of mutual purpose between her unconscious perceptions and the therapist's unconsciously empathic interventions could be formed rather readily. The dream, however, also gave some evidence that a budding transference relationship could be rapidly infused with inordinately conflicted regressive wishes.

By way of contrast, a 14-year-old girl had the following dream on the eve of her first therapeutic session:

> I had a baby boy. My mother sedated me so she could take it and control it. I screamed in anger that it was mine. The baby grew rapidly and was becoming attached to her. I felt enraged because I was losing the bond.

This manifest dream was based upon a more primitively organized structural foundation, with the dreamer having less good self experience available for anticipating an unconsciously empathic therapeutic experience. There were some prognostic implications in the symbolic representation of her being overpowered by a need supplying object and of losing contact with her baby. The prospect of entering treatment seemed to have acted as a spur to a malignant regression, and presaged the need for accurate interpretive help early in the ensuing relationship. It raised concern as to whether an effective therapeutic alliance could be established and signaled the therapist to be on the alert for any authoritative attitudes that could be readily perceived as destructively controlling.

The capacity to represent containment and safety symbolically before engaging in the actual therapeutic experience is a sign of latent stabilizing forces in the personality, which can be mobilized in response to an unconsciously empathic environment and allow a therapeutic regression. The prospect of a helping relationship can activate these dormant structured representations of good-self experience, even when destructive forces are extreme.

This was evident in the dream of a 9-year-old girl after overhearing her parents' telephone call to arrange an appointment:

I was chased by a gorilla in a hall outside of your office. I ran into your office to be safe, and knew as long as I was there I would be all right.

The manifest dream symbolized the dangers rampant in her internal world, and represented a haven of safety in the as-yet-unknown therapist's office. It showed a latent capacity to feel contained, and stressed the need to establish well-regulated ground rules and boundaries.

The particular psychological disturbance motivating the search for therapeutic help has undoubtedly interfered with the full realization of self potentials. The stimulus of moving toward a potential source of help in some measure involves an act of self assertiveness, amplifying latent or atrophied psychic functions.

This was reflected in the manifest dream of a 30-year-old woman prior to her first appointment:

When my father died he left a drawer full of Barbie dolls behind, and I discovered that Barbie dolls were now worth $1,000. I noticed that I had a Skipper doll, and since fewer of them had been made, they must be more valuable. The dream shifted and I was walking with friends near a river on a country road. I was aware of having trouble walking and I lagged behind. They turned to ask if I was okay and I said I was fine. We came to a point where they turned to walk along the river. I walked calmly into the water and was not scared. It was a good feeling.

The symbolic imagery in the dream gives expression to the discovery of unrecognized resources in the form of the Skipper doll, and the dream then shifted. It portrayed the dreamer's difficulty in keeping up with others and the need for entering a regression that would take her away from the mainstream of her life for awhile. Her acceptance without anxiety was a statement of readiness to confront regressive infantile experiences and an important prognostic indicator of a good potential for the therapeutic relationship.

At times, seeking psychotherapeutic assistance intensifies a psychic disturbance, jeopardizing the individual's ability to sustain whatever balance has been achieved and threatening to expose what has heretofore been intolerable. In such a situation the prognosis for successful therapeutic intervention is somewhat more questionable, or at least heralds the difficulty that may be encountered in forming a therapeutic alliance.

This was illustrated in the dream of an 18-year-old boy the night before his first session:

I was in a TV show, "The A Team." There was a lot of fighting and violence. I was terrified because people were cut up, injured, and their organs were all bloody and exposed.

The manifest content symbolized the aggression carefully guarded within his personality and his apprehension that it would be exposed in a traumatic fashion. An immediate question emerged concerning his ability to tolerate a therapeutic regression, pointing to the need to proceed slowly.

A manifest dream may give valuable information as to whether the impending relationship is sought out to gain an unconscious understanding or whether it is looked to for reenforcement of a pathological defense. A dream may be the only means of communicating this kind of motive, since it is impossible to articulate it directly, and it can be vital when an immediate decision is called for.

The following dream of an extremely depressed adolescent boy is an example. He was considered to be suicidal, had been hospitalized, and was referred for a second opinion. He was sullen, quiet, could only say he felt silently enraged most of the time, and hesitantly described his wish to leave the hospital. He put emphasis on his inability to convince anyone that he should be allowed to do so, which left him feeling totally ineffective and defeated. After a long silence he remembered a dream from the night after he had arranged the appointment:

I was with my friends and we were goofing around. Another friend drove up, chased by the police. They jumped out of their car, arrested us, and put us in jail. We were innocent and angry for being judged superficially. The police looked like rookies who were frightened and needed to look tough in each other's eyes and like they were doing their job.

The manifest content showed the dreamer locked up by frightened, inept authoritarian figures. This characterization of an empathic failure

left him feeling helplessly angry. Apparently the idea of another therapeutic contact had aroused the anticipation of a repetition, which in all
likelihood was resonating with infantile traumas. The dreamer's reaction
to being misunderstood on the basis of an external object's anxiety and
need for narcissistic enhancement underscores the debilitating effect of
having pathological defenses reenforced, and implies that he is unconsciously searching to be understood.

Although it is certainly not decisive, the appearance of efforts to
gain reenforcement of pathological defenses in the manifest dream
can be the first indication of a bleak outlook for treatment.

This was exemplified in the dream of an 18-year-old boy whose
primary motive for seeking help was at the behest of others worried
about his explosive behavior:

I was on the arch on the outside, holding on but unsteady. I looked
down to see how high I was, and I was very scared. I looked for
anything I could find to hold onto.

Reporting the dream in the initial session gave some evidence of a
willingness to communicate his internal concerns, and in that sense had
some positive prognostic meaning. The dream itself, however, reflected
his tendency to find internal exploration especially dangerous and to
look for any means possible to reenforce a pathological defense. A true
picture of his unconscious motivation could not be forthcoming until the
effects of an unconsciously empathic therapeutic environment could
exert an influence, in which case there might be enough containment to
enable a therapeutic regression to unfold without undue anxiety.

## Prognostic Implications in the Manifest Dream
## at the Outset of Therapeutic Contact

When a therapeutic relationship has been initiated the experience
can serve as the day residue, and a more accurate picture of its
growth-promoting properties is obtained. A patient's unconscious
perception of the specific attributes of the treatment environment can
elicit latent resources, otherwise unavailable, that possess positive
prognostic significance even in the presence of severe pathology.

This was demonstrated in a dream reported by a 7-year-old boy after
three evaluative sessions, during which it was decided to continue on a
regular basis. He had been referred because of his hyperactive, frag-

mented, and overcontrolling behavior. Previous efforts at finding help had been totally unsuccessful.

> We were all on earth and it was freezing. My family was covered with ice and turning blue. My mother and I jumped to the sun and got all warm and thawed out.

The great emotional distance in his attachment to love objects was graphically symbolized in the ice-covered scene of the opening dream segment. Nevertheless, he was able to represent a maternal relationship that was warmed by the sun, implying that the conditions of the treatment were unconsciously empathic. The resulting mobilization of latent resources gave a more favorable outlook.

In the earliest stages of a psychotherapeutic interaction it can be extraordinarily difficult for a therapist to achieve enough of an understanding for the relationship to be unconsciously empathic. Consequently, the indications of a questionable prognosis may subsequently be modified, as inadvertent failures in empathy are rectified and their effects interpreted, and the therapist's grasp of what is required is deepened.

This was shown in the following sequence of two dreams reported by a young woman who had been referred following a period of hospitalization precipitated by an abrupt rupture in a previous therapeutic relationship. The first dream took place after the initial appointment:

> I went to see my sister's therapist and she said it was amazing that in one hour she had gotten to know me better than she had my sister in years. I had a sore on my knee. It was very deep and bad and I was showing it to her. As I left, I thought my sore wasn't healing. I went to my apartment, went from room to room to turn on the lights, they wouldn't go on, and I felt frightened.

During the course of the session the therapist had reacted to the severity of her illness with conscious concern about the extent of self damage, uncertainty as to what would be required, and a vague feeling of uneasiness triggering a less conscious defensive attitude. The manifest dream was constructed around a derivative of her unconscious perception of the therapist's emotional distance, and rather than mobilizing latent resources, it evoked despair over the value of revealing her illness. The symbolic imagery reflected the sense of being understood very quickly, but then of experiencing an empathic failure. It suggested that exposing her self damage to the therapist had been of no help, and implied that she had been left too much on her own. At the time the dream tended to strengthen the therapist's doubts about a favorable prognosis.

In subsequent sessions it was possible for the therapist to identify the source of his defensiveness, acknowledge her unconscious perception of the empathic lapse, and interpret its destructive impact. Thereafter, the treatment revolved around diminishing the distorting influences in her internal world, revealing the extent to which good self experience had been preserved. A second dream was reported two years later, after there had been a relatively continuous period of constructive therapeutic work:

> I'm in therapy with a woman. I'm on the couch and getting smaller and smaller. I am amazed because I don't feel frightened.

This dream was founded upon representations of good self experience solid enough to symbolize a controlled, benign regression, demonstrated her emerging capacity to enter into a therapeutic symbiosis, and was indicative of the progress that had occurred. Thus, when the therapist was able to filter out personal anxieties, the conditions conducive to expressing good instinctual self experience carefully preserved in the deeper layers of her personality could be discovered and provided. The potential for healing self splits could begin to be realized. What had initially seemed to be evidence of a questionable outlook gradually evolved into an increasingly positive outcome.

Seeking psychotherapeutic help may carry with it a feeling of hope and excitement, which is fueled by unconscious instinctual wishes searching for a means of attaining gratification. The experience of the ensuing interaction may then evoke a deep inner feeling of disappointment. Instead of being an indication of a doubtful prognosis, because it seemingly does not express a search for unconscious understanding, it may be a sign of the readiness for a regressive transference experience and have positive prognostic value.

This was reflected in the manifest dream of a young woman who had eagerly looked forward to her first appointment, had felt understood, but was surprised at the feeling of disappointment that enveloped her afterwards. That night she had a dream:

> I got a phone call from a friend excitedly describing some sea anemones that she wanted me to come over and see. I went, looked, saw the aquarium had lost its water, and they were drooping. I felt very disappointed.

The thought of making a new attachment had activated unconscious instinctual drives. The actual conditions of the treatment aroused a profound transference response to her infantile wishes not being realized. It was the beginning of an intense genital oedipal transference heralded in the manifest content.

The theme of being disappointed was also reflected in the following dreams of a 15-year-old boy after beginning treatment, but here it was the consequence of a lapse in empathy.

> I was in a train surrounded by war refugees. Everything was desolate. We came through a tunnel into the glitter of a modern, remodeled train station. It was all a sham, like leading people to a gas chamber. The refugees cried out in happiness and excitement, and I wandered off very sad.

After reporting the dream he was reminded of an earlier repetitive dream:

> I go to the freezer and all that was there were quick awful fast foods dressed up to look great. I angrily threw them out looking for good food. Another part of me was off to the side amused.

Both dreams symbolized the effects of strengthening false hopes by reenforcing a pathological defense, and hinted at the infantile traumas that had resulted from empathic failures. The despair of finding the unconscious understanding he was looking for was pictured in the first dream, while the second dream gave expression to his rage and revealed his characteristic style of using humor to ameliorate disturbing affects.

## Prognostic Implications in the Manifest Dream During Therapeutic Contact

The dream report is best understood within the overall context of the unfolding transference relationship, and its use must be consistent with the required conditions of the treatment situation. Interventions that facilitate the expression of contents in the deeper layers of the personality are called for, whereas those that reenforce a pathological defense are contraindicated. Having an accurate picture of the structural organization of the personality is of inestimable value in determining the answers to such complex questions as when to interpret and when to request associations to specific dream content. The manifest dream itself has the potential for providing this vital information, thereby guiding a therapist in how to utilize the dream to enhance the growth-promoting properties of the relationship.

The following dream is an example:

> I am alone in a beach house. Teenagers are having a party on the
> beach. They suddenly threaten to invade the house. As they try to
> enter, a man corrals them, talks to them, and I feel safe.

This manifest dream suggests that at those moments when the
dreamer is confronted with regressive, instinctually overstimulating
experiences, interpretive interventions are essential to enable a therapeutic regression to continue. Conversely, the following dream is
illustrative of a different message:

> My mother has come back to life. I am with her but she is sick and I'm
> trying to help. An older man is after me. I try to hide but he finds me.
> I went back to help my mother, but it was too late.

The manifest content represents a concerted effort to remain attached
to a maternal imago emerging from repression. The symbolic portrayal of
running from a figure trying to reach her interferes with this important
connection and implies that any active intervention by the therapist
would intensify her need for defense. It would therefore be inadvisable
to either ask for associations, interrupt the flow of material, or offer
interpretations prematurely.

It is always essential to keep in mind that a manifest dream is
representing unconscious forces seeking expression, and is thereby
dominated to a greater or lesser extent by defensive responses.
Unconscious instinctual drives cannot be determined directly from
the manifest content, but the dream imagery offers some guidance
for gaining access to these underlying repressed, infantile wishes.

A therapist's interventions can be a much needed source of
support, facilitating the expression of contents in the deeper layers of
the personality. They may interfere with the unfolding of the
regressive transferences necessary to accomplish this aim, or they may
be used to shore up defenses working in opposition to constructive
growth. A great deal depends upon the specific constellation of
intrapsychic forces most in the ascendency. A manifest dream can
provide information often unavailable through other means. The
following dreams are illustrative:

> I was on a tightwire feeling restless, like I wanted to move and
> couldn't. Out of the corner of my eye I could see a battlefield with
> explosions, shooting, and fighting. If I tried to look closer I might fall
> and my whole body shook.

The manifest content symbolically represented the dreamer's precarious position in relation to dangerous instinctual forces that could only be seen peripherally. His effort to look implied that he could use interpretive help in integrating inordinately threatening drive derivatives, and thereby alleviate the defensive immobilization.

I was trying to reach my parents to get some important information and every effort I made was interfered with by David Green. It was never clear who or where he was, but his presence was always in the way when I tried to make a phone call or to find my way there.

The symbolic imagery was a reflection of the therapist's interventions, distracting the dreamer from the process of recovering repressed infantile experiences. By implication, silence was the most facilitating attribute for furthering a therapeutic regression.

I was searching for something hidden—like a treasure hunt. It was extremely frustrating and I was very anxious. Then the dream shifted and I was in my bed at home. My mother came in to talk to me and climbed on top of me. I struggled to get free. It was intensely sexual and I was wondering about it. I was most frightened, not of the sexuality, but of being trapped.

The first dream segment, involving the search, depicted the frustration and anxiety associated with the attempt to recover what has been repressed. It instigated a shift to an intensely sexual attachment preventing freedom of movement. It appeared to capture the effects of reenforcing a pathological defense, which entrapped the dreamer within the confines of a fixed characterological position. In his sessions the dreamer was constantly striving to engage the therapist in interpreting the erotic meaning of his relationship with his mother, and periodically succeeded. His immediate association to the dream was a comment upon her presence being like a blanket covering up the frustration and anxiety of the first part of the dream. It emphasized the importance of allowing the buildup of frustration and anxiety when the therapist was silent, vividly showed how interpretations were being received, and implied that requesting associations would most likely have a similar effect.

Finally, the manifest dream may be an important indicator of the strength and solidity of the structural changes achieved in the course of treatment. It will then have prognostic significance in regard to continuing progress.

This was exemplified in the dream of a 35-year-old man who had originally sought psychotherapeutic help three years earlier because of an obsessive fear of contracting AIDS. He was constantly on the alert for possible symptoms, and terrified of contaminating his loved ones. His ability to function was almost totally disrupted by the ruminative, compulsive, ritualistic thinking that dominated every moment of his waking and sometimes sleeping life. On the eve of finishing his therapy he had a dream:

> I was in a chemistry lab pipetting blood samples by mouth. I accidentally took in some serum and was astonished at both the fact that I did it and my reaction in not being overcome or overwhelmed.

The internalization of an unseen, potentially dangerous object was symbolically represented in the imagery of the dream, reflecting his new found capacity to integrate the unseen aspects of instinctual experience. It was indicative of a functional, structured pathway of instinctual integration, which had previously been inordinately conflicted with no access to sublimatory activities or secondary autonomy. The dreamer's reaction to taking it in without being adversely affected was expressive of the stability of this structure and of the extent to which infantile, intrapsychic conflicts had been resolved. It boded well for ongoing self expansion.

The inclusion within the body of a manifest dream of symbolic references to guidelines for the conduct of a therapeutic relationship is in itself a positive prognostic sign. It is generally a product of the continuing viability of the thrust for developmental progression and the growth-promoting properties of an unconsciously empathic relationship.

# 5

# Perception and Dreaming

The manifest dream possesses another unique feature, placing it in a position of special importance among all psychic productions. This feature involves the differing perceptual agencies required in registering a dream and in communicating its form and content. Perceptual functions operate both at the surface and in the depths of the personality, and though they are apparently on a continuum, their characteristics are at variance. It is reminiscent of the changes in self observation during the course of a therapeutic regression, when advanced psychic functions are suspended. This suggests that the alterations in perception are the result of more regressive mental structures assuming dominance as they move to the forefront of psychic activity.

Phenomena such as a dream within a dream and the persistance of the dreaming state into waking life point to the existence of perceptual agencies sufficiently discrete as to be separate. Developmentally perceptual processes activate the representational and organizational functions of the ego, an interdependent relationship with mental structure formation evolves, and a self boundary is defined. The content of a manifest dream has the potential for illuminating the manner in which the self boundary is established and for explicating the specific mental structures that incorporate perceptual functions. One perceptual agency registers a dream, another is utilized to observe the contents remaining in memory, and the two acts of perception reflect the dynamic interplay of forces in the transition from sleep to wakefulness.

## From the Dream Experience to the Dream Report: The Relationship of Perception to Differing Self Boundaries

Dreams are highly symbolized mental productions registered by a discrete area of internally focused perceptual functioning, which, in turn, has an effect upon their form and content. The actual dream experience, the dream imagery, the way it is remembered upon awakening, the content as the dreamer organizes the memory, and what is reported are all mental constructs existing on a continuum. The initial dream experience and the final product, although extremely different in form and substance, have an obvious connection to each other. The connection is related to the nature of perception registering mental activity during sleep, and the perceptual functions involved in observing the end result.

The shifts and fluctuations in the qualities of perception reflect the presence of two distinctly separate, but intimately related, perceptual agencies. One is an area of consolidated perceptual activity within the conscious system organized at the surface of the personality, the other is a consolidated area of perceptual activity within the preconscious system organized in the deeper layers. These two focuses of perception maintain continuity with each other, are monitored by regulatory principles consonant with the predominant mental structures operating in each locale, and possess the capacity for registering mental impressions consistent with the functions that are available. The movement from the dream experience to the formation of the manifest dream to reporting what is observed reflects the transition from a regressive perceptual agency, functioning in the deeper layers, toward the advanced function of self observation at the surface of the personality. The traversal of this perceptual pathway is accompanied by an increasing accessibility of integrative ego functions.

The changes that take place from the dream experience to the remembered manifest dream are largely due to and determined by these differing qualities of perception. They are not necessarily the consequence of a continuing need for defense. This is best illustrated by considering the significance of the dreamer whose self image is portrayed in a dream. A well-delineated visual representation of a dreaming self is registered, with a variety of symbolic representations localized outside this self boundary. These same psychic contents are contained within a self boundary in a waking state in nonsymbolic forms, which indicates that the self in a dream and the self in wakefulness have a different boundary.

The functioning of perceptual processes is inextricably bound to and interrelated with mental structure formation from the outset of development. With each advance in psychic structuralization, perceptual functions participate in establishing an ever-expanding self boundary. The outlines of the self in a waking state encompass the most advanced functions predominant, which are suspended in the regression induced by sleep. Consequently, more primitively organized psychic structures rise to the ascendancy in sleep, and their incorporated perceptual functions establish the boundary of a sleeping and dreaming self.

The exceptions are seen in individuals manifesting severe developmental arrests and primitively organized personalities. In this situation a regressive mode of functioning predominates during waking life. Limited forays into advanced levels of psychic organization are present but incapable of being sustained under stress or adaptive demand, and they rise to the forefront in sleep. Under these circumstances the severity of the pathology interferes with the interweaving and continuity of perceptual functions, making their role in defining a self boundary more explicit and noticeable.

This aspect of the dreaming process was revealed by a 25-year-old woman who suffered acutely from the impact primitive splitting mechanisms had on her ability to lead a full and productive life. She was terrified of intimacy in a relationship, was drawn to extremely destructive interactions to reinforce uncaring, unfeeling attitudes, and soft, tender facets of herself were thereby made more distant and inaccessible. While describing her despair of ever realizing these valued attributes she reported a dream:

I was with two cats. One was a cold, callous, unfeeling alley cat that drifted off into the night. The other was a tender cat with a human face that I tried to push away, encouraging it to go with the first cat. It persisted in staying with me, and I gave it strict rules to follow if it was going to remain. The cat's face became more and more human as it conformed to my rules.

She associated the two cats with the two parts of herself and felt sad that the tender cat lost its identity by conforming to her strict rules. She remembered a second dream:

I was observing a figure in the distance, felt strongly drawn toward it, and was terrified I would be pulled inside and lose myself. I had the thought that it was only a dream and I could wake up and be myself. To be absorbed in the other figure only meant I was trying to reach a part of myself I had lost contact with.

Her primitive level of psychic structuralization was revealed in the fear of loss of differentiation. It was only under the special conditions of sleep that she could allow this movement toward approaching the split off and vulnerable aspects of her good self experience. The advanced mode of perception characteristic of self observation at the surface of the personality could not be suspended with the regression induced by sleep and continued to be operative in defining the boundary of her self in the dream. The idea of losing herself by being drawn inside a distant figure gave expression to the existence of a regressive mode of perception, and to the lack of continuity in her personality. It also suggested that the regressive self boundary was not structured enough to sustain a separate image.

The infantile origins of psychic contents observed outside the dreaming self are highlighted by the process of symbolization. These same elements exist within the waking self but their derivations are in a less recognizable form.

This was graphically portrayed in the dream of a 5-year-old boy, referred for treatment due to night terrors arising in response to his parents' divorce. He was constantly preoccupied with emphasizing his strength and prowess: he reassured himself endlessly of his invulnerability and repeatedly commented upon his bravery and fearlessness. Periodically, infantile longings would surface and immediately precipitate a loud protest that he could do everything himself. Separations elicited tears, angry attempts to deny their presence, irritability, and hostile interactions designed to justify his attitude. His great distress led him to identifying these tearful longings as his "baby parts," which he wanted to leave with the therapist so they would no longer plague him. He appeared greatly relieved when the therapist welcomed his "baby parts" and agreed to hold them until he was ready to have them back. Shortly afterward he reported a dream:

I was lying in my bed and my nightmares jumped right out of my head and into the closet. The first was a big monster. I got my sword, attacked him, and he began to cry. I was surprised, put him in my bed, and he became my friend. Just then a second nightmare jumped out of my head. This one scared me. He was a big angry tiger and he ate up all my toys.

He spontaneously stated that he thought the nightmares were like his "baby parts"; he was trying to take them back but there just wasn't enough room.

The imagery in the dream delineated the perceptual pathway by which various aspects of self experience are extruded when the boundary of the self is regressively narrowed. The therapeutic relationship was making it possible to integrate increasing dimensions of instinctual activity, though he was having particular difficulty with oral aggressive drive derivatives. The first "nightmare" symbolically represented archaic prohibitions, which were inordinately threatening when he was awake. The regression induced by sleep established a different self boundary, and with it this nightmare moved out of his head into the closet. From a regressed position he was able to face the danger, achieve some degree of mastery, and the nightmare was brought closer to him as an ally. It still remained outside the boundary of a dreaming self, but no longer possessed threatening properties. At this point, another nightmare, symbolically representing oral greed, was extruded. This instinctual figure could only be perceived at a distance and was extremely frightening, and the dream could only continue by virtue of his ability to represent its devouring qualities.

## The Origin of the Perceptual Agencies Involved with Registering and Reporting the Dream Experience

I have previously described the interrelationship of perceptual processes and mental structure formation, the manner in which perception functions to establish the expanding boundary of the self, and the evolution of two separate but continuous perceptual agencies operating as a foundation for the function of self observation (Mendelsohn 1987). The eye of consciousness is the predominant perceptual agency operating at the surface of the personality. It is regulated by the reality principle, and is consonant with the conditions of secondary process thinking. The superego eye is the predominant perceptual agency operating in the deeper layers of the personality. It is regulated by the pleasure principle and is subject to the conditions of primary process thinking.

The function of self observation initially evolved with the internal search for, and discovery of, a separate good object's influence. This developmental event takes place during the key period of separation and individuation, resulting in the formation of new mental structures and a more advanced level of psychic organization. It represents a step forward in self differentiation, leading to the anchoring of object constancy. The boundary of the self is expanded by extending perception, which is a facet of good self experience, to include the mental impressions of a separate good object. The representation of this recognition is structured to support a focused area of internally directed perceptual attention, the eye of consciousness, thereby establishing a foundation for the function of self observation.

This consolidated area of perceptual activity, based upon the search for a separate good object's influence, necessitates the inward direction of perceptual attention. The extension of self experience is identified as the introjective arm of perception, since it is the pathway for internalizing and registering the stimuli of the external world. The connection to the impressions of an object is identified as the projective arm of perception, since it is the pathway to the influences of an object. The projective arm of perception is stabilized by the formation of a fixation point, based upon an awareness of the good object's bad prohibitive qualities. This fixation point functions as the cornerstone for ensuring object constancy by sustaining a differentiated bond to the influences of an object and must be maintained throughout the life cycle. The stability it provides is necessary to allow phase and stage specific needs to be the determining factor in the timing and composition of new mental structure formation and to assure the firmness of structural unions between the self and object. Separation and individuation is accomplished through the recognition of a separate good object, but in the early stages the pull of fusion and merger becomes dominant under stress or fatigue and the differentiated linkage is lost. The awareness of a good object's bad qualities, through a line of continuity of prohibitive experience, places differentiation on a secure foundation and solidifies object constancy.

In forming the eye of consciousness, the structured remnants of reactions to impingement are an obstacle that must be bypassed to discover the impressions of a good object. These defensive self experiences are associated with a focus of attention directed toward the external world. The eye of consciousness thereby possesses two borders. One is internally directed and patterned after the internal search for a good object, the other is externally directed and patterned after the alertness to impingments from the external world. Initially, the eye of consciousness has a greater capacity to register the influences of an object, since attention is focused in that direction. Later, when mental structures are formed to unite and differentiate the representations of self and object, they incorporate these perceptual borders, and attention is directed into the self system.

A mental structure is composed of a relatively permanent differentiated union between representations of the self and object, with fantasy elaborations that are capable of this degree of cohesion serving as the linkage. The first mental structure is formed to balance the vulnerability and helplessness associated with separateness. It is instinctual in nature, since it requires the binding function of libido to establish an effective union. Good instinctual self experience is linked to the fantasy of a good instinctual object and structuralized, incorporating the inwardly and outwardly directed perceptual functions. This structure can be called the grandiose self because it involves participation in a fantasy.

The resulting depletion in adaptive capacities and disturbance in instinctual balance motivates the formation of a second structure based upon selective identifications. Deficient self potentials are elaborated in fantasy and linked to the qualities of an object that are needed and admired, again incorporating the inwardly and outwardly directed perceptual functions. This structure can be called the ego ideal because it involves including the influences of an admired object within self experience. These two unifying and differentiating structures, the grandiose self and ego ideal, are the precursors of an organizing superego. They form the boundaries within which the superego can ultimately develop into an independently functioning agency. Their incorporated perceptual functions are consolidated to register mental impressions from deeper within the personality. This focus of perceptual attention can be referred to as the superego eye.

The superego eye exists on a line of continuity with the eye of consciousness. It is capable of registering contents of the transition from the unconscious to preconscious when directed inward, and of the superficial layers of the preconscious when directed outward. The eye of consciousness is firmly structured at the surface of the personality closest to perceptual contact with the external world, and is predominant in registering the mental contents of the conscious system. The superego eye outlines the boundary within which the superego is organizing, and is predominant in registering the mental contents of the preconscious system. The eye of consciousness and superego eye, although functioning in discrete sectors of the personality, possess continuity with each other. The interrelationship is initially mediated by the fixation point in the object system and the grandiose self and ego ideal; later by character defenses and the superego.

## The Fixation Points

The fixation point on the projective arm of perception stabilizes the system of object representations, and the grandiose self and ego ideal are structured to strengthen cohesiveness. The grandiose self balances the vulnerability of separateness at the expense of depleting adaptive capacities. The ego ideal utilizes selective identifications to strengthen self experience. When increasing degrees of regulation are necessary, the prohibitive influences of a bad object can be included. This process of identification with an aggressor is an early phase of superego organization, at the foundation of reaction formations, and an integral part of the formation of character defenses.

Structuring the ego ideal directs perceptual attention into the self system. A fixation point is established on the introjective arm of perception, based upon a recognition of the good self's bad instinctual qualities. The introjective arm of perception has had to remain open and unobstructed by the effects of memory during the pregenital period in order to register the experiences necessary to enable developmental progression. In health, a fixation point in the self system is only transiently maintained during the period of oedipal organization to create the stability required for structuring the transition from narcissism to object relatedness. With the resolution of the oedipal conflict, instinctual demands that have previously been overstimulating are integrated, and the fixation point is relinquished. Consequently, stimuli from the external world can be registered without the distorting influence of memory, and the effects of unseen objects can be represented for the first time.

The fixation point in the object system must be continuously maintained, and in health expands through the advancing phases of psychosexual development. It is then strengthened and freed from its exclusively infantile attachment by a gradual process of depersonification. Eventually, it is replaced by memory traces of new and independent attachments. The result is in the dominance of a conflict-free sphere within the ego, operating in harmony with an independently functioning superego.

Structuring the ego ideal directs perceptual attention into the self system. The fixation point that is established is based upon the memory traces of pregenital instinctual overstimulation. Enough stability is provided for the genital oedipal fantasies to flourish and form new object related structures. The oedipal conflict is resolved through selective identifications, and the superego is consolidated to operate in harmony with the interests of the ego. These advances in development are reflected in the functioning of the eye of consciousness and the superego eye.

Perceptual functions are monitored by the superego. The nature of the mental contents being perceived gives an indication of the predominant perceptual agency in the ascendancy. Immediate perceptions, depersonified mental impressions, ideational symbolizations, and internal language occupy the conscious system and are observed by the eye of consciousness. Regressive memories, fantasy images, instinctual derivatives, and the derivatives of unconscious perceptions occupy the preconscious system and are observed by the superego eye.

The fixation point in the object system is expanded through undergoing a process of depersonification in which a good object's bad prohibitive qualities are symbolized in a form that parallels the infantile attachment. Object constancy is thereby strengthened and the exclusive attachment to an infantile object is loosened. The groundwork is prepared for infantile attachments to be replaced by attachments to new and independent objects. The fixation point in the self system is gradually relinquished in concert with the resolution of the oedipal conflict. The infantile experiences of instinctual overstimulation on which it is based no longer require defense, have attained secondary autonomy, and are available for sublimatory activities.

In the neurotic disorders, pregenital development has not been synchronous with stage and phase specificity, which in turn affects the composition and function of the fixation points, the grandiose self and ego ideal, the structure of castration anxiety, and the configuration of the oedipal conflict. The fixation points remain tied to their infantile origins and are at the foundation of fixed character traits and pathological defenses. The structural precursors of the superego are not adequately consolidated and operate in opposition to the interests of the ego. Castration anxiety is harshly prohibitive, and the new object related structures formed by oedipal fantasies are inordinately conflicted. The interrelationship between the two perceptual agencies at the surface and interior of the personality is subsequently interfered with by these defensive responses. It creates a barrier to the smooth transition from one to the other which occurs in conjunction with regressive movements. In nonneurotic disorders, either fixation points are highly unstable and incapable of successfully monitoring a controlled regression, or continuity of experience and cohesiveness have not been established and fixation points are nonfunctional. Splitting mechanisms predominate, and the function of self observation is severely impaired or deficient.

The perceptual function of the eye of consciousness is predominant in the waking state and participates in defining the boundary of an enlarged and complete self. The perceptual function of the superego eye is predominant in the act of dreaming and participates in defining the boundary of a more regressive self. When the function of the eye of consciousness is suspended, as occurs in sleep and dreaming, the superego eye assumes dominance. What then constitutes a self is encompassed within that perceptual agency. The other elements in a dream are the mental contents that have undergone a process of symbolization and are registered by the superego eye. This more regressive mode of perception, in conjunction with the process of symbolization, registers these psychic productions in a form that is closer to their infantile roots.

The contents of the conscious system display the effects of the secondary process and emerge as people, events, dialogue, and defined structures. The contents closer to the boundary of the unconscious system display the effects of the primary process and emerge as primitive, symbolic representations showing the influence of infantile experience. The very same contents are registered by the eye of consciousness and are altered because of the advanced functions to which they are exposed. The contents of the unconscious system cannot be observed directly, since they reside within a non-perceptual boundary. They are only identifiable by inference from the derivatives they evoke.

## The Interrelationship between the Eye of Consciousness and Superego Eye

The perceptual agencies involved in registering a dream and in remembering and reporting it, although they exist on a line of continuity with one another, possess different and distinct properties. This is best exemplified by the manner in which a self boundary is defined within the context of the dream imagery and the manner in which it is defined in the waking state. The shift from one to the other is involved in moving from dreaming to waking and becomes more discrete as the dream is remembered and reconstructed. This interrelationship is sometimes reflected in the dream itself, when the dreamer is aware of both dreaming and observing.

The following dream was introduced by a young man with the statement that it had been remarkably clear and distinct:

I am with a girl who I know is going to die. It has something to do with the X-ray machines in an airport terminal. The dream shifts and I am with the same girl. I know she will die within three weeks. I make plans to be with her and she dies. At the same time I am dreaming, I am watching the dream from above. In the dream I am also trying to figure out what it means.

The dreamer made reference to the two perceptual agencies and their role in defining a self boundary by describing his position of being in the dream and at the same time observing and trying to understand its meaning. The advanced psychic functions associated with the eye of consciousness had not been fully suspended in the course of falling asleep. The more regressed superego eye registered the dream while still affected by their activity. The dreamer, in not relinquishing these advanced psychic functions, is indicating a fear of regression and has instituted a highly defensive response.

The readiness with which the functions of the eye of consciousness are carried into the dream to become intertwined with the functions of the superego eye gives expression to either an absence or ineffectiveness of character defenses. Character defenses are based on the memory traces of pregenital attachments to an object and pregenital instinctual experience, and when inordinately active stand as an obstacle to the smooth transition from one perceptual agency to the other. The manner in which the eye of consciousness and superego eye are interrelated in this dream can either be the consequence of highly unstable fixation points incapable of supporting well structured character defenses or the result of the undoing of well-established character defenses during the course of a benign, therapeutic regression.

The symbolic representation of the loss of an object is indicative of repressive, defensive responses being emphasized. This suggests that in this situation character defenses are not operative because of a lack of sufficient structuralization leading to the need for advanced functions to serve a defensive purpose during the process of dreaming. The eye of consciousness is thereby accessible to the regressive mental structures involved in constructing the dream, two separate images of the dreamer are represented, and the regression is effectively curtailed.

The interrelationship between the eye of consciousness and superego eye is also in evidence on those occasions when, in recalling a dream, the dreamer has the sensation of being drawn into the confines of the dream. The threat is of losing self differentiation as it is known in the waking state while being pulled toward what has been a self in dreaming. It sheds light on the role of the structures that support self observation in creating a self boundary, since the eye of consciousness is based upon perceptual functions embodied in structuring self object differentiation. Conversely, the representation of the self in a dream gives an indication of how firmly consolidated the superego has become.

The superego eye, founded upon regressive structures, is more subject to the distorting effects of defense, making it consonant with the needs of the dream work. Therefore, when the feelings in a dream are carried into waking life, it may augur an out-of-control regression.

The following dream of a young woman beginning treatment is an example. She awoke in the middle of the night crying. The feelings from the dream persisted, and they continued to encompass her as she entered the session.

I was in a totalitarian society facing a firing squad. I was shot a number of times and could feel myself dying. The dream changed and I was in a place where I could see a light through a window. As I was dying, I said that my boyfriend and parents were the most important things in my life. I died and awoke crying.

The perceptual agency registering the dream is the same agency most dominant in the midst of a regression. The eye of consciousness, an integral part of advanced psychic functions, is under the dominance of the reality principle and is a facet of secondary process thinking. The superego eye, an integral part of more regressed psychic functions, is under the dominance of the pleasure principle and a facet of primary process thinking. The two perceptual agencies are on a line of continuity. As the function of one is in the forefront, the other is dormant. The eye of consciousness is gradually suspended in a free associative process, secondary process thinking gives way to more regressive mental imagery, and the superego eye is highlighted as the predominant agency of perception. Character defenses function to obviate against this regressive movement by forming a firm barrier between the two perceptual agencies, creating distance between the emotional and intellectual aspects of an experience.

In this case study, treatment had just been initiated. The dreamer emphasized the retention of the dream experience, and hints that a regression is threatening to get out of control. It points to an absence, instability, or ineffectiveness of character defenses and calls attention to the status of the two perceptual agencies. Narcissistic disturbances consistently display this lack of demarcation because character defenses are not well structured or are highly unstable. An individual's capacity to regulate a regression is roughly equivalent to the extent to which the interrelationship between the eye of consciousness and superego eye can be monitored.

When psychoanalytic treatment has successfully intervened with character defenses, one consequence is in the ready shift from an advanced to a regressed perceptual modality. At the height of a transference neurosis, this phenomenon is anticipated. There is a long period of time during which character defenses are gradually relinquished, the interrelationship between the eye of consciousness and superego eye then flow freely, primal scene fantasies and integrative functions are extremely active, and a benign regression is in evidence. A benign regression, if well regulated, facilitates the discovery of previously defended and repressed psychic content, is an integral part of a transference neurosis, and enables the dissolution of character defenses.

A free associative process fosters the suspension of advanced psychic functions associated with the eye of consciousness, enabling the perceptual agency of the superego eye to become ascendant. When the superego eye is predominant, dream imagery can be more readily traced to latent dream thoughts, and the distortions are accessible to integrate psychoanalytic work. Fixed character attitudes serve a defensive function by maintaining stability under conditions of instinctual overstimulation and obstruct continuity between the eye of consciousness and superego eye.

The regression induced by sleep, together with the lack of reenforcement from stimuli of the external world, substantially reduces the effectiveness of pathological defenses and the degree of stability they offer.

> This function of character pathology was dramatically exhibited in an old dream recalled by an 8-year-old girl who had been sent for therapeutic help for a number of hysterical symptoms she referred to as "growing pains." She gave them this name because it felt like something was trying to grow but met opposition, causing her pain. The therapeutic relationship gradually lessened the need for her pregenitally structured character defenses, genital instinctual drive derivatives emerged, and she remembered a dream that had stayed in her mind since the age of 4.

> This wild and excited girl jumped right out of my chest, and I just floated and bumped into the furniture. I couldn't regain my balance.

> She was intrigued with the idea that her balance was secure as long as the girl remained inside her. It was only when she moved outside the boundary of her dreaming self that the ability to remain steady was weakened. The image of a wild and excited girl captured the essence of instinctual impulses, which provoked a need for character defenses and underscored their relationship to the perceptual agency registering the dream. This symbolic representation of instinctual overstimulation was ejected from within a self boundary and with it the need for character defenses dissolved. The dream imagery then reflected the consequence of losing its stabilizing effects. She went on to describe the way events in a dream are perceived, stating that she could see both better and worse

in a dream. "It's like looking with your eyes squinting"; a single object could be seen more distinctly at the expense of blocking out a wider view.

## The Significance of a Nightmare

A nightmare signifies that in the state of dreaming the ability to institute defense has reached its limit, and the only avenue available is to invoke a new set of perceptual boundaries. The superego eye, registering the dream and establishing the dreamer's self boundary, does not have the advanced functions associated with the eye of consciousness readily available. The unconscious forces giving impetus to the dream are beyond the capacity to regulate their intensity; the level of anxiety reaches panic proportions, the dreamer's self integrity is threatened, and it becomes necessary to bring into play the advanced functions that have been suspended in sleep. It is important to identify the circumstances creating this traumatic situation in order to illuminate the therapeutic task.

The following dream reported by a young woman is an example. She referred to it as a nightmare.

I was in a foreign country in a hotel built inside of a cliff. It was a very steep path down, although it was covered by foliage and flowers. I was a captive in the hotel and they wouldn't let me go. I kept trying to leave, but couldn't. Then there was something about John Lennon letting me know he was sexually available to me, and I awoke in a state of panic.

The unconscious instinctual wishes fueling the dream were able to be represented symbolically until a specific point was reached. The mental structures upon which the manifest dream rested were not in jeopardy. There was sufficient material accessible in the preconscious system to continue the dream work until genital instinctual demands entered the picture. At this juncture the degree of instinctual regulation required to allow the dreaming process to continue was no longer adequate, the integrity of the dreaming self was endangered, and the high level of anxiety invoked the need to introduce more advanced psychic functions by awakening the dreamer.

Enough of a genital consolidation of the component instincts was available to represent the nature of the threat, but it was not on firm enough ground to continue the dream. The ensuing state of panic could only be contained within the expanded self boundary established by the eye of consciousness. It was indicative of the dreamer moving toward an advance in development without the defensive wherewithal to manage the associated increase in instinctual activity.

A nightmare may also result when there has been an extreme narcissistic injury such as occurs with an illness or accident. The impact upon bodily processes may then occupy the center of perceptual attention, depleting the capacity to regulate instinctual demands. A breakdown of bodily processes, or a body reaction to invasive illness, is then often experienced and represented as a threat to self integrity, eliciting a dream with nightmare qualities. The unconscious perception of this body ego experience may then serve as the nidus of a dream and at times be an early indicator of the disturbance in bodily function.

This was demonstrated in a young male exhibiting the tenaciously held, anally derived, fixed attitudes of obsessive character pathology. Intellectualizations and the overuse of mechanisms of isolation supported the effectiveness of repression. Over a period of time he had dreams symbolically representing instinctual dangers, usually in the form of distant battles or explosions, but there was never an inordinate degree of anxiety or any indication of a dream being interrupted as a consequence of inadequate regulation. He developed a symptom of numbness in his fingers that was inconsistent with the structural organization of his personality, and at the same time he had a series of dreams in which he was in a leaking boat, awakening in a state of panic. Neurological examination showed a leaking vertebral artery, which was then surgically repaired.

Individuals who have not attained sufficient superego consolidation for it to function independently, and who are thereby excessively dependent upon external objects for regulation, may have a nightmare when there is an impending loss or separation from a loved object.

This was exhibited in the dream of an 8-year-old girl referred for treatment because of severe obsessive rituals interfering primarily with her school performance, but also affecting all facets of her life. Overt signs of difficulty were first noticed, at the age of 4, after the birth of a brother, when she became sullen, hostile, and intensely jealous. The following dream took place just prior to a two-day trip away from home and after a session in which she talked at length of a visiting cousin who had usurped parental attention, making her feel left out, angry, and sad.

I was in a car driving with my mother, feeling pleased my brother wasn't there. A robber appeared at the window with a gun in his hand.

My mother screamed. We were able to drive on, but the farther we went the more robbers we ran into. Then I was in a room. My mother was all taped up looking like she was dead. I ran looking for my father to get help, couldn't find him, became panicky, and woke up scared with my heart beating fast.

The dream implicitly reflected her wish to retain exclusive possession of the mother, in the image of being with her in an enclosed space. It also eliminated competition from the hated younger brother, expressed directly through the pleasure at his absence. The dreamer was then confronted with an escalating series of hostile, dangerous, impinging objects, threatening both herself and the mother. An attempt to escape this mounting threat of aggression was symbolically represented and eventually led to the immobilization and implied destruction of the mother. The frantic search for, and inability to find, the comforting presence of the father represented a last ditch effort to contain the eruption of unmanageable instinctual activity. The regressive state of sleep was then disrupted, instituting a new perceptual position with an expanded self boundary and enabling more advanced functions to be accessible.

The arousal of anal sadistic impulses directed against the hated, rivalrous figure of the brother was being actively but ineffectively defended against, with any protective influence included in the parental imagoes immobilized and unavailable. The anticipation of the impending separation was evocative of the loss of external reenforcement of her defensive posture, revealed her deficiencies in instinctual regulation, and contributed to the nightmare situation in the dream.

Extreme empathic lapses in a therapeutic situation may have the same effect upon the dreaming process. A failure in empathy can generally be symbolically represented, and the foundation of unconscious perceptions registering their impact is usually firm enough to support a dream. A particularly destructive, impinging lapse in empathy, however, may so undermine the containing influences in the personality that an imbalance is created, making lower intensities of instinctual demand potentially traumatic.

## Dreaming and Other Regressive Experiences

The function of self observation is accomplished by two separate, distinct areas of internally directed perceptual activity on a line of continuity with each other, whose harmonious interrelationship is interfered with by any stimulus invoking an inordinate need for defense. In the more primitively organized personality, these areas of perceptual functioning may be impaired or incompletely developed, which is reflected in the body of a dream. The registration of the dreaming process, and the reporting of the end product retained in consciousness, gives expression to the interrelationship of these perceptual agencies and of the structural foundations upon which they operate.

This was strikingly exemplified in a dream reported by a 37-year-old woman responding to the regressive pull induced by a therapeutic regression:

I am in a leaking boat. The boat sinks and I feel myself on top of the water. I can use all of my resources to swim when I feel the tide pulling me down. I fight very hard to stay on top so I can retain my ability to swim. I am terrified I will be overcome, lose my ability to function as I am pulled down, and eventually be suffocated and drown. All of a sudden I realized it was best to not fight, to go to the bottom, conserve my strength, and then push off to return to the top. I do that, am drawn to the bottom and mobilize my resources to push myself back. I reach the top, and as I do, my ability to swim returns. I break the surface of the water and feel able to breathe, relaxed, and confident.

The dreamer is symbolically representing the advanced psychic functions available at the surface of the personality, embodied in the sensations and imagery at the surface of the water. The regressive pull is accompanied by the threat of losing these functional capacities, eliciting a fear of being drawn into the loss of a self boundary. The manifest content expresses the recognition that moving into the the depths of the personality requires a regression. In addition, instead of being enveloped by the regressive structures in operation at that locale, the dreamer is able to reinstitute the advanced structures held in suspension. In this way a regression can be instructive, can be encompassed rather than enveloping, and can facilitate growth. A continuous interplay between the two perceptual agencies, and the ability to move from one to the other, is essential for both the processes involved in a therapeutic regression and the regressive conditions embodied in dreaming.

Regressive transference experiences occurring during waking life are accentuated in a psychoanalytically conducted treatment relationship and possess many of the underlying characteristics of a manifest dream. This is especially apparent when a transference neurosis has evolved, since the processes utilized in the dream work of transforming an unconscious force into representational imagery are also at work in constructing this new edition of an infantile conflict. Condensation, displacement, representation, and secondary revision are all involved. The therapeutic task is similar. The differences concern the greater emotional distance when reporting a manifest dream, whereas a transference neurosis is immediate and much like a waking dream

The act of suspending the eye of consciousness in a therapeutic regression facilitates the ascendancy of the superego eye. All experience is then registered by this more regressive perceptual agency. It is also involved with registering a dream, and is behind the similarity between a dream, regressive experience, and a transference neurosis. The concept of transference as an intrapsychic process in which an unconscious impulse is transferred across a repressive barrier onto a preconscious day residue fits all of these situations. Differences are created by the mental structures accessible in sleep, in wakefulness, and at varying levels of regression. These regressive events all lend themselves to revealing their structural composition in varying degrees. The manifest dream is unique in this regard because it comes closest to giving a more accurate portrayal of the original infantile experiences at its foundation.

# 6

# The Day Residue

A consistent and noteworthy component of a manifest dream is the day residue. When this representation of a current life experience is examined closely, it meets the criteria of a derivative of the unconscious perception of an emotionally important event.

Unconscious perceptions are based upon the structured representations of good self experience, which provide the stability and containment essential for supporting advances in self differentiation. Their derivatives are thereby anchored to the foundation of the personality. They are stable enough to enable the dream work to be accomplished and to retain the end product in consciousness with the attribute of a memory.

The internal sense of having dreamt, with no available content, can be easily explained as a consequence of repression. Although this explanation is readily validated from the frequency with which unremembered dreams are recovered when defensive opposition is alleviated, other dreams are never recalled even under conditions where resistance and repression are at a low enough level to expect their emergence. It raises a question as to whether dreams incapable of being retained have a slightly different composition than a remembered dream, suggesting that they utilize preconscious contents without including a day residue and are inaccessible with the transition to wakefulness.

The day residue seems to be a necessary ingredient to serve as the nidus around which a dream is constructed, in order for it to be retained in consciousness. Because it consists of the derivative of an unconscious perception, the manifest dream represents "the truth of reality" and the dreamer experiences "the reality of truth." This does not mean distortions are not created by the dream work, but that the focal point centers around an unconscious truth.

## Dreams and the Therapeutic Relationship

During the time that I was becoming aware of the powerful impact of the therapeutic relationship on a patient's unconscious perceptions, I noticed that the way in which conditions of psychoanalytic treatment were introduced had a profound effect. Sometimes the effect determined the entire course of the treatment. This was particularly evident in regard to the fundamental principle of free association, for when it was presented as instruction or suggestion it violated the essence of the principle itself. Instructions immediately become authoritative and are unconsciously perceived as demanding conformity, whereas suggestions have a seductive quality and are unconsciously perceived with distrust. Individuals manifesting nonneurotic transferences reacted negatively, revealing directly the absence of unconsciously empathic responsiveness when the conditions of treatment were presented in this fashion. Individuals manifesting neurotic transferences expressed similar reactions, but in a more subtle fashion, primarily through derivatives. When these derivatives of their unconscious perceptions were treated like transference fantasy distortions, the whole thrust of the ensuing relationship was occupied with conflicts around autonomy, seductiveness, and submission to authority. Resolution was made difficult because of the consonance with similar attitudes on the part of the therapist, which then dominated the treatment situation.

It became apparent that this basic principle, operating as a cornerstone for the uniqueness of psychoanalytic treatment, was best introduced through the vehicle of the therapist's manner of participation. The consequence was to foster a therapeutic alliance that consisted of a bond of mutual purpose between the patient's unconscious perceptions of the growth-promoting factors in a relationship and the therapist's unconsciously empathic interpretations and management of the framework. Broadening the concept of transference to include unconscious perceptions, expressed through derivatives, provided a means for applying the basic principles of psychoanalysis across a wider range of pathology. The author's increasing recognition of this important phenomenon gradually led to a change in how the conditions of psychoanalytic treatment were defined and presented (Mendelsohn 1987). The author no longer presented the fundamental rule as a direction to report all available psychic content without exercising censorship or judgment, first, because it placed the groundwork of treatment on an illusory basis since it was impossible to follow, and second, because it contained the emotional atmosphere of authority and depended upon submission or conformity for its success. These were the very attitudes it was important to eliminate in order to create the proper conditions for a therapeutic regression. Therefore, he adopted a listening posture and introduced the principle of free association by interpreting unconscious messages to encourage this mode of communication.

In the midst of this change in approach, a 31-year-old man sought help with what he initially described as a mild case of impotence. It later emerged that he had been suffering from total ejaculatory impotence, and the humiliation was so extreme he could only barely admit it to himself. The early sessions were filled with his frantic, escalating pleas for direction and guidance. He constantly complained about a lack of defined purpose, and angrily insisted that left to his own devices, he would travel in never-ending circles leading him to an overwhelming state of frustration and despair. These demands were understood and interpreted to be an expression of his fear of regressing, of following his spontaneous associations, and of some as yet unspoken fantasies concerning the therapeutic relationship. The patient's loud protest against what was consciously experienced as a lack of guidance stirred doubts, questions, and uncertainty about the efficacy of this method. It mobilized concern that the treatment might be more effectively conducted under the standard, classical psychoanalytic position of presenting explicit and clearly stated directions. At this point he reported a dream:

> I was traveling on a road, lost and confused, desperately needing to get to Williamsburg. At first the road was deserted, but I noticed a raggedy-looking hobo standing at the side of the road. He appeared familiar with the surroundings and was seemingly at home. I asked for directions to my destination. He simply replied that I should follow the road. I saw many roads and asked which one. With quiet conviction he told me to take any road, they would all get me there; I was surprised that my fear lessened, and I knew he was right.

The dream reflected his unconscious perception of the therapist's attitude and although he attempted within the context of the dream to depreciate and devalue the therapist, its correctness in leading him toward the center of himself was portrayed. The town he was searching for carried his own name, and the dream gave some assurance that the treatment was embarking on the right track.

Psychoanalytic clinicians have long noted the consistency with which dreams contain some overt feature displaying the influence of the treatment relationship. There are times when it is elusive and has to be inferred, but on almost all occasions it can be found. It may involve a symbolic reference to some aspect of a therapist's name, a particular facet of the therapist's personality or physical characteristics, an attribute of the therapeutic relationship, or a specific property of the surrounding environment. These are generally interpreted to represent transference manifestations incorporated into the body of the dream, and though not always identified as such, fit the description of the derivative of an unconscious perception. Frequently, they are identified as the day residue, while on other occasions they are seemingly unrelated to a current life experience.

Upon closer inspection, the psychic contents serving as the day residue invariably show a direct or indirect symbolic attribute of the treatment relationship. Their presence is so constant, it suggests that they play an essential role in the construction of a remembered dream. Recent dream psychophysiological studies have pointed to the vast amount of dreaming and the small number that are retained. The discrepancy cannot be adequately explained on the basis of repression, although it has been demonstrated often that many dreams return when defensive opposition is alleviated. Nevertheless, these dreams also include the derivatives of an unconscious perception. The day residue, rather than representing an insignificant event, turns out to depict an experience of contact with the external world that is either hurtful or enhancing. A day residue thus refers to an event having had a powerful emotional impact that is unconsciously perceived and expressed in this derivative form.

In practice, every clinician is acquainted with the influence of unconscious perceptions on a manifest dream, but their role in dream formation has not been fully appreciated. In part this has been due to the absence of a theoretical substrate on which to distinguish between transference distortions based upon fantasy and unconscious perceptions based upon body ego experience. Although all mental events are multidetermined and exposed to numerous influences, ultimately it is the manner in which they are perceived that has the most potential for revealing the forces that shaped their formation and those that continue to affect them. Perceptual processes activate the representational and organizational functions of the ego, determine the composition of the body ego experiences and object impressions that are registered and represented, and play an integral role in establishing the self boundary within which these mental contents are contained. In order to understand the role of unconscious perceptions in the construction of a manifest dream, and how the day residue must consist of their derivatives, it is essential to trace unconscious perceptions to their very beginnings.

## The Developmental Line of Unconscious Perceptions

The nuclear self emerges with the dawning of perceptual functions during intrauterine life. The stimuli of the intrauterine environment, in combination with the stimuli emanating from biophysiological demands, are registered by the anlage of perceptual processes and begin to delineate a primordial self boundary. The boundary is limited by the nature of perception and by the ego's capacity to represent it.

Initially the ego is a body ego and each perceptual activity arouses its dual functions of representing a stimulus as a mental impression, and of organizing mental impressions into an identifiable unit. Distant receptors such as hearing and sight have a low capacity to evoke representational functions, whereas close receptors such as touch, taste, and smell have a high capacity. Close receptors have little effect upon organizing functions, and the stimuli are represented under primitive conditions with an inability to organize them as emanating from a given source. The mental representation of these primitive perceptual activities then gradually coalesces according to the nature of the stimuli and the capacities of the developing infant. These are the beginnings of psychic structuralization and of what will become a self representational system.

The representation of body ego experiences forms within the boundary of a nuclear self and reflects differing responses to varied stimuli. Advances in development, together with the maturation of the autonomous ego functions, consolidate these part self representations into a totality that is accelerated as the organizing influence of distant perceptual processes comes into play. The stimuli of the external world occur at the surface of the personality and are either empathic and containing or prohibitive and impinging. The stimuli of biophysiological demands occur at the interior of the personality, and whether they are enhancing or impinging, carry an instinctual cast. The body ego experiences of contact with the external world differ from those that are a consequence of biophysiology, and the way they are represented varies according to the locale at which they were perceived.

The first perceptual contact with the external world is intrauterine, and the primordial nuclear self registers the buffering, physiological, metabolizing functions of the maternal intrauterine environment. This is represented as the background object of primary identification and is then expanded through the containing regulating interactions with a mothering external object in postuterine life. The background object of primary identification is present at birth, establishes the basic groundwork for an ongoing interrelationship between perceptual activity and mental structure formation, and is responsive to those factors in a relationship that promote growth. Good qualities of experience are those that need no defense, whereas bad qualities are those that elicit or require defense. At the outset of development, the facets of goodness have to be represented at the interior to buffer the disruptive impact of biophysiological demand, allowing the processes of internalization and structure building to take place. The foundation of unconscious perceptions is composed of these body ego experiences, and their derivatives are thereby anchored to the very foundations of the personality.

The attributes of an external object resonate with these developmental underpinnings, so that if a therapeutic environment is empathic with unconscious communications it will be validated by derivatives expressing qualities of goodness. Containment, regulation, optimal gratification, and optimal frustration are most powerfully introduced by the conditions of a treatment situation. A patient's unconscious perception of these particular characteristics provides guidelines for what is growth-promoting in a relationship. When the stimuli of the external world are excessive, or possess impinging and depriving features, they are immediately evocative of the defensive responses associated with bad qualities of experience.

In the early phases of development the consolidation of part self representations into an entity is accompanied by the concurrent integration of the varying perceptual modalities. The maturation of perceptual processes and the interrelated formation of self and object representations increase the availability of the organizing functions elicited by distant receptors. Consensual validation refers to the integration of perceptual processes, enabling the dual ego functions of representation and organization to be available through all perceptual avenues. Visual and auditory stimuli can then be registered and represented by other sensory modalities and vice versa. The capacity to register and express the effects of unconscious perceptions is dependent upon attaining this developmental step. With consensual validation established, the various perceptual modalities function in unison, and emotional nuances in an interaction can be unconsciously perceived through one perceptual modality and evoke a total response.

Unconscious perceptions are manifested either by derivatives expressing their meaning or by the internal state reactively evoked by an external stimulus. The body ego experiences at the foundation of unconscious perceptions react to the stimulus, and the derivatives or internal state expressing their activity reflect the nature of its attributes. A stimulus is initiated at the point of perceptual contact with the external world, evoking derivatives or reactions, depending upon the mental mechanisms and structures available, that reflect the way it is unconsciously perceived. Perceptual contact with the external world will be of greater or lesser intensity in proportion to its nature and impact. Stimuli of diminished intensity, or with little evocative connection to the memory traces of meaningful body ego experiences have a minimal effect, whereas stimuli of great intensity, or with a high degree of resonance with the memory traces of meaningful body ego experiences, have a powerful impact. A stimulus occurring at one locale is unconsciously perceived by its effects upon the mental representations in another sector of the personality, making it important to delineate the original developmental events incorporating this feature of perception.

The underlying body ego experiences upon which unconscious perceptions are based occur during the earliest phases of development. The intermeshing of inner demand and outer metabolic response, registered in an ongoing interaction with the buffering physiological functions of the intrauterine environment, establishes a body ego experience by which a stimulus outside of the self is included within the self. It is the original mental representation of a primary identification and at the foundation of the psychological symbiosis of postuterine life, and ultimately evolves into the more differentiated forms of identification necessary to foster constructive growth. Stimulation is continuously present at the interior of the personality from the demands of biophysiology, and intermittently at the periphery from interactions with the external world. The intensity of biophysiological demand is variable, depending upon the status and composition of the representational world. Perceptual processes register a certain quantity not requiring defense as phase specific instinctual gratifications, and these are enhanced by containing, need-satisfying interactions with external objects.

The resulting body ego experience is evocative of the background object of primary identification, while at the same time the autono-

mous ego functions are amplified by the optimally frustrating properties of an empathic interaction. Initially these good part self
representations consolidate into a whole at the interior, although the
point of perceptual contact is at the periphery. A certain amount of
the continuum of biophysiological demand has an intensity that is
overstimulating, mobilizing the need for defense, and this aspect is
represented as the instinctual facet of a bad self. The body ego
experiences resulting from nonempathic interactions with an external
object are registered at the periphery, and these reactions of fight,
flight, and withdrawal are represented as another facet of a bad self.
The impingements of overstimulating instinctual demands, along
with these external impingements and the representation of sensory
deprivations, organize into a whole at the periphery. Thus, an
evolving bad self consolidates at the surface of the personality,
although the point of perceptual contact with the instinctual aspect is
at the interior.

This translocation of perception, in which the representation of a
stimulus occurs away from its source, is the basis for the mechanism
of splitting. Splitting is the major defensive activity of the primitively
organized ego, and is essential for enabling good and bad qualities of
self experience to consolidate into unified entities. Good self experience is needed at the interior to buffer the impact of biophysiological
demand until it is sufficiently structured. Bad self experience is
needed at the periphery for protective and differentiating functions
until the influences of an object are sufficiently organized to occupy
this role. Only then can good self experience move to the surface
leaving structured remnants behind to stabilize the foundation of the
personality. Bad self experience recedes into the interior, and splits in
the ego are replaced by the emergence of repression proper as the
primary ego defense.

A pathway has thereby been laid for the reactions touched off by
unconscious perceptions to traverse from one locale to the other. The
containing influences of the background object of primary identification are amplified by interpretations and management of the
treatment framework that are responsive to a patient's unconscious
communications. Their empathic qualities are unconsciously perceived by virtue of the effect on this basic mental representation.
Unempathic responses are also internalized, and are unconsciously
perceived from the adaptive reactions to impingement that are
mobilized. Derivatives are then aroused that express the unconscious
significance of what has been received.

## The Role of Unconscious Perceptions
## in the Manifest Dream

The construction of the mental imagery of a manifest dream necessitates a stable background for it to be retained in consciousness with the characteristics of a memory trace. Regressive mental structures, which are available for psychic functioning during sleep, do not possess the stability required to accomplish this. Therefore, the preconscious psychic contents utilized as a nidus for the dream work must be anchored to the foundation of the personality. The derivatives of unconscious perceptions, remaining as a residue of memories from the most powerful emotional experiences of the day, operate most effectively in this regard. Those that resonate with prominent unconscious strivings become the focal point for constructing a dream. Unconscious perceptions are based upon the structured representations of good self experience at the root of all advances in psychic organization and possess an anchoring and stabilizing influence. Their derivatives are included in the manifest content as the day residue.

In a psychoanalytically conducted treatment situation, an individual is engaged with powerful and intense infantile emotions, which are activated in the deeper layers of the personality. On most occasions the unconscious perception of that relationship will be the focus for constructing a dream.

This was demonstrated in a dream reported by a young woman who had sought therapeutic help in understanding her pattern of establishing turbulent, ambivalent love relationships that consistently ended with her being abandoned. From the outset of therapeutic contact she expressed conscious concerns about being seen as seductive, which seemed to emanate from a hidden world of instinctual overstimulation. She utilized face to face contact to avoid introspection, recognized the need for the couch, was frightened of it, and after much discussion put herself in that position to deepen her self understanding. On one occasion she entered the session in a shirt and no bra, exposing her breasts to the therapist's view, and associated to the unworthiness of people who notice things silently without bringing them into the open. The therapist commented upon her distrust of his silence in the presence of her posture. At first she became extremely humiliated, then heard the therapist's breathing as evidence of sexual arousal, and was flooded with childhood memories of seductive experiences with her father. That night she had a dream:

I was alone in a beach house. Some teenagers were having a party on the beach and threatened to invade my house. An older man corraled them, took them aside to talk to them, and I felt safe.

The dream was constructed around the derivative of an unconscious perception of the therapist's intervention, which, in recognizing her unconscious communication of distrust, had amplified the containing function of the background object of primary identification. This enabled instinctual demands, symbolized in the imagery of the wild teenagers, to be represented without undue anxiety. (This dream was presented earlier to demonstrate the positive prognostic implication of the feeling of containment elicited by empathic interpretive interventions.)

The day residue of a dream, in being founded upon the derivative of an unconscious perception, will reflect in some measure how the therapeutic environment is being received. Although an unconsciously empathic environment amplifies the containing influences of the background object of primary identification, empathic lapses and failures are also unconsciously perceived at the foundation of unconscious perceptions. The derivatives are connected to unconscious perceptions inextricably bound to structuralized good self experience. They serve well for retaining the resulting dream within consciousness, and are symbolized to portray the unempathic attributes of the therapeutic relationship and the specific nature of its disruptive effects.

This was illustrated in the dream of a 22-year-old woman complaining of severe episodes of vomiting instigated by her presence in social situations or by any impending heterosexual contact. In the early sessions she spoke relatively freely of her internal experiences, was thoughtful and introspective, and seemingly expected little from the therapist. She maintained an unyielding view of the therapeutic situation as a helping process, did not seek responses either directly or indirectly, and appeared content for the relationship to deepen within the context of the therapist's listening attitude. The therapist's office was located in a hotel, where the public address system could be dimly heard in the distance. There were periodic, repeated requests for the maintenance person to report to the front desk. She was apparently oblivious to this soft, barely recognizable sound. Any attempt by the therapist to gain clarification or to offer an interpretation of the material being presented met with a subtle tone of irritability. There was a three week period during which the therapist remained in total silence. The therapist finally interrupted to ask a question, to which, once again, the patient reacted with irritability. That night she had a dream (used previously to show how a therapist's interventions are symbolized, and provide guidance to what is needed to further a therapeutic regression):

I was trying to reach my parents to get some important information and every effort I made was interfered with by David Green. It was never clear who or where he was, but his presence was always in the way when I tried to make a phone call or to find my way there.

After reporting the dream she was puzzled about the person interfering with her progress, since the name was totally unfamiliar. At just this moment the dim sound of the PA system was directing the maintenance person, David Green, to report to the front desk. This time she registered the sound of the name and recognized its presence in the back of her mind. It represented a derivative of her unconscious perception of the intrusiveness of the therapist's question, was used as the nidus around which the dream was elaborated, and symbolized the interference with her attempt to reach repressed infantile memories and experiences. The therapist's silence had been an important adjunct in her regressive journey, and the question impinged upon the unconsciously empathic qualities of the relationship. The intrusive PA system was registered in her preconscious, and was resonant with her unconscious perception of the relationship.

The opposition of repression may prevent a given dream from being recalled, but it is likely that there are many more in which it is not the sole reason responsible. Dreams may not be remembered because the day residue does not consist of the derivative of an unconscious perception. Most, if not all, remembered dreams seem to contain such a day residue, giving a picture of the status of the treatment at that moment.

This was vividly exemplified in the following dream presented by a young man after a session in which the therapist had inadvertently introduced personal information by leaving an identifiable package in the waiting room.

I am in a dormitory area at work. Someone pointed out that the wall dividing the bathroom from the sleeping area was leaking. I went to inspect it and water was seeping down between the bricks. I went into the bathroom, noticed a hole in the roof, and thought I could patch it from the inside though I would need a roofer to patch the outside.

The therapist's office had a brick wall separating it from a bathroom and the sound of a flushing toilet could be heard in the office. The patient did not appear either to react to or notice the noise, and had no conscious awareness of the wall and bathroom behind it. Nevertheless, the stimuli were registered and represented in the preconscious system, and were available to serve as a derivative expressing his unconscious perception of the therapist's lack of containment. They provided a firm enough foundation for constructing the manifest dream, giving uncon- scious instinctual drives access to representation through the dream work, and for it to be retained with the characteristics of a memory.

The manifest dream reflects the underlying structural organiza- tion of the personality, gives a picture of the particular intrapsychic difficulties in the forefront, and is a starting place for unraveling the unconscious forces at work. A remembered dream must be con- structed around the derivative of an emotionally important uncon- scious perception in order to be retained. This derivative, included within the dream as the day residue, is resonant with unconscious forces. It possesses the stability necessary to be utilized for the dream work. Psychoanalytic treatment is involved with strong infantile emotions. Since treatment is designed to facilitate a therapeutic regression, the resulting transference relationship is a powerful stimulus for derivatives of those unconscious perceptions that are most affect laden. It is thereby a major factor in instigating a dream and generally is the primary source of remembered dream activity.

There may be other events in an individual's life that periodically have that effect, as indicated in the dream of a 9-year-old girl whose obsessive ruminations, severe obstinacy, and controlling behavior were causing her family great distress. Therapeutic contact was initiated and she spent the early sessions reassuring herself of her love for her mother, suffering pangs of extreme guilt in response to any negative or hostile feelings, and plagued with the internal compulsion to engage in repetitive ideational rituals. She slowly began to recognize her difficulty in man- aging aggressive impulses and became increasingly assertive in her relationships. This triggered her parents to seek additional family ther- apy. At the first family meeting the mother bombarded her with ques- tions concerning her behavior. The child screamed a demand for her mother to give her room, and her mother continued as though she had not spoken. The father mildly intervened to state that her mother was just interested in understanding better and that it was nothing to get excited about. She then had the following dream:

A lady or a girl grabbed me and I was very scared. My father was there smiling in a funny way, as if it was nothing to be afraid of and was just a game. I hoped he was right. He was trying to reassure me but wasn't sure himself. I bit down on her hand gently but she didn't get the message. I then bit with all of my strength and my teeth went through her hand. At first she didn't feel it, but then she let go of me, holding her hand and screaming in pain. My father and I ran away very frightened.

The powerful emotional stimulus created by the family session was registered in her preconscious as a day residue, and was the nidus around which the manifest dream was built. The dreamer symbolically represented the mother's suffocating, destructive invasiveness, the father's anxiety in confronting it, and her own efforts to gain separateness. It clearly revealed the unconscious truth she perceived of the dynamics operating in her family. The implied unconscious impulses, condensed into the dream imagery, could only be inferred. It would require considerable undoing of defense to bring the latent dream thoughts into view. They seemed to encompass oral aggressive, anal sadistic drive derivatives, along with more hidden genital oedipal strivings. The manifest content, however, did give almost direct expression to her unconscious perception of an emotionally important event.

The derivative of an unconscious perception possesses the stability to allow the dream work to be retained in consciousness and is incorporated in the body of the dream as the day residue. The resulting symbolic imagery takes on the characteristics of reality and presents a picture of its unconscious truth. The dream represents the truth of reality, as it indicates the truth the dreamer has unconsciously perceived in the external world. The dream itself is real to the dreamer, due to the reality created by an unconscious truth. In identifying the day residue, a patient's unconscious perception of the therapeutic relationship is highlighted, illuminating the status of the treatment and any existing obstacles.

This was shown in the dream of a 41-year-old woman who had been in psychoanalytic treatment off and on over a period of eighteen years. She had seen a number of different therapists and described herself as driven to present a chameleon-like image of herself to elicit approval. Looking back, she thought the time was spent polishing her "false self." She was now making one last effort. She felt as if she could no longer spend her life this way, was filled with hopelessness and despair, and was considering suicide. Her entire existence seemed empty and false. This drove her to extreme eating and drinking binges. The only bright spot involved her wish to become an engineer. She loved to create and manipulate objects, observing a concrete result from her efforts. Although she had started out on this course, early in her education she had been diverted by a love relationship. Attempting to please her partner, she had moved into a different career that was very unsatisfying. She identified this time as a crucial turning point in her life when anything real had been totally shattered, and she could no longer pick up the pieces. The therapist, unconsciously responding to the depths of her desperation, implicitly encouraged this one spark of interest by wondering what prevented her from continuing on a path that seemed to carry a measure of hope. That night she had a dream:

> I applied to Harvard and was taking a test. The idea was to design a building. We were shown a drawing on a screen for forty seconds and then had to draw it. Paper was passed out to draw on. Mine was embossed with the outline of a flapper girl. It was very bumpy and impossible to draw on. I was puzzled as to how I was to go about it.

After reporting the dream, she described her amazement at not being frustrated and defeated, just puzzled. This immediately led her to the same feeling of puzzlement she had in response to the therapist's question about picking up on her interests. It felt to her as if the therapist was imposing his own agenda upon her, and reminded her of how she had always wanted to engage in boys' activities but was forced into a mold of parental expectations as to what constituted feminine pursuits. It prevented her from realizing herself, and she had continually repeated this pattern in her previous treatment.

This dream initiated an exploration of the distinction between the derivatives of unconscious perceptions and those of transference fantasy distortions. She had unconsciously perceived the therapist's detrimental attitude, and the derivative was symbolized and incorporated into the manifest dream as the day residue. It then became possible to acknowledge her perception, rectify the empathic lapse, and interpret its effects. In the past, when unconscious perceptions were treated as fantasy distortions, it so reenforced her "false self" that she had felt totally trapped within its confines.

The emotional impact of a therapeutic relationship is particularly evocative of a patient's unconscious perceptions. The derivative of the experience is most likely to serve as a day residue around which the manifest dream is constructed. Consequently, a facet of the dream will include a symbolic picture of how the relationship is unconsciously perceived and by implication how the treatment is progressing. When a therapist appears in a dream without being symbolized, it is indicative that the features of the relationship are an exact replica of what is unconsciously perceived. There is little fantasy distortion, although the figure of the therapist is utilized as a derivative.

This was portrayed in the dream of an 18-year-old girl who sought therapeutic help when on the eve of her graduation from high school, her parents announced an impending divorce. In the initial contact the therapist silently listened to her anguished expressions of feeling torn apart and distraught. At the end of the session the therapist commented that he could certainly see the great distress this traumatic event produced, but it sounded like it was all interwoven with a revival of other traumatic events in her life and this one had special meaning because of her imminent move toward greater independence. Her response was to become quietly contained, and to spend the next few sessions talking about an earlier time in her life when she was closely attached to her mother. This was disrupted by the birth of a sibling and by a change in her mother's attitude. She had reacted by becoming excessively independent, prided herself on an ability to manage her own life, and worked hard to keep harmony in the family. Following a session in which she was surprised at the strength of her attachment to her mother and the pain of being rejected, she reported a dream:

> You were with me watching my mother and father arguing. My father disappeared and my mother turned on me and tried to take my makeup. I fought to hold onto it and she hit me. She began to scream at me about how jealous she was of my materials and wanted them for herself.

She awoke from the dream with a strange sensation that she had understood something without being able to articulate what it was, as if her mother, in the dream, was a mirror image of herself. The therapist's unconsciously empathic attitude had been evocative of the good self experiences structured at the foundation of her personality, and was consonant with the qualities in a relationship most needed to facilitate her growth. The containing influence it provided was reflected in the therapist's presence in the dream, allowing oedipal rivalries to be symbolically represented and projected onto the image of the mother. Genital instinctual impulses were previously associated with overwhelming anxiety, but the day residue of this dream consisted of a derivative expressing the unconscious perception of empathic qualities, offering enough regulation for the dream to continue. The figure of the therapist did not require the disguise of symbolization because his posture was consonant with what was unconsciously perceived, and negative oedipal strivings were in the ascendancy. The disappearance of the father hinted that her positive oedipal attachment had been successfully repressed.

The concept of transference refers to an intrapsychic process in which an unconscious impulse is transferred across a repressive barrier and attached to appropriate psychic contents in the preconscious system. The interpersonal manifestation of that underlying process is expressed in the transference aspect of a therapeutic relationship. The identical process is involved in the formation of instinctual derivatives and the derivatives of unconscious perceptions. An unconscious force exerts a demand for expression, meets an oppositional barrier, and evokes resonant mental activity in the preconscious system parallel with the essence of the demand. This movement of an unconscious instinctual demand-seeking expression is the force fueling and instigating a dream, which is then put together using mental contents having accessibility to consciousness.

The dream work embodies the transformation of an unconscious force into a new and different mental configuration. Symbolization limits the particular contents in the preconscious system that can be utilized. For a dream to be retained it must be built around mental impressions capable of supporting this intricate process. Recallable dreams are thereby based upon the derivatives of unconscious perceptions, which are the only psychic contents possessing enough stability to be registered with the characteristics of a memory. The manifest content of the resulting dream can then be a starting point for unraveling the latent dream thoughts. In interpreting a dream, an attempt is made to reconstruct the nature of the dream work retrospectively. This gives a more penetrating view of the dynamic interplay of conflictual forces in the personality and of the mental background against which they take place.

The day residue can play an essential role in exposing the associative linkages that are necessary to reveal the latent dream thoughts, as was shown in the following dream of a 45-year-old man. He sought treatment because of the limitations imposed upon his functioning by reaction formations against anal sadistic aggression, which dominated his thinking and adaptations. He was meticulous, ruminative, and suffered acutely from pangs of guilt with any expression of aggression or self assertiveness. Following a session in which he blurted out an angry, frustrated reaction to the therapist's silence, he had a dream, and introduced it by mentioning the day residue. Several days before, while driving, he had inadvertently grazed a black man riding on a bicycle.

> I was accused of the crime of bumping into the man and was put in jail. It was a crime I didn't commit, but I was to be executed in the morning. I escaped. The jailers came after me, and I woke up in a cold sweat.

He was immediately struck by how the incident in real life was woven into the fabric of the dream, and it reminded him of the many times he had done something without it having the intent others put into it. This made him mad. He held it in and when it erupted he attacked himself. He then became aware of the similarity between the black man on the bicycle and an unspoken sense of the therapist's surprise at his outburst of anger.

The black man on the bicycle represented a derivative of his unconscious perception of the therapist's reaction to his outburst. It provided a focal point for unraveling the dream work to gain access to the underlying infantile wishes. The manifest dream captured the essence of his harboring repressed, sadistic impulses, not granting them discharge, and standing accused by a harsh, punitive superego. The content of the dream was an available pathway toward exposing the latent dream thoughts centered around the derivative of his unconscious perception of the therapeutic relationship. The transference distortions that were elaborated could then be identified, and their manifestations within the subsequent free associative process became more apparent.

After delineating the structural foundation of the manifest dream, the groundwork is prepared for determining the nature of the dream work and latent dream thoughts. A direction toward uncovering the underlying unconscious forces being given substance and expression is indicated by the context of associations in which the dream appears, furthered by identifying the day residue. The particular day residue selected, since it consists of the derivative of an emotionally important unconscious perception, contains implied meaning with the potential for revealing the specific unconscious forces that are most active. The day residue most suitable for inclusion in a dream is one that is most resonant with the instinctual drives in the ascendancy. In most instances it involves the therapeutic relationship, and a guideline is then available for maintaining the proper conditions necessary to foster a benign regression.

This was portrayed in the dream of a 7-year-old girl, referred for treatment because of extreme fits of temper, bizarre behavior, difficulty in school, and increasing isolation from all relationships. In her first session she spoke of her light side, which was mischievous and fun-loving, and of her hidden dark side, which was ominous and frightening. That night she had a dream:

> I was in a strange school. The teacher was kind but firm. There was a second floor that couldn't be explored. I was very curious. I wanted to see what was there and thought it was something like a computer that affected everything I did. The teacher led the class in a prayer and stated emphatically that nobody was to open the door to the second floor.

After reporting the dream she emphasized its strangeness because it was an amalgamation of her room at school with the therapist's office. The door to the second floor in the dream was exactly like a door to a closet in the therapist's office. She laughingly spoke of her curiosity about that door, wanted to examine its contents, and was fearful that it was off limits.

The preconscious day residue was embodied in the closet door and the kind yet firm figure of the teacher. It enabled her to build a dream implicitly hinting at dangerous, voyeuristic impulses striving for expression. The prohibitive needs of the manifest dream were met by the teacher's admonition against exploring hidden spaces. The dream pointed to the importance of maintaining firm therapeutic ground rules and boundaries in order to facilitate a therapeutic regression safely. It presented a guideline for the therapist to aid in exploring her hidden dark side, which stood as an obstacle to constructive growth.

A therapist may also construct a dream around the derivative of an unconscious perception of a therapeutic encounter, and it will also portray the attributes of the relationship. When this occurs it is indicative of a countertransference-based obstacle existing in the treatment. Ideally, a patient should not occupy the center of a therapist's emotional stage or be the focus of regressive fantasies and identifications. It is the unevenness of the emotional attachment in the therapeutic relationship that gives impetus to the regressive transference, and it is essential for a therapist to be of greater emotional importance to the patient than the patient is to the therapist. The imbalance is crucial for the growth-promoting properties of the relationship, and will be unconsciously perceived by both parties.

Nevertheless, there are moments when a patient will occupy a place of prime emotional significance, reflecting the loss of ideal therapeutic functioning. It is a sign that the flow of associative linkages to unconscious meanings has been disrupted within the therapist during the course of a session. A patient's pathological defenses function to alter the imbalance in the relationship in an attempt to protect against regressive dangers. When successful, the destructive influences of infantile objects are recreated in the transference. This often serves as the day residue of a therapist's dream, which can then be welcomed as a source of material to better grasp the unconscious forces at work and spotlight the therapeutic obstacle.

# 7

# The Manifest Dream as a Diagnostic Instrument

The manifest dream is a particularly useful means for verifying, and at times determining, an accurate diagnostic assessment. Although it has undergone secondary revision, it represents imagery more closely approximating the lines of structural development. The particular construction of a dream makes it especially advantageous for defining the status of evolving or already established id, ego, and superego structures and the intrapsychic conflict or developmental arrest being highlighted at the moment.

## Sequence of Major Developmental Steps and Their Relationship to Categories of Psychopathology

When the diagnosis of psychopathology is approached from a developmental perspective, it can be seen that all pathological distortions evolve against a background of a specific developmental task that has not been successfully negotiated. Each of these tasks centers around a crucial point, when a new level of psychic organization must be achieved for progress in self differentiation and for self expansion to continue. Stage and phase specificity refers to the manner in which instinctual representation and mental structure formation provide a perfect match for meeting a developmental need. In each category of

101

pathology there is a lack of synchrony in stage and phase specificity, which either adversely affects the way a given task is negotiated and a more advanced level of psychic organization reached, or obviates against that accomplishment.

## Autistic Disorders

The first crucial step involves the entry into a psychological symbiosis. Developmentally, this has required the presence of sufficient empathic responsiveness from an external object to amplify the representation of the background object of primary identification, enabling the lack of differentiation necessary for the internalization of a good object's influence. The movement into a psychological symbiosis represents a developmental advance, and the autistic disorders reflect the pathological result of an inability to negotiate this initial step.

An autistic child's representational world is composed of fragmented part self and part object configurations, with a predominance of impinging, destructive object imagoes. Symbiotic attachments to the mental impressions of bodily processes are formed, and primitive autistic withdrawal remains as a primary defense. The dearth and fragmentation of good self experience, the destructive impact of a bad object's influence, and the primitive level of psychic organization are such that it is highly unlikely for a dream to be retained within the realm of conscious experience. The internal reaction elicited by unconscious perceptions is not sufficiently organized to form derivatives, mental content is not anchored enough for a manifest dream to be constructed, and the dreaming that takes place is unavailable as a source of communicable mental content.

On those rare occasions when a therapeutic relationship has been successful in offering an unconsciously empathic experience, it leads to the building of new mental structures and an autistic organization is no longer in evidence. It is then possible to engage in the processes involved in the dream work, construct a manifest dream, and report it in the context of a therapeutic relationship. The new level of psychic organization is most in evidence, although the impact of the earlier disturbance will be reflected in the body of the dream.

> This was displayed in the dream of a 22-year-old man who had been in intensive psychotherapy for a period of seventeen years. At the outset of treatment his infantile autism was predominant. He had been able to make advances in psychic structuralization and was capable of functioning at a much higher level. While talking about a forthcoming move away

from home and treatment in order to attend college, he reported a dream:

> I was driving down the street in the middle of the night expecting the traffic lights to be off so I could drive straight through without stopping. I was very upset because the traffic lights were working, all of the stores were open, and there was an enormous amount of traffic. I had to wait for all of the cars to pass before I could move. A new store was opening and the number of cars kept increasing. I was furious.

He had successfully structured a new level of psychic organization during the course of his treatment, which was evident in his adaptive functioning and in the composition of this manifest dream, but the dream also reflected the extent to which early oral rage continued to pose an obstacle to his progress. He associated the traffic with his anticipation of difficulties in dealing with new relationships. The store opening made him think of his impending move, and he expected an upsurge of frustration and unbridled rage. He had certainly achieved considerable self expansion, but the structural composition of his personality was infused with the impact of his earlier pathology, which then entered into the dream content.

Dreams in the autistic disorders either are not sufficiently anchored to be retained within consciousness or are not recognized as content to be communicated. With progression beyond this primitive state, dreams are reported and often symbolize the earlier devastation in the representational world.

This was shown in the dream of a child who had begun therapy at the age of 4 exhibiting all of the characteristics of infantile autism. He engaged in a therapeutic symbiosis, represented new experiences to enable a new level of psychic organization to be achieved, and when approaching his thirteenth birthday had the following dream:

> I was building a tall skyscraper and had almost completed the thirteenth floor. I looked up to see how high it would go and couldn't be sure. I looked around and noticed a beat-up, old, ramshackle shed that had to be torn down to make room for the new building.

He had now developed enough mental structuralization to construct a manifest dream, retain it within consciousness, and include it within a communicative modality. The dream gave expression to the growth he had attained, the uncertainty as to how much further he could go, and the residuals of his fragmented representational world.

## Schizophrenias

The second crucial step involves negotiating the symbiotic interaction itself. This requires a relatively adequate balance of good and bad qualities of self experience and prepares the groundwork for initiating separation and individuation. The schizophrenias reflect the pathological result of an inability to negotiate this step. Identifiable quantities of phase-specific instinctual gratification have been represented, but the pathological features of the symbiosis have created the necessity for them to be split off in order to be preserved. This split in the self is possible since instinctual experience is based upon attachment to an object. It is the only facet capable of detachment, and primitive withdrawal is still available as a response. The consequence is in the evolution of a basic schizophrenic process in which an infantile realm of good instinctual self experience is split off, a depleted, advanced realm of psychic functioning continues to be in contact with the external world, and a defensive organization is constructed around the core representation of a pathological symbiosis that functions to maintain the split.

The infantile realm, split off during the symbiotic period, is then elaborated into fantasies of an adequate symbiosis. The defensive structure, organized around the representation of a pathological symbiosis, enlarges its distorting influence with poorly differentiated impressions of a bad object and bad self experience to function as an internal saboteur. The advanced realm of psychological experience continues to develop, and is engaged with the external world on the basis of submission and conformity to the expectations of others. This basic schizophrenic process evolved when what was necessary for survival was equally the source of destruction, and is the ultimate of a true and false self as described by Winnicott (1965).

The infant's solution to an impossible dilemma resulted in an advanced realm of overdeveloped autonomous functions operating on a substrate of brittle mental structures, a pathological defense composed of fused bad self and object imagoes, creating distortions that threatened to repeat the original trauma, and a split-off realm of orally determined instinctual experience exerting a constant regressive pull. Effective therapeutic intervention must be guided by a patient's unconscious perception of what is growth promoting in a relationship, which, in this situation, requires that the distortions created by the internal saboteur be eliminated or diminished while simultaneously presenting the specific conditions of an adequate symbiosis. The depth of the ensuing regression has a fragmenting effect on the advanced realm of psychic functions, accentuating the need for a differentiating influence, which is provided by maintaining a firm therapeutic framework. The defensive organization of the internal saboteur can then be gradually differentiated and realigned into bad self and bad object entities, and an attachment made to the previously split-off representations of good instinctual self experience.

A schizophrenic break takes place when the original split in the self can no longer be successfully sustained, initiating a malignant regression under the distorting influence of the internal saboteur. The two disparate worlds of psychological experience merge in a traumatic collision, and there is an internal state of fragmentation and chaos with a momentary period of total detachment from all contact with objects. With each such episode, good self experience is damaged to some extent, making it essential to institute a schizophrenic process of repair.

The reparative process encompasses a narrowing of self boundaries to focus perceptual attention upon a narcissistic overevaluation of fantasied potentials and the reconstruction of an object world that combines the fragmented consequences of a schizophrenic break into sometimes bizarre new unions. The various symptoms usually associated with schizophrenia, such as hallucinations, delusions, and bizarre self experiences, are the product of a compensatory attempt to repair the self damage. A schizophrenic break is threatened with every incident of stress, adaptational demand, or potential love relationship, and once it has occurred, immediately instigates a process of repair. Successful therapeutic intervention is proportional to the extent that the split-off representations of good instinctual self experience have not been damaged, since this realm has to be preserved in sufficient quantities to direct and support a growth-promoting therapeutic symbiosis.

All three stages on the continuum of schizophrenic pathology may co-exist simultaneously in a given individual, making the determination of treatability extremely difficult. The degree to which good instinctual self experience has been preserved is vital to ascertain, for when self damage is extensive, a basic schizophrenic process is not viable and psychoanalytic treatment is ineffective or contraindicated. A dream can be an invaluable aid in the assessment, since the availability of good self experience will often be reflected in the symbolic imagery.

This was illustrated in the treatment of a young adult woman displaying all three stages of a schizophrenic disturbance. She had a number of schizophrenic breaks for which she had been hospitalized, and could only vaguely recall being out of contact. A schizophrenic process of repair was manifested in the presence of hallucinations emanating from a background world to which she was periodically drawn alternately feeling safe and in enormous danger. Nevertheless, she was searching for a relationship that could provide the regressive healing she knew was needed, and she reacted negatively to any reenforcement of her pathological defenses. This suggested that she had also split off and preserved a sufficient quantity of good infantile instinctual experience to maintain a basic schizophrenic process.

She had a series of vague dreams in which she was lying on a couch very frightened, which made her think about using the therapist's couch. She was convinced it would not be a good idea for her; it would be too distant. The therapist would be out of sight and disconnected from her; she would get lost in an uncontrolled regression, have a schizophrenic break, and end up in a hospital. It seemed too frightening—as if it would remove her from contact with the external world. Her words were reminiscent of similar statements as to why psychoanalytic treatment is contraindicated in the schizophrenias, and the therapist stated that he had a different view of the couch. It seemed to him that he would be much closer to her inner experiences and more in touch with the deeper parts of her. The present position of face to face contact felt as if it held him at a distance, where he was frequently out of touch with what she experienced.

In the following session she described feeling dizzy after she left, like the sensation of spinning around, and she couldn't explain it. The therapist remarked that he was reminded of the two different ways in which they had talked about the couch, and it made him think of her being spun around in response to his words. She then recalled a dream from the night before:

> I was on the couch and a woman was my analyst. I became smaller and smaller, and was very surprised that I wasn't too frightened, and felt I was in the proper hands.

The manifest content was symbolically representing her capacity to regress to a position of total vulnerability and helplessness, without the overwhelming threat of annihilation. It would require a significant amount of good self experience to construct such a dream and have it retained within consciousness, giving validation to what was emerging in the treatment situation. Although there had been many schizophrenic breaks and enough self damage to put her ability to sustain a healing therapeutic symbiosis in question, the search for the conditions of an adequate symbiosis was in the background of all of her communications. The dream was indicative of sufficient quantities of good instinctual self experience remaining preserved. This served well as a map illuminating the status of the treatment and added verification to the diagnosis of a basic schizophrenic process being functionally available.

When a schizophrenic process of repair is the dominant feature structured in the personality, it signifies that good infantile instinctual self experience has been damaged to such an extent that to all intents and purposes it is inaccessible to the healing properties of a relationship. Such individuals rarely remember or report a dream, and when they do, the compensatory process of repair is reflected in the manifest content. Unconscious perceptions may still be functional and their derivatives can serve as a nidus for the construction of a dream, which makes it possible for the dream to be retained. The total personality has been restructured, however, to maintain a compensatory narcissistic focus of attention upon fantasied self potentials, with an object world consisting of bizarre unions of fragmented mental representations and fantasy elaborations, with no regard for the distinction between them.

This was shown in the dream of a 24-year-old man exhibiting the delusions, hallucinations, and bizarre self experiences expressive of a schizophrenic process of repair. He sought therapeutic help primarily to satisfy the demands of others who were increasingly disturbed by his strange behavior. Any attempt at internal exploration was extremely disruptive, and he looked for the therapist's participation only in reenforcing his restrictive psychotic character. In the context of his annoyance at the therapist's search for unspoken meaning in his communications, he remembered a dream:

I saw a neighbor lady naked with a long dick between her legs. I took out a knife, sliced it into pork chops, and ate it.

The mental contents available to be utilized in the dream work display the readiness with which object impressions can be shaped into bizarre configurations. The dream imagery portrays the dismantling of an instinctual part object and incorporates it for the narcissistic enhancement of the self. The intermixture of memory trace with fantasy elaboration and the fusion of oral and genital components all are consonant with a schizophrenic process of repair.

Psychoanalytic treatment is applicable with the schizophrenic only when a basic schizophrenic process is predominant. The principle of free association facilitates the expression of the deeper layers of the personality, which in this situation are the split off representations of orally determined instinctual experience. The principle of abstinence requires that a pathological defense not be reenforced, which involves interpreting the distortions created by the internal saboteur and rendering them ineffective. The principle of anonymity and neutrality directs a therapist to filter out personal reactions so as not to project them onto a patient. This is especially relevant since the pressure exerted to confuse and distort meaning is an exaggerated defensive maneuver, and the regressive fantasies a therapist must confront without becoming defensive or withdrawing are often of a frightening nature. Psychoanalytic treatment is applicable to a small number of schizophrenic patients, particularly those who have sustained a basic schizophrenic process over an extended period of time. It is indicative that the split-off realm of good infantile instinctual experience has been preserved undamaged and in sufficient quantities to direct and support a constructive, growth-producing therapeutic symbiosis. Psychoanalytic treatment is ineffective in the presence of a schizophrenic break, and is contraindicated when there has been extensive self damage.

## The Borderline Personality

The third crucial step involves the negotiation of separation and individuation. This requires that good self experience be represented in sufficient quantities to be structuralized at the interior of the personality. The impact of biophysiological demand can then be adequately buffered, and the internal search for and discovery of a separate good object's influence can take place. Bad self experience must be in balanced enough proportions to serve differentiating and defensive functions and not exert a fragmenting effect on mental structuralization. A differentiated connection to the influences of an object can then be continuously sustained through the formation of mental structures uniting the self and object systems of representation.

The borderline personality reflects the pathological result of an inability to negotiate this step. Splitting mechanisms within the ego, essential for the coalescence of separate entities of self experience during the symbiotic period, persist as a primary defense. Whole entities of good and bad self experiences have consolidated, good self experience is deficient and remains organized at the interior, bad self experience is organized at the periphery to serve a protective function, the impressions of an object are not coalesced and are highly unstable, and distorted structural unions are formed to maintain differentiation.

The borderline individual is in an intermediary position between initiating self differentiation by forming discrete entities of self experience and discriminating the influence of a separate good object. The organization of the borderline personality is such that the conditions of psychoanalytic treatment enable structural change by virtue of progression to a more advanced level of differentiation. It is not until cohesiveness is structured and borderline features are no longer in evidence that a therapeutic regression can evolve. A free associative process facilitates the expression of the deeper layers of the personality, which in this situation fosters a progressive rather than a regressive movement since good self experience is buried in the deeper layers. An unconsciously empathic therapeutic relationship enables the recognition of a separate good object's influence, and leads to a more advanced level of psychic organization.

This was demonstrated in the dream of a 7-year-old hyperactive boy whose wild, uncontrollable behavior and persistent aggressive efforts to control his environment led his family to seek therapy. (In chapter 4 the dream illustrated how latent resources are portrayed in the presence of severe pathology.) He could not concentrate, his thinking was fragmented, he had frequent eruptions of rage, and yet at moments he could be charming and lovable. Shortly after beginning psychotherapy, he reported the following dream:

We were all on earth and it was freezing. My family was covered with ice and turning blue. My mother and I jumped to the sun and got all warm and thawed out.

The manifest content pictured a separate good object's influence, a recognition that could not be sustained in the face of adaptive demands during waking life. The symbolic imagery of the frozen objects gave expression to the borderline organization of his personality, and the two positions showed the progressive movement that had to take place before a therapeutic regression could be growth promoting. It also was indicative of a thin thread of cohesiveness existent in his personality, for in the borderline personality consolidated entities of good self experience are incapable of connecting to the impressions of a separate good object's influence.

The borderline individual's tendency to devalue the qualities of a good object is partly a product of the need to find external support for the unstable, distorted means by which differentiation is structured, and partly a product of bad self experience being consolidated at the periphery of the personality to serve a protective function. When the search for reenforcement of pathological defenses is unsuccessful, the devaluation may become so extreme that it threatens the alliance necessary to sustain a psychoanalytically conducted therapeutic interaction. In addition, unempathic qualities in a relationship may instigate a malignant regression and lead toward a psychotic episode. This combination of factors makes it difficult to provide the containment required to support effective therapeutic intervention, which is reactively sensed by a patient, furthering the internal instability.

The danger associated with this position was reflected in a dream reported by a 40-year-old woman seeking help for a lifelong inability to establish meaningful relationships, and for the anguish she suffered in being drawn to sadistic partners. In discussing the use of the couch, she recalled this dream:

> I was lying on a bed of words, and as long as I remained perfectly still I was safe. I knew that if I moved, the words would turn into sharp knives and cut me to pieces.

The dream was founded on a level of psychic structuralization characteristic of the borderline personality, captured the threat posed by an overloading of orally derived, poorly neutralized aggression, and pictured the imminent danger of an uncontrolled regression.

It was earlier discussed as an example of a questionable prognosis and now also points to the enormous need for a well-contained, unconsciously empathic therapeutic environment. The manner in which the structural organization of the borderline personality operates to undermine developmental progression was manifested in the dream of a 14-year-old girl. She had been referred because of parental concern about the intensity of her fight for independence. She was constantly involved in episodes of drinking, she took drugs, and she frequently engaged in promiscuous relationships. She spoke tearfully of having grown up alone, of pushing longings for closeness aside, and of her concern now that she was losing her ability to be tender. She then recalled a dream:

> I had a baby boy and my mother sedated me so she could take it and control it. I screamed in anger that it was mine. The baby grew rapidly and began to become attached to my mother. I felt enraged because I was losing the bond I had made.

The manifest dream was constructed against the background of a pathological structure designed to maintain differentiation. It consisted of a union of good self experience with the impression of a bad, overpowering instinctual object. Although this borderline organization was necessary to sustain differentiation, it was debilitating and destructive to growth. The image of the mother taking control of a young baby originally connected to the dreamer captures the essence of this pathological differentiating structure. The attachment to the baby gave expression to the highly overvalued but deficient representation of good self experience protectively held at the interior of her personality, and the detachment of the bond reflected the loss of contact with this vital growth-promoting aspect of herself. The dream also hinted that a malignant regression was accelerating, and the dreamer was in danger of a suicidal depression and imminent psychotic episode.

When a borderline patient perceives a therapist as bad, it can be easy to confuse this projective identification of bad self contents and understand it as a projection of transference fantasies. It is based on the mistaken idea that a differentiated whole object can be perceived, and unwittingly places a therapist in the role of reenforcing a pathological defense. In overlooking the borderline individual's general inability to discern the impressions of a whole object and his specific inability to recognize a separate good object's influence, unnecessary deviations from the clear cut framework required for a well-contained relationship are introduced. The consequence is in an escalation of pathological regressive cravings and a more concerted effort to rupture therapeutic ground rules and boundaries.

A therapist must internalize the pressure to deviate, in order to unravel the makeup of the underlying distorted structures behind pathological defenses and then interpret their significance. It is important for interpretive interventions to contain the therapist's perspective, and in this way supply the faulty, deficient, or missing function of self observation. The effect is to strengthen latent strands of movement toward separation and individuation that have been vulnerable to destruction, or to outline a pathway to the heretofore unrecognized impressions of a separate good object.

The basic principle of free association facilitates expressing consolidated good self experience, which has been protected in the deeper layers, and ultimately leads to structuring cohesiveness. The principle of abstinence directs a therapist to avoid reenforcing pathological defenses that involve distorted, highly unstable unions of good and bad qualities in the self and object. These are the source of the projective identifications fueling the transference relationship, and the principles of anonymity and neutrality assure that they will flow freely allowing adequate interpretations to be made. Once separation and individuation have been negotiated, cohesiveness and continuity of experience are established and there is a change in the composition of the deeper layers of the personality. Repression proper emerges as a primary defense, and there must be a corresponding shift in the therapist's posture. The ingredients required for continuing growth are structured within the personality, though they may be weak, inhibited, or engaged in conflict. It is no longer necessary for a therapist to provide a missing, deficient, or arrested function, and to do so would be infantilizing.

## Narcissistically Determined, Object Related, Phobic Disorders

The fourth crucial step involves negotiating the shift from narcissism to object relatedness. This requires cohesiveness and continuity of experience to be well established, the component instincts to consolidate into a genital drive, and the regulatory forces in the personality to be organized under the aegis of a developing and functional superego. The conditions are then present for oedipal fantasies to flourish, and new structures are formed that enable object related perceptions to be registered. The narcissistically determined, object related, phobic disorders reflect the pathological result of an inability to negotiate this step. Cohesiveness and continuity of experience are established, but on an unsteady foundation, and the threat of fragmentation is a constant presence. The fixation points are based on a phobic avoidance of the prohibitive impressions of a bad object and of overstimulating instinctual experience, which makes them very unstable. Although there are some limited advances in instinctual representation, and some movement toward a genital consolidation and object related orientation, a narcissistic fixation persists.

The phobias represent different stages in the progression toward forming an oedipal conflict, which is overwhelming, rather than being symbolic of the conflict itself. A phobic attitude toward the prohibitive influences of an object does not permit identifications with an aggressor, reaction formations are not possible, castration anxiety has not been consolidated into a signaling and regulatory structure, the superego remains dependent upon external objects for its regulatory function, and perceptual attention is directed away from the source of a threatening stimulus. A mixed neurotic symptom and character picture is commonly exhibited, which is a product of the instability of the fixation points and the structures maintaining cohesiveness.

The following dream (already cited to shed light on the process of symbolization) of a young adult man shows the problem of managing instinctual activity in the phobic disorders.

> I was driving in a car in my childhood neighborhood. I was both inside and outside the car, and as I got out I noticed a mist surrounding and suffocating me. I had the thought in the dream [that] it was my own feelings both outside and inside me.

The unsteady foundation upon which cohesiveness is structured was manifested in the dreamer's position of being in two places simultaneously. He had entered treatment because of his avoidance of close interpersonal contact, which made him feel trapped and claustrophobic. The manifest dream revealed that instinctual experience was a threat to self integrity rather than representing a specific danger.

A phobic avoidance of the prohibitive impressions of a bad object was demonstrated in the following dream of a 16-year-old boy who had sought therapeutic help when he was unable to attend school.

> I was trying to see my enemy and face him once and for all. I did and he was so monstrous and terrifying that I awoke in fright.

This manifest dream (used in Chapter 3 to illustrate how potential barriers to effective treatment may appear in a dream) symbolically portrays the phobically avoided impressions of a self-threatening prohibitive object, making the identifications with an aggressor essential for instinctual regulation impossible. The dreamer's effort to confront this potentially fragmenting internal presence resulted in a nightmare, creating the need to invoke a whole new set of perceptual functions.

The compromises required for the formation of a neurotic symptom depend upon the capacity to represent an instinctual danger. The phobias in representing a threat to self integrity are a transitional step in that direction.

This was shown in the following dream of a young man, reported early in his treatment:

> I was searching for something hidden—like a treasure hunt—and was extremely frustrated and anxious. Then I was home in bed. My mother came in to talk to me and she climbed on top of me. I struggled to get free. It was intensely sexual and I was wondering about it. I was most fearful of being trapped, not of the sexuality.

The dreamer symbolically represented the threat to the loss of self functions from being enveloped by an overpowering instinctual object, clearly indicating that the instinctual aspect, though present, was not the primary danger. Earlier, the dream exemplified how the therapeutic relationship may be pictured in a dream.

In an unconsciously empathic therapeutic environment with the phobic individual, the therapist emerges in the transference as an instinctual object possessing attributes consonant with the degree of advancement toward the evolution of an oedipal conflict.

> This was evidenced in the dream of a 10-year-old girl who had entered pubescence early and was enmeshed in an intense ambivalent relationship with her mother whom she alternately clung to and angrily attacked. The therapist had commented upon her strong wish for independence that was obstructed by a fear of her budding sexuality, and in the following session she reported a dream:
>
> > I was in love with a rock star and felt excited and alive. I went to a concert, where he announced he had just gotten married. I was absolutely crushed and heartbroken. He introduced his wife; I killed her and felt tremendous relief.
>
> The therapist's interpretation enabled some beginning movement toward representing the genital instinctual wishes associated with an oedipal situation. The manifest dream symbolized the gradual escalation in intensity of a genital attachment, and the introduction of a rivalrous object. The overstimulation was reaching a level that was potentially overwhelming, the emerging conflict could no longer be tolerated, hostility was directed into destroying the oedipal rival, and the dreamer was relieved. It was indicative of her need for consistent and active interpretive help in integrating the impact of her evolving genital sexuality. The movement toward a genital consolidation and object relatedness was a transference repetition, whereas the full flowering of genitally determined oedipal fantasies is a new experience.

The phobic's early development has been characterized by an effective symbiotic period, abruptly interrupted by a profound change in the empathic conditions of the external world at the point that individuation becomes viable. It results in a precocious and defensive movement into the separation-individuation process, and is behind the subsequent instability in psychic structuralization. Empathic lapses are thereby reacted to in an exaggerated fashion. When a therapist is perceived as a phobic object, it is indicative of an empathic failure rather than exclusively a transference fantasy distortion. It signifies that the therapist's behavior is in some fashion resonating with the traumatic events of early development, making it imperative to at least implicitly acknowledge a patient's unconscious perception of the therapist's role, and to then rectify the lapse and interpret the unconscious meaning of its effects.

A dream can be helpful in identifying the existence of a failure in empathy, as in the dream of a 10-year-old boy referred because of quiet, withdrawn behavior, difficulty in adapting to the demands of school, and parental concern about his general unhappiness. He found it very difficult to talk, and would often sit in silence for long periods of time. Although he mentioned a fear of ghosts and of nuclear war, he was unable to go beyond these limited statements. It was equally hard for the therapist to find usable material for interpretive interventions. The sessions were filled with long silences. He appeared to be immobilized, could not allow any free play of his thoughts or feelings, and at this point reported a dream:

I was walking on a tightrope and was very restless, like I wanted to move and couldn't. I was aware of standing over a battlefield like in Vietnam, with explosions, shooting, and fighting going on. Although I was drawn to watching, I couldn't, and my whole body shook.

This dream was mentioned briefly in a prior chapter, to emphasize how the content may provide a therapist with directions that are otherwise unavailable. Here the dream reflected the underlying phobic organization of his personality, and gave expression to his efforts to observe mental contents that were extremely explosive and frightening. The degree of instability was symbolized by his position on the tight-rope, and the act of internal exploration was threatening his sense of balance and integrity. The content of the dream suggested that the therapist's silence was not addressing his need for help in modulating the disruptive effect of the prohibitive influences of a bad object or with managing the dangers of instinctual overstimulation. The therapist was thus alerted to the empathic failure, acknowledged his role in perpetuating the silence, and interpreted the way it had been elaborated into fantasies of an excessively prohibitive attitude. In this way, unconscious empathy was reestablished.

The narcissistically determined, object related, phobic disorders are the first in which the application of the basic psychoanalytic principles approaches the conditions usually associated with classical psychoanalytic treatment. Infantile instinctual conflicts are enacted in the transference relationship and can be resolved by insight with the aid of unconsciously empathic interpretive interventions. These phobic disturbances are equivalent to what are often described as cohesive narcissistic personality disorders. In an unconsciously empathic environment the overwhelming trauma of an evolving oedipal constellation is recreated.

## *Neuroses*

The fifth crucial step involves negotiating a resolution of the oedipal conflict, which establishes the superego as an independent agency functioning in harmony with the interests of the ego. This requires alterations in the fixation points and the replacement of infantile objects with the representation of new and independent attachments. The fixation point anchoring object constancy is gradually depersonified, loosening the tie to its infantile, narcissistic origins, and ultimately is replaced by an object related attachment. The fixation point in the self system, which is necessary during the oedipal period of new structure building, is gradually integrated and relinquished. The resolution of the oedipal conflict through selective identifications creates a well-regulated pathway of instinctual integration, and the stabilizing function of this fixation point is taken over by a consolidated superego.

The neuroses reflect the pathological result of an inability to negotiate this step. The fixation points are defensively bound to their infantile roots, having undergone little alteration. The superego remains at an immature level of organization, with its functions polarized and in conflict with the interests of the ego. The new boundary for the unconscious system based upon incestuous fantasies is defensively overdeveloped, whereas the structured pathway for instinctual integration based upon primal scene fantasies is highly conflicted. Object related experiences are potentially traumatic, and obsessive or hysteric pathology is determined by the particular asynchrony in stage and phase specificity that transpires during the pregenital period. Repression proper predominates as the primary ego defense, and identifications with an aggressor and reaction formations are available to increase its effectiveness. Prohibitions and character defenses are anally derived in the obsessive, and have either a phallic or genital derivation in the hysteric.

The anal derivation of mental structures is disclosed in the dream imagery of the obsessive, demonstrated in the dream of a 45-year-old man entering treatment because of a repetitive pattern of marrying one woman and seeking warmth and companionship with another. He was dominated by reaction formations designed to protect any expression of anal sadism, and was constantly ruminative and intellectual in his description of internal events. The therapist's interpretations acquainted him with the defensive function of his fixed attitudes, which led to the emergence of anally influenced, genital instinctual derivatives. While talking about a fight with his wife because of his involvement with another woman, he remembered a dream:

I was out walking the dog and he ran into the street. It was a very busy street with lots of fast cars. I screamed and yelled at him. He froze and this put him in greater danger. I finally got to him and he ran away again. I got so furious I kicked him hard and he ran down the street yelping. I went into the house and called the vet, trembling with fear. I woke up very frightened at this loss of control of my anger.

In recalling the dream it felt as if he and the dog were one entity, and he could feel himself become detached in order to be on the sidewalk yelling. The increasing ineffectiveness of anally derived character defenses was symbolically represented in his efforts to control the animal, and the newfound awareness of anal sadistic aggression left him shaken. Although the specific latent unconscious wishes cannot be fully outlined without the associative material necessary to unravel the dream work, the call to the doctor seemed to express his appeal for help in managing genital drives that had previously been held under repression and were now incorporated in the image of the uncontrollable dog.

Phallic and genitally derived mental structures are utilized in the construction of a dream in the hysterical personality, which is explained in the dream of a 30-year-old woman beginning treatment because of a conflicted wish to become pregnant. While describing the importance of having a baby, she remembered a dream:

I was in the baby's room with my husband and there were others present who I could not see. I knew we were going to be beheaded. I accepted it, but I wanted us to be together. I couldn't stand the idea of seeing his head cut off and the blood running. I decided to simply hold his hand and not look.

The dream symbolically represented the genitally determined prohibitive responses characteristic of castration anxiety, which by implication suggests the latent dream thoughts concerning forbidden genital instinctual wishes. It hints that her desire to be impregnated was connected to an unconscious infantile fantasy.

In the neurotic individual, incestuous fantasies are overdeveloped, expressing the inordinate need for defense, and their derivatives will frequently be symbolically represented in a manifest dream. The relatively open expression of incestuous fantasies is not accompanied by high levels of anxiety or excessively prohibitive responses, which is reflective of the effectiveness of their defensive function.

The following dreams are illustrative:

I am at a hotel with my mother. I am sexually aroused and rubbing my erection against her. I am aware that it is wrong and of my father's absence, and I'm surprised it really doesn't bother me.

This first dream was reported by a 32-year-old man concerned about episodes of impotence and premature ejaculation, and was presented with an attitude of surprise at its openly incestuous content.

I was kissing my neighbor, was sexually aroused, and curious about my reaction.

This second dream was reported by a 40-year-old woman after a session in which she spoke positively about her treatment. The openly oedipal nature of the dream was immediately apparent to her, and she could only express puzzlement about her lack of anxiety.

Incestuous fantasies structure a new boundary for the unconscious system and when hypertrophied, serve well as the foundation for defense transferences and protect against the emergence of more threatening primal scene fantasies. Anxiety and prohibitions are more in evidence in response to primal scene fantasies, which represent the unseen dimension on the continuum of biophysiological demand and consequently involve an unseen instinctual object.

The following dreams symbolically represent the danger associated with this source of instinctual overstimulation:

I was in a strange school. The teacher was kind but firm. There was a second floor that could not be explored. I was curious, wanted to explore it, and sensed there was something there. The teacher led the class in a prayer, stressing that the second floor was off limits.

The dream was reported by a 7-year-old girl after a session in which she talked about her hidden dark side. It was referred to in another chapter to show the significance of the day residue. The symbolization of a hidden, unseen, implicitly instinctual object mobilized prohibitions, giving expression to the obstacles that prevented any movement toward integration.

A girl on a private golf course is putting. As she strokes the ball a bolt of lightning hits her and the ball rolls in the hole. A lighthouse on a point of land speaks, "Next time you'll play on a public course."

In this manifest dream, reported by an obsessive man, the derivative of a primal scene fantasy is symbolized as a bolt of lightning. It captures the intensity with which this powerful stimulus is registered as it gains access to representation.

The obsessive and hysteric neurotic disturbances have negotiated the transition to object relatedness and have attained the structural organization necessary to develop a transference neurosis. An oedipal conflict has formed, but remains in an infantile state without having achieved an adequate resolution. The conditions enabling psychological growth are those making it possible for repressed infantile instinctual drives to become accessible to the integrative forces in the personality. A benign regression guided by the basic psychoanalytic principles leads to a gradual unfolding of the continuity of transference experience, ultimately creating a new edition of the infantile neurosis in the treatment relationship. Interpretive interventions foster its development and resolution, infantile instinctual experience is integrated, infantile attachments are replaced by new and independent objects, and the superego then functions independently in harmony with ego interests.

## Composition of Mental Structures and Their Appearance in the Manifest Dream

A mental structure is composed of the representation of a body ego experience, its object impression counterpart, and a fantasy linkage capable of the degree of cohesion necessary for it to be permanently sustained. The manifest dream is constructed to represent unconscious forces symbolically and thereby has the potential for revealing the underlying structural organization of the personality and occupying a special place in illuminating the foundation of a psychological disorder. The particular level of psychic functioning accessible to the process of dreaming presents a picture that can be of great value in determining an accurate diagnostic evaluation, in following therapeutic movement, and in furthering the view of therapeutic needs.

In order to delineate the structural composition of the personality from the manifest dream, an assessment must be made of the self system of representations, the object system of representations, the manner in which they are united and differentiated, the degree of stability at the foundation of the personality, and the nature of conflicting forces. The makeup of the mental structures accomplishing the psychic functions most in evidence gives a portrayal of the level of psychosexual development at which the dreamer is primarily operating and the degree of developmental progression that has been attained.

Attachments to an object are effected through fantasies, which contain both affect and cognition. Any process that is destructive to a fantasy is equally destructive to the vehicle by which connections to an object are maintained. The attachments to an object that structuralize cohesiveness in the personality take place at three specific locales. The first is based upon a recognition of the good object's bad prohibitive qualities and anchors object constancy. Separation and individuation are initiated with the healing of splits in the ego, as the ongoing consolidation of good self experience moves from the interior to the periphery of the personality. The first moment of cohesiveness occurs when a separate good object's influence is recognized, registered, and represented, which is accomplished by extending self experience around structured remnants of reactions to impingement to locate the impressions of a good object.

This advance in psychic organization expands the boundary of the self by forming two arms of perception and a focused area of internally directed perceptual activity. The extension of self experience is at the foundation of what becomes an introjective arm of perception. The connection to the impressions and influences of an object is at the foundation of what becomes a projective arm of perception. The focused area of perceptual activity establishes a foundation for the eye of consciousness and function of self observation.

A good object's influence has been present in the form of fusion and merger experiences, which at this early stage of individuation exerts a strong regressive pull. Therefore a separate good object's influence must be stabilized by the differentiating effect of its bad qualities, so as not to entail a loss of functional capacities. The good object's bad qualities are perceived through the line of continuity of prohibitive experience, as optimal frustration shades into prohibitions and impingements. A fixation point is then formed on the projective arm of perception that serves to anchor object constancy. To lose that attachment to an object is to lose differentiation.

The second attachment to an object that structuralizes cohesiveness involves the formation of the grandiose self and ego ideal, which unite and differentiate the self and object systems of representation at the surface of the personality. The grandiose self unites good instinctual self experience with the fantasy of an optimally gratifying object in order to balance the vulnerability associated with separateness. It is called the grandiose self because it is founded upon the participation in a fantasy. The ego ideal utilizes fantasied self potentials to unite with admired and needed qualities of an object, which then serves to strengthen adaptive capacities and the sense of identity. It is called the ego ideal because it is founded on including the influences of an object within self experience via a process of selective identification. These structures maintain cohesiveness, form a boundary within which the superego is organized, and incorporate perceptual functions within the boundary that become focused into the superego eye. This perceptual agency is in continuity with the eye of consciousness, registers regressive psychic contents in the preconscious system, and establishes the boundary of a dreaming self.

The third locale structuring cohesiveness takes place at the interior and involves the oedipal linkages. These structure a new object related boundary for the unconscious system of mental activity and a pathway for instinctual integration. The oedipal conflict is comprised of overstimulating genital instinctual attachments to an object linked by primal scene and incestuous fantasies. The self and object systems are only united at the surface of the personality until an oedipal conflict is structured. Therefore cohesiveness remains in jeopardy, since there is little available to regulate the demands of biophysiology in the deeper layers of the personality. Primal scene fantasies involve an attachment that structures a pathway of instinctual integration, and are accompanied by the movement of instinctual demand from the interior realm of biophysiology toward integrative sublimatory functions localized at the periphery. Movement and impulsion is the predominant feature in dreams representing this activity, which is then symbolized as a powerful, mobile force in action eliciting strong prohibitions. Incestuous fantasies involve an attachment that structures a boundary for the unconscious system, and are accompanied by a defensive alignment in opposition to instinctual activity. There is a relative absence of movement in dreams emphasizing incestuous fantasy derivatives.

A dream symbolically representing the loss of an attachment to an object, in addition to its specific unconscious meaning, has diagnostic significance. A loss or threatened loss of attachment to an object encompassed in the structure of the grandiose self or ego ideal will not allow the dream to continue. The perceptual functions operative in a dream are those incorporated in the grandiose self and ego ideal, since the eye of consciousness is suspended during sleep. Any process that engenders an attack upon these linkages places the integrity of the dreamer's self in jeopardy and precipitates the need to invoke a different set of perceptual conditions. The dream then becomes a nightmare and the dreamer is awakened in a state of extreme anxiety. The following dream already referred to in regard to its structural organization and to its implications for what is needed in treatment, shows the nightmare qualities when prohibitions threaten an attachment to a good object's influence.

> I was trying to see my enemy and face him once and for all. I did see him and he was so monstrous and terrifying I awoke in fright.

A loss involving an oedipal attachment at the interior of the personality is indicative of the extent to which genital strivings are in the ascendancy, and that prohibitive opposition has gained dominance. This dream was used previously to demonstrate the interrelationship between the two agencies of perception, and also depicts an object loss.

> I'm with a girl who I know is going to die. It has something to do with the X-ray machine at an airport terminal. The dream shifts. I'm with the same girl, only this time I know she'll die in three weeks. I make plans to be with her, and at the same time I'm watching the dream trying to figure out what it means.

The loss of an oedipal attachment does not threaten cohesiveness or place the integrity of the self in danger, and consequently does not assume nightmare proportions.

## Character Defenses, Perceptual Functions, and the Manifest Dream

Character defenses can only be functional when cohesiveness is established, and they are based upon the memory traces of an infantile attachment to a prohibitive object and upon pregenital experiences of instinctual overstimulation. In healthy people these memory traces, which have established stabilizing fixation points to enable new structure formation, undergo alterations as a necessary accompaniment to continuing self expansion. The fixation point in the object system must be retained to anchor object constancy and support projective processes. It is expanded through gradually being symbolized and depersonified, and is eventually replaced by the impressions of new and independent objects.

The fixation point in the self system is integrated in conjunction with the resolution of the oedipal conflict, and its stabilizing function is taken over by the conflict-free sphere of the ego operating in harmony with a consolidated and independent superego. Character pathology results when this fixation point is maintained defensively beyond stage and phase specificity and when the fixation point in the object system retains its original infantile attachment. Subsequently, fixed character attitudes evolve that reenforce the repression of oedipal strivings, and continuity between the two perceptual agencies is then obstructed by the need to defend against a regression.

When psychoanalytic treatment is successful in facilitating a benign regression, pathological defenses are rendered ineffective and continuity between the eye of consciousness and superego eye is more readily accessible.

The following sequence of dreams, occurring over a period of three years in the treatment of a 17-year-old boy, elucidates the effect upon the two perceptual agencies when character defenses are no longer required and the pathway toward instinctual integration is relatively open.

He sought therapeutic help for what he described as episodes of severe depression, panic, and an inability to meet adaptational demands. He was extremely obsessive in his attitude toward the internal and external world, had established reaction formations against anal sadistic aggression, and was constantly afraid of losing control. In the early sessions he spoke of his family, making a slight reference to his father, who had died when the boy was 9 years old. He had always been puzzled about his lack of feeling in response to the loss. Afterward he reported a dream:

> I walked into a store to buy a shirt and saw a television set. A wall of dirt appeared on the screen with gun barrels buried in it. A zombie covered with mud emerged as though it was struggling to get loose, and I felt responsible for its coming into existence. It had a bright red opening in its chest. A woman was connected to the zombie and she agreed it was my fault. The zombie came after me and scared me. I began to run because I was fearful I could be influenced by the zombie.

After describing the dream he was amazed that the symbolic imagery had an obvious connection to his father. The gun barrels in the mud and bright red opening in the zombie's chest immediately brought to mind how his father had died of a heart attack while being held up by a gunman.

The zombie, symbolically representing unconscious forces striving for expression, could only be responded to with great anxiety in the dream; yet his attitude while reporting it was of intellectual surprise with little affect. Thus, his character defenses were functioning to prevent an unobstructed interchange between the two agencies of perception. The superego eye, engaged in registering the dream content and establishing the boundary of a dreaming self, had little access to the integrative functions associated with the eye of consciousness. The dreamer was then confronted with the emergence of repressed instinctual dangers that could only be portrayed as instigating a flight. The eye of consciousness, engaged in reporting the dream and establishing the boundary of a wakeful self, was clearly demarcated and the affective components of the dream were totally unavailable. He could observe the dream from a great emotional distance, but the regressive experiences incorporated in the dream and linked by associations to their unconscious determinants were inaccessible because of the effectiveness of his character defenses.

One year later he reported the following dream:

> I was living in a huge dam holding back an enormous river. The house was awesome. I was at the top and I had just discovered a government plot to destroy the dam so the water would surge through. I was excited at the prospect, not frightened, because it seemed that the water would rush through and cleanse the house. I looked up and saw yellow stains as though it was beginning. The dream shifted and I was on an airplane on a special mission to Washington. The plane landed, the brakes failed, and it looked like it would go off the runway. Again I was excited and not scared, and the plane stopped right at the edge.

The manifest dream symbolized the beginning breakdown of his character defenses and an anticipation of being flooded by the eruption of unconscious instinctual drives no longer able to be held under repression. The sense of not being frightened appeared to be the product of a benign therapeutic regression, which was responsible for his gradual relinquishment of these pathological defenses. There was also some evidence of more advanced integrative functions operating in the construction of the manifest dream, indicative of a freer flow between the two perceptual agencies. Repressed unconscious wishes that had previously been represented as a frightening, potentially trau-matizing zombie were now symbolized as a powerful surging river and an airplane. The dam leaking and brakes not working were both received with excitement.

Further validation was present in his associations to the dream. Homosexual secrets in relation to his father came into the open, as did childhood memories of being frightened and overstimulated. The appearance of homosexual fantasies had previously elicited a panic reaction, but they could now be explored, and he even tentatively entertained the idea of their presence in the transference relationship. In a waking state it was increasingly possible to suspend the eye of consciousness, observing internal events through the more regressive posture accompanying the ascendancy of the superego eye.

Sometime later, while describing his anxiety and excitement at the prospect of an impending sexual contact, he remembered this dream:

> I was in a bathroom looking at a naked boyfriend in the bathtub. I felt sexually aroused, and smiled with recognition. I had the thought in the dream that this was what I had been fighting against for a long time.

He immediately recalled his first dream, became deeply immersed in derivatives expressing a negative oedipal transference attachment, and noted how his fixed character attitudes had protected him from feeling the impact of these underlying fantasies. Accompanying the dissolution of his fixed, anally derived character defenses was a freer interplay between the eye of consciousness and superego eye. His genital instinctual demands became more accessible to the integrative forces in his personality.

The ready passage from one perceptual agency to the other is also observable in the cohesive, narcissistic personality disorders. In this situation, however, it is not the product of having attained a more advanced level of psychic structuralization, but is the result of highly unstable fixation points. The superego is inadequately consolidated and incapable of any significant degree of independent functioning, and the eye of consciousness and superego eye, rather than operating in well-defined sectors of the personality, blend into each other with little discrimination. In waking life such individuals readily lose perspective when regressive experiences are dominant, and in a dream the same fusion of perceptual functions is often exhibited. This phenomenon is illustrated in the following dreams: This one had been presented previously to show how symbolic processes operate and how instinctual activity is managed in the phobias.

> I was driving in a car in my old neighborhood and I was both inside and outside the car. As I got out I noticed a mist that surrounded and suffocated me. I had the thought in the dream that it was my own feelings.

The mixture of advanced and regressive modes of perception places the dreamer in two places simultaneously. Perceptual functions establish a self boundary; two separate boundaries are created that are both continuous and separate. They flow into each other with no demarcation, and they are accompanied by a blending of regressive and more advanced psychic functions. The dreamer is thereby capable of symbolically representing an experience of suffocation, suggestive of early oral fusion and merger wishes, and at the same time is observing the scene and denoting its meaning. This dream was used before to demonstrate how the unconscious perception of an empathic lapse is symbolized.

> I went to the freezer, and all that was there were quick, awful fast foods dressed up to look great. I angrily threw them out looking for good food. Another part of me was off to the side amused.

The dream symbolizes the aggression associated with early oral disappointments, and at the same time places the dreamer off to the side observing with perspective. The appearance of two separate selves, each with a different set of characteristics, reflects the existence of two separate and functional perceptual agencies operating in concert with each other. One is not in suspension as the other assumes dominance, but both are continuously active and blend into each other. These two dreams were founded upon the structural organization of a cohesive, narcissistic personality disorder, and displayed the readiness with which the two perceptual agencies combined to act in unison.

Firmly bound pathological character defenses prevent a regression, act as an obstacle to the projective identifications fueling the transference relationship, and maintain genital instinctual wishes under repression. They operate on the foundation of fixation points rooted to infantile experience, create fixed attitudes and distortions, and remain tied to the structures that unite and differentiate the representations of self and object. These structures, the grandiose self and ego ideal, are an integral part of the superego eye. Therefore, when character defenses are effective, experiences of instinctual overstimulation cannot be projected outside the boundary of a dreaming self.

In the hysteric, the grandiose self is phallically derived, linking instinctual experiences of phallic exhibitionism to the fantasy of an admiring object; the ego ideal is also phallically derived, linking the fantasy of needed regulation to the impression of a humiliating prohibitive object. The fixation point that anchors object constancy is based upon the memory trace of an infantile attachment to an object possessing bad, prohibitive, humiliating qualities, and the fixation point stabilizing the self system is based upon a memory trace of the good self's bad voyeuristic qualities. In a dream, the grandiose self and ego ideal retain overstimulating instinctual qualities within a self boundary. They are symbolized as being held in check by an opposing force.

> This was brought out in the dream of an 18-year-old boy after his first sexual encounter:
>
> > I was in a condo in Florida with a friend and my parents. Two beautiful girls came and my parents invited them in to talk. I couldn't stand the temptation but was immobilized by the presence of my parents. My friend masturbated, said "the hell with it," and took the girls into the bedroom.
>
> The manifest dream was constructed on an underlying foundation with character defenses working to hold unconscious genital instinctual drives in abeyance. When such drives threatened to be expressed, the

attachment to prohibitive parental objects represented an oppositional force. The tenacity of this infantile attachment was gradually loosened, which was reflected in the appearance of a friend who was capable of overcoming the prohibition.

Character defenses tend to be more solidly entrenched in the obsessive, but when they are ineffective, the projection of pregenital impulses on which they are based creates an inordinate threat. The obsessive's grandiose self is anally derived, linking instinctual experiences of mastery to the fantasy of an omnipotent object; the ego ideal is also anally derived, linking the fantasy of needed regulation to the impression of a sadistically impinging prohibitive object. The fixation point that anchors object constancy is based upon the memory trace of an infantile attachment to an object possessing bad, prohibitive sadistic qualities, and the fixation point stabilizing the self system is based upon the memory trace of the good self's bad anal sadistic qualities. Character defenses do not allow bad self experience to be projected outside the boundary of a dreaming self, but if the underlying sadism cannot be contained, it is either symbolized as a very dangerous sadistic figure or the dream may be interrupted.

This was manifested in the following two dreams. The first was reported by an obsessive adolescent boy whose waking life was occupied with ruminative and ritualistic thinking.

I was in a TV show with a lot of fighting and violence. I was frightened because people were being cut up and injured, and I sensed they could turn on me at any moment.

The manifest dream was founded upon anally derived character defenses that were undergoing a breakdown in their effectiveness as anal sadistic impulses were projected outside the dreaming self and symbolically represented as overwhelmingly dangerous.

The second dream was reported by a 22-year-old man suffering acutely from a periodic upsurge of intolerable guilt whenever anally determined character defenses were unsuccessful in maintaining reaction formations against sadistic impulses. He was the fourth of six boys, was intensely competitive with his brothers, often felt like a "wimp," and was concerned that he appeared effeminate. After a session in which he talked about an older brother, feeling a great deal of discomfort with the depth of his hostility, he had a dream:

I was with my brother and I suddenly have a gun in my hand. I shot him in the head, felt attacked by guilt, and awoke screaming as I tried to take it back but it was too late.

The dream symbolically represented the breakthrough of anal sadistic impulses and the delayed opposition of his character defenses. Consequently these bad instinctual qualities were unable to be successfully projected, and the dream ended in a nightmare.

When a manifest dream contains no evidence of the functional existence of character defenses, it signifies that a fixation point in the self system has either not formed or is not solidly anchored. Under these circumstances the grandiose self and ego ideal can narrow the boundary of a dreaming self to include only those aspects involving good self experience. Any facet of self experience outside this narrow boundary can then be symbolized and although it may take the form of an object, it will possess self attributes.

This was exemplified in the following dream of a 5-year-old phobic boy:

My nightmares jumped out of my head and into the closet. The first was a big monster. I attacked him with my sword and he cried. I put him in my bed and he was my friend. Then a second nightmare jumped out of my head. This was a scary one. It was a big angry tiger that ate up all my toys.

Aspects of bad self experience were readily projected outside the dreamer's self, vividly portrayed as jumping out of his head, and then symbolically represented as monstrous objects though they clearly possessed self attributes.

## The Level of Psychosexual Development, the Nature of Anxiety, and the Firmness of Identity Reflected in the Manifest Dream

In delineating the structural organization upon which the manifest content of a dream is founded, it is important to identify the particular stage of psychosexual development that is symbolically represented. In this previously presented dream, an orally derived object possesses either nurturant or incorporative qualities.

I had a baby boy, and my mother sedated me so she could take it over and control it. I screamed in anger that it was mine. The baby grew rapidly, began to become attached to my mother, and I felt enraged because I was losing the bond I had made.

An anal object fosters mastery or exerts sadistic control:

> I'm in school and a boy begins to beat me up. Just then a table wiggles and Baby Godzilla comes to life. He attacks the boy, protects me, and teaches me how to fight. He carried me home in his arms. On the way he set me down and I became afraid that he was going to dominate and control me. I ran away with him chasing me. While looking over my shoulder to see him, I ran into a pole, was stunned, and woke up.

A phallic object is approving or humiliating:

> I was with a girlfriend, talking, laughing, and having a good time. She gave me her phone number. Later I dialed it, and just as I got to the last number I hung up. I was very uneasy, tried again, and this time I got her father who accused me of sexual intentions. I was horribly embarrassed and hung up.

A genital object supports independent genital activities or is castrating:

> I was in the baby's room with my husband. There were other people present but they were unseen. I knew we were going to be beheaded. I accepted it but wanted us to be together. I couldn't stand the idea of seeing his head cut off and seeing all the blood. I decided to hold hands and not look.

The nature of the anxiety present in a dream is of diagnostic significance, but it is the quality rather than the intensity that is important. From the point of view of the ego, the primary anxiety in a phallic or genital organization is of castration.

> I had gone away to camp. I had mosquito bites on the inner side of my thigh and was going to the doctor. A lot of other children in the camp had poison ivy and the doctor was giving them shots. I was on a conveyor belt with three other children and was moving toward the doctor. The doctor said if the first three children had poison ivy, the fourth did too. The first three had poison ivy. I didn't want to get a shot. I started to scream and my mother came to hold me.

Anally it is of a loss of control:

> I was out walking the dog and he ran into the street where there were many fast cars. I screamed and yelled at him. He froze, which put him in more danger. I got him and he did it again. I got so furious I kicked him hard and he ran down the street. I was in the house calling the vet and shaking. I woke up trembling at the loss of control of my anger.

Orally it is of losing functional capacities:

> I'm in a leaking boat and fighting to prevent it from going down. All of a sudden I realize it is best to not fight. I can go to the bottom and push off to get back above water. I do get back above water, and it felt real good.

From the point of view of an attachment to an object, the primary anxiety in a genital organization is of the superego's disapproval:

> I'm at a hotel with my mother. I'm sexually aroused and rubbing my erection against her. I'm concerned and aware of how wrong it is, and also aware of my father's absence.

In a phallic organization it is the disapproval of the object:

> I'm in a condo in Florida with a friend and my parents. Two beautiful girls come by and my parents invite them in to talk. I can't stand the temptation, but I'm immobilized by the fear of my parents' disapproval.

Anally it is the loss of the object's love:

> My mother and father are arguing. My father disappears as my mother tries to take my makeup. I fight to hold onto it and she hits me and hurts me. She screams at me and is jealous of my cosmetics. She wants them all for herself.

Orally it is the loss of the object:

> My mother has come back to life and I'm with her. She's sick and I'm trying to help. An older man is after me. I try to hide but he finds me. I go back to help my mother but it is too late.

The manner in which the dreamer is presented within the context of the dream has a bearing on the sense of identity. Identity may rest upon an uncertain foundation, which will then be reflected in rapid fluctuations in the dreamer's position:

> Men were robbing a bank and I got a chain to stop them. Suddenly I was one of them, and a woman bank teller was a hostage with her hands chained. I had to get away and ducked into a pipe system with no way out. I tried to get over a fence but it was endless and had barbed wire. I kept looking for a way out and knew I would find one.

When identity and the integrity of the self are in danger, the threat will be symbolically represented.

> I was enveloped by a huge spider and was so afraid I would suffocate. I slipped away and ran to my grandfather's house. He had a big shotgun and shot the spider. I yelled, "He's a dead duck."

Or the dream may be interrupted:

> I was looking for my penny in the grass. A car came toward me with the lights on. It was both in control and out of control. It was trying like the devil to hit me but was skidding. Just before the impact I shook and woke up.

The dreamer's self may be firm even in the presence of potential danger, revealing a relatively solid sense of identity:

> I'm pipetting blood samples by mouth. I accidentally took in some serum and was astonished at the fact that I did it and that I was not overwhelmed.

The dreamer's self may also be firm when its integrity is in jeopardy and must be carefully protected. Under those circumstances, however, the danger will be present in the setting of the dream:

> I am in a house with my parents and brother. A kind old man invites me to come out and play. There are other kids there and I go to a clubhouse built in a tree. I am excited and it's fun, but I suddenly realize it is in a swamp. There are crocodiles all around, I can't climb down, and I'm separated from home.

## The Symbolic Representation of Defenses in the Manifest Dream

The nature of a defense symbolized in a manifest dream can be helpful in determining whether the impinging stimulus emanated from an internal instinctual demand, or whether its source was an unconsciously significant failure in empathy. It can be crucial to distinguish between the way instinctual impingements and the impingements of the external world are defended against, in order to aid in identifying those derivatives expressing the activity of unconscious perceptions. Internal instinctual stimuli cannot be evaded or made to disappear and hence are always attended to in some fashion, whereas external stimuli can be made to disappear primarily through motility. Nevertheless, unavoidable instinctual dangers must be represented as avoidable for a dream to continue, while avoidable external dangers must be represented as unavoidable for their unconscious meaning to be symbolized. In the dream itself there is no escape but to awaken. Therefore, the stimuli of instinctual activity, which cannot be evaded, utilize the representation of an ability to escape as the basis for their defense; and external impinging stimuli, which can be evaded, utilize the representation of an inescapable danger as the basis for their defense.

Instinctual demands are on a continuum that attains a level of intensity having the qualities of an impingement. There is a dimension not requiring defense, a dimension included within the realm of self experience with the aid of defense, and a dimension with the qualities of an independent, instinctually impinging object. With the dawning of perceptual functions and the emergence of a nuclear self *in utero*, the accompanying primitive state of lack of differentiation does not allow these discrete nuances to be clearly defined. The impinging dimension on the continuum of instinctual demand is poorly localized, leaving only a vague mental impression. The massive external impingement at birth is immediately reacted to, is well localized, and is evocative of and shaped by the instinctual impingements at the interior. External impingements are thereby colored by the phase of psychosexual development in the forefront at the time they are represented. They are devouring during orality, sadistic in the anal phase, humiliating in the phallic period, and castrating with a genital consolidation. Once cohesiveness has been established, as is the case in a dream, these impinging impressions of an external object are utilized for prohibitive responses and are an important source of defensive opposition to instinctual overstimulation.

Primary repression, which is the model for all internally directed defensive operations, refers to the transition from biophysiology to mental representation. It is the boundary for unconscious mental activity during the earliest phases of development, and is the only defense that functions as a wall. Once instinctual demand gains access to mental representation, the wall of primary repression is no longer available as a defense. The representation of attending to a stimulus is founded upon the need to do so with instinctual demands, and is the basis for the effectiveness of reactions to impingement as a defensive response. The reactions to impingement are body ego experiences of fight, flight, or withdrawal. They are nondiscriminatory in nature and are the major source of defensive opposition to external impingements.

Within a cohesive personality, repression proper, which functions by directing attention away from the source of a threatening internal stimulus toward mental contents that are less threatening, is the major defense against instinctual activity. The representation of a turning away is founded upon the ability to do so with external impingements, and is the basis for repression proper being effective in directing attention away from a potential internal danger. External impingements require the use of perceptual functions to mobilize the necessary defensive response, and attention is thereby not directed away from the source of a threat. During sleep, external stimuli are only registered to a very limited extent, motility is markedly reduced and largely unavailable, and the stimuli of the internal world are highlighted. The symbolic representation in a dream of either a turning away or of invoking prohibitions is indicative of a defensive response to the impact of internal instinctual stimuli, whereas the symbolic representation of fight, flight, or withdrawal signifies a defensive response to the unconscious perception of an emotionally important external impingement.

The following two dreams, presented earlier to illustrate different points, emphasize the impact of an internal instinctual impingement, identifiable in the manifest content primarily from the nature of the defensive response.

> I was in a strange school. The teacher was kind but firm. There was a second floor that could not be explored. I was curious and wanted to explore it and sensed something was there. The teacher led the class in a prayer, stating that they absolutely should not go there.

> I was trying to see my enemy and face him once and for all. I did. I saw him and he was so monstrous and terrifying I awoke in fright.

Both dreams symbolize an impinging stimulus and a defensive response. In both there is an attempt to discover the source, and the defensive maneuver includes a prohibition. The extent of the danger is proportional to the intensity of the stimulus and the strength of the prohibitive response, which are more extreme in the second dream.

By way of contrast, the following two dreams emphasize the impact of an external impingement, identifiable in the manifest content by defensive responses that are symbolized quite differently:

> I was with friends and we were goofing around. Another friend drove up chased by the police. They jumped out of their car, arrested us,

and put us in jail. We were innocent and angry for being judged superficially. The police looked like rookies who were frightened and needed to look tough in each other's eyes, as if they were doing their job.

A lady or a girl grabbed me and I was scared. My father was smiling in a funny way, like there was nothing to fear and it was just a game. I hoped so, but he was trying to reassure me, though unsure himself. I bit down on the lady's hand, gently at first, but she doesn't get the message. I bit down with all my strength and my teeth went right through her hand. At first she didn't feel it, but then she let go of me, holding her hand in pain. My father, brother, and I ran away.

The first dream symbolized an impinging stimulus, which elicited a defensive response of angry withdrawal. In the second dream an impinging stimulus is symbolized that elicited a defensive response of fight and flight. In both, the impingements appear to represent an experience of unempathic contact with the external world, and serve as the derivative of an emotionally important unconscious perception around which each dream was constructed.

# Part II

# The Manifest Dream across the Spectrum of Pathology

# 8

# Dreams in the Schizophrenias

A dream examined for the structural foundations of its manifest content can only reveal what is in the ascendancy at a given moment. In the healthy and in the object-related hysteric and the obsessive neurotic, this will appear fairly consistent over a long sequence of time, since the foundation of the personality is solidly established and change is gradual. Neurotic forms of pathology have attained advanced levels of psychic structuralization. They are manifested in a fixed, consistent interrelationship of the self and object systems of representation and symbolized in the manifest dream. The appearance of relatively rapid shifts and fluctuations can be extremely significant in reflecting the degree of stability in the personality. This is often seen in the narcissistically determined, object related, phobic disorders. When cohesiveness is unstable, though developmental progression may be evidenced within a particular dream, it cannot be sustained under a variety of conditions.

Although the seeds of any pathological entity are sown in childhood, in the cohesive disorders there is enough advanced development for healthy modes of functioning to be available under the proper conditions for extended segments of time. A neurotic character or symptom disturbance may not be manifest until stressful circumstances are present. This is not the case in the noncohesive disorders, since the influences of an object are not available to

137

strengthen self experience. The resulting pathology is existent from its inception in childhood.

The more cohesive the personality, the less vital dreams are for furthering therapeutic work. The less cohesive the personality, the more vital dreams are for accomplishing this task. The individual without continuity of experience structured in the personality has a difficult time revealing the composition of the internal world, and dreams aid greatly in illuminating this often shadowy area. In the more cohesive personality, dreams are an effective means for exposing the unconscious realm of mental activity, which is accomplished by utilizing a free associative process to unravel the latent dream thoughts and dream work. In the less cohesive personality, the impact of splitting has a disruptive effect upon associative connections, but the dream can act like a map to guide a therapeutic journey. When cohesiveness is not structured, dreams are more valuable as a signpost of therapeutic progress and less effective as a pathway to the unconscious.

The manifest content of a dream, presented in the context of a therapeutic relationship, has the same significance as does any flow of associative material. When that flow is interrupted, the reasons need to be as clearly explicated as is possible. Frequently, when a patient is asked to associate to a dream, the response is to elaborate on the manifest content. A fuller picture of the dream imagery may then be brought forth, creating the impression of gaining a more complete version of the dream and of broadening the base from which a deeper understanding can unfold. What may be more relevant though is that the patient has been encouraged to amplify and enlarge advanced psychic functions, which must be utilized to translate the more regressive content of a dream into a communicative modality. This form of associating to a dream is a continuation of the process initially involved in the dream work itself and may or may not be useful in unveiling latent dream thoughts. It is certainly helpful in determining the underlying structural composition of the manifest dream, since it provides more content to work with that may be elucidating. Unfortunately this approach can be in opposition to the esssence of free association. A dream may contain many gaps that can conceivably be filled by such an exploration, but in the meantime the dreamer's characteristic style of presenting internal experience would be bypassed. It is not necessary to have this information in order to determine the structural foundation of the dream, and its absence is an important part of the dreamer's character.

In the schizophrenias, good self experience is split off from attachment to an object, so that the most reliable source for validating the growth-promoting properties of a therapeutic relationship is obscure. In addition, the lack of continuity of experience in the personality does not permit derivatives to be expressed without extreme interference, and the distorting influence of a primitive defensive organization creates confusion and uncertainty. A therapist must rely on an intuitive grasp of what is largely unspoken and unspeakable, leading to many stormy episodes in a transference relationship.

The manifest dream offers a vital contribution toward guiding a therapist in the conduct of the treatment, though it is less useful in revealing the specific unconscious wishes being granted symbolic expression. The very fact that a dream is retained within consciousness and communicated is in itself indicative of a search for unconscious understanding and suggestive of a potential for healing self splits.

## The Nature of Schizophrenic Pathology

Schizophrenic pathology is manifested in three separate yet interrelated phases: the basic schizophrenic process, the schizophrenic break, and the schizophrenic process of repair (Mendelsohn 1987). All three phases may coexist. Each contains a different structural configuration, and the task of treatment varies depending upon which is predominant. The basic schizophrenic process is the most significant because it is at the root of the disorder and determines its course.

The structural foundation of a basic schizophrenic process is formed within the symbiotic period. Early experiences of phase specific instinctual gratification are gleaned from isolated fragments of empathic responsiveness and are threatened with destruction by the invasive qualities of a pathological symbiosis. The impact of the destructive interaction evokes the primitive, reflexive response of withdrawal. Instinctual experience is dependent upon attachment to an object, withdrawal continues to the point of its being split off, and these aspects of good self experience are thereby preserved. Nevertheless, they remain in an infantile state, exerting a constant demand for attachment to an object. Simultaneously, a defensive constellation must be organized possessing enough oppositional force to maintain the split. At this primitive level of development the representation of the pathological symbiosis necessitating the split is all that is available, and it serves as the nidus around which a defensive alignment is constructed. From that moment two separate and disparate realms of psychological experience evolve: one is an infantile realm of instinctual experience totally divorced from contact with an object or with the external world; the other is an instinctually depleted realm of advanced psychic functions in contact with the world of external objects. The schizophrenias bear an intimate relationship to the autistic disorders in that both are the consequence of a pathological symbiosis. The incipient schizophrenic has managed to experience sufficient empathic responsiveness, limited though it is, to engage in a symbiosis, but has been unable to attain the degree of structuralization necessary to negotiate self differentiation successfully.

With each advancing step in development, the separation becomes wider and more disparate. The psychic contents of the deeper layers of the personality are composed of the split-off representations of good instinctual self experience and their fantasy elaborations. The momentary period of empathic attachment to an object prior to the split has left a trace of the influence of a good object. This enables the fantasy of an adequate symbiosis to be elaborated. The object seeking desires of this split-off infantile realm are intense and require a state of lack of differentiation in order to be realized. The advanced instinctually depleted realm at the surface of the personality is composed of the remaining aspects of good self experience that continue to develop. The motive for progression is based upon submission to, and conformity with the expectations of external objects. Mental structures evolve that are fragile, brittle, and rigid, and differentiation is primarily maintained through the hypertrophied activity of autonomous ego functions.

The defensive structure built around the representation of a pathological symbiosis must become more effective in sustaining the separation, since the pressure for an infantile attachment becomes more extreme. All elements of bad self experience and of a bad object's influence are fused and consolidated into this powerful defensive force, which operates to distort any experience of contact with the external world that resonates with the conditions of an adequate symbiosis. The potential for making an infantile instinctual attachment threatens the ability to maintain the split, and it must be transformed into a repetition of the original traumatic symbiosis. For this reason I have called this defensive structure an internal saboteur.

The split-off realm of infantile experience is constantly in search of an object for attachment, and when the stimuli of the external world are resonant with the qualities needed, they pose a threat. The internal saboteur functions to enforce the split by creating distortions reminiscent of the original trauma. When this defensive effort is unsuccessful a regression quickly gets out of control, but under conditions where distortions are rampant. The resulting instinctual attachment, in a regressive state of lack of differentiation with distorting influences active, is experienced as a submission out of need to the invasive power of a pathologically symbiotic object. The rigid, fragile advanced realm of psychological experience is fragmented by the malignant regression, and previously preserved representations of good infantile instinctual experience are distorted, injured, or destroyed. A schizophrenic break refers to the specific instant when the two separate worlds merge with a traumatic and fragmenting collision, under the distorting influence of the internal saboteur. Good infantile instinctual self experience is damaged by the pathologically distorted attachment, and there is an immediate reaction of withdrawal from all contact with objects.

With the onset of a schizophrenic break, the two disparate realms of experience fuse, shattering all aspects of mental representation. The depth of the regression, the fragility of the advanced realm of psychological functioning, and the unleashing of primitive aggression combine to create chaos and fragmentation. Good instinctual self experience is damaged or destroyed, and there is an immediate reflexive withdrawal from all contact with objects. A schizophrenic break may be total, or it may be isolated to a small sector of the personality. It is, however, a transient state that instantly instigates a schizophrenic process of repair.

A schizophrenic process of repair is designed to compensate for the damage and is initiated by narrowing the self boundary to enable a narcissistic focus of perceptual attention upon fantasied self potentials. A new object world is reconstructed with the fragmented psychic contents resulting from the consequences of a schizophrenic break. Strange and bizarre new unions are established without regard for whether they represent a body ego experience or a fantasy elaboration.

This compensatory organization is at the foundation of the symptoms usually associated with the diagnosis of schizophrenia, such as hallucinations, delusions, and megalomanic self experiences, and is unaffected by the influences of the external world. If a schizophrenic break and the ensuing process of repair only involve a small portion of good instinctual experience, a basic schizophrenic process may still predominate. All three stages will then be manifested in the same individual simultaneously. There may be repeated episodes until the damage is so extensive that the process of repair is all encompassing. Once this occurs, a split in the self is no longer possible, and the entire personality is organized to maintain a narcissistic overevaluation of a damaged self. A reconstructed world of persecutory objects binds the primitive aggression, and together with the unyielding focus upon compensatory fantasies, fixed attitudes reminiscent of character pathology are established.

An individual maintaining a basic schizophrenic process lives with a depleted, fragile, submissive manner of adapting and also has the internal awareness of the effects of the split-off infantile realm of experience. This takes the form of fleeting moments of intense longing for an infantile attachment, which is both foreign and familiar, accompanied by anxiety of panic proportions based on the constant threat of imminent annihilation. There are numerous episodes of losing perceptual contact with the external world, as the processes of withdrawal and regression are extremely active. Transient regressions into the infantile realm are both attractive and frightening, and the individual's life is severely crippled. An unstable hold on perceptual contact with the external world is reflected in recurrent sensations of imbalance and loss of orientation, which are often experienced as moving walls or floors.

The ability to sustain a basic schizophrenic process over extended periods of time is usually associated with a vast potential for autonomous ego functioning. The use of these capacities, however, is extremely narrow and limited, since so much is absorbed in warding off the regressive demands of an infantile world. Under stress, anxiety is inordinately debilitating, and there is little wherewithal to absorb narcissistic injury. The rigidity, inflexibility, flatness of affect, and preoccupation with control may bear a slight resemblance to the obsessive, but the resemblance is superficial. The obsessive has a rich instinctual life, has established object constancy and continuity of experience, and exhibits a stable sense of identity. Love relationships are either impossible or can only be viewed from a distance because the regressive pull toward an infantile attachment and the threat of a schizophrenic break are constant companions. Some will do anything to halt the regression, even going so far as to injure or destroy themselves. Any increase in adaptational demand, instinctual intensity, or potential love relationship may trigger a schizophrenic break.

An individual can live without an instinctual attachment to an object for only so long before even a pathological attachment is accepted. The ability to sustain a basic schizophrenic process depends a great deal upon the extent to which good instinctual self experience has been preserved. The greater the amount, the longer the split can be maintained, and the more it is possible to accept only a good object for attachment. The developing infant is faced with an impossible dilemma, in that what was needed for growth destroys and finds an answer by splitting off those aspects already formed. It requires a quality of strength, in a state of weakness, vulnerability, and need, to accomplish this act of preservation. The totality of existence depends upon the integrity of preserving good self experience from destructive influences, which frequently expands into a relentless commitment to exposing distortions. Over time it evolves as the core of an identity guiding all future relationships and is constantly in jeopardy. Although this is a shaky basis for identity, it is strengthened as long as the position is held.

Maintaining the split involves an enormous expenditure of defensive effort and is exhausting. It may reach a point where the slightest provocation can instigate a schizophrenic break, and whenever that point is reached there is an accompanying recognition that the temptation could have been resisted a moment longer in time. This awareness leaves an impression of having submitted out of neediness to the power and control of a pathological engulfing, invasive object. The sense of having participated in the corruption of integrity creates a deep inner conviction of basic badness. The hunger of instinctual need erodes the foundation of an identity that has been relied upon as a source of strength, and it is a devastating experience. Whenever a schizophrenic break is imminent, the defensive structure is losing its effectiveness, and the primitive aggression bound into the fused self and object images may be directed into self destructive acts to halt the repression. It is not so much an expression of self destructiveness as it is an attempt to stop the infantile longing. The aggression, being primitive and inadequately neutralized, stands ready to be unleashed in this desperate defensive response.

## Structural Composition of the Manifest Dream in the Schizophrenias

A young adult woman made an appointment to find help with a long-standing and serious disturbance. Her early life history was filled with extremes of sexual, emotional, and physical abuse, as well as periods of abandonment. She was taken from and returned to a psychotic mother on several occasions during her childhood and was hospitalized, receiving medication and shock treatment, in adolescence. At that time she was deeply involved in a private fantasy world, was largely out of contact with the world surrounding her, and her behavior was dictated by powerful hallucinated voices. Hospitalization occurred when she actively hallucinated, spoke in gibberish, and was totally disoriented. These episodes came about whenever she was separated from familiar surroundings, confronted with an adaptational demand, or anticipated a potential love relationship. Throughout, she was constantly seeking a therapist who could understand her internal world, and though she felt defeated by her efforts, she persisted in looking for what she described as someone capable of standing firm and at the same time nurturing an infantile part of herself. Following her first session she reported a dream:

> I went to see my sister's therapist and she said it was amazing that in one hour she had gotten to know me better than in the years she knew my sister. I had a very deep sore on my knee and was showing it to her. When I left her office I thought my sore wasn't healing. I went to my apartment, went from room to room to turn on the lights and they didn't go on. I felt frightened and woke up disoriented and on the edge of losing contact.

This manifest dream represented a clearly defined self and an object, and a differentiated connection between them. It reflected her awareness of a severe, deeply penetrating illness, symbolized by the sore on her knee, which was shown to a doctor and was not healing. It also pictured a separation from the doctor, along with an unsuccessful attempt to shed light on her own private space, culminating in a high level of anxiety that extended into wakefulness and threatened her ability to remain in contact with the external world.

The dream gave expression to her search for therapeutic understanding and to her anticipation of an empathic failure. The manifest content implicitly captured the position she was in, the questionable circumstances surrounding this latest venture toward finding therapeutic help, the need to expose and reveal the depth of her illness, and her inability to discover a cure through self understanding when left to her own devices. Upon awakening she was in even greater danger, since the level of psychic structuralization required to construct the manifest dream was less effectively maintained as she entered a waking state. It was indicative that the mental structures underlying the manifest dream were more advanced than those available to her when confronted with the demands of adapting to the external world. This apparent paradox requires an explanation, for the process of dreaming takes place in a regressive state of sleep and would seemingly have to use less organized mental structures.

A basic schizophrenic process does not encompass every aspect of the personality. There may be threads of healthy mental processes latently present, but they are so vulnerable to destruction they can only be manifested under circumstances in which there is no potential for narcissistic injury and at the same time no threat of effecting an attachment to an object. They cannot be viable when there is the potential for engagement in a relationship, since the opportunity for an attachment is especially dangerous. These healthy processes are inadequately supported and highly unstable, and they are unable to contain either instinctual activity at levels of intensity requiring defense, the effects of impingements, or adaptational demands. They can be used as a foundation for a dream because the potential for narcissistic injury or attachment to an object is significantly reduced, and the boundary of a dreaming self can be narrowed to exclude traumatic elements.

The operative conditions in the state of sleep involve a relative disengagement from the stimuli of the external world and more specifically, from the powerful demand to effect an attachment to an object. It enables the schizophrenic individual to make use of the split-off representations of good self experience and the threads of healthy processes dormant in the personality as a foundation upon which a dream can be constructed. The structural organization behind a dream will thereby be much more advanced than is evident while the individual is awake.

This was demonstrated in the dream of a 30-year-old woman who had desperately sought help when she felt compelled to destroy herself. This self-destructive impulse was designed to halt an all encompassing internal pull threatening her contact with the external world and creating episodes of extreme disorientation. In the therapeutic relationship, she was drawn to making an infantile attachment, which was associated with anxiety of panic proportions, and it mobilized an unyielding effort to convince the therapist that the treatment was destructive to her ability to grow. In the midst of her despair over finding a way to integrate split-off infantile aspects of herself, she reported a dream:

I was in a leaking boat, fighting to prevent myself from going down. All of a sudden I realized it was best not to fight going to the bottom. I could hold my breath and retain my ability to swim. When I got to the bottom I could push off and get back to the top. I did that and as I broke the surface with water on my face it felt very good.

The manifest content symbolically represented her fear of and need for a regression in order to heal the split-off infantile world clamoring for an attachment. It also implied that this process was in motion and that the distortions created by an internal saboteur were operating to disguise its occurrence and thereby prevent its continuation. The dream presented a picture that she was unable to portray or articulate in her waking life, and provided the therapist with validation of the growth-promoting properties of the treatment. Threads of healthy functioning, in conjunction with derivatives of her unconscious perception of the relationship, were capable of serving as a nidus around which the dream could be constructed. A more advanced level of psychic structralization was functional while dreaming, when the stimuli of the external world and the threat of an instinctual attachment were to a large extent diminished.

The act of constructing a dream depends upon a background of cohesiveness, since there must be a differentiated connection between the representations of self and object in order to symbolize the unconscious forces pushing for expression. This higher level of psychic organization at the foundation of a dream can be manifested by the schizophrenic during sleep, but the severity of the pathology will be in evidence in some form in the body of the dream. The manner in which the schizophrenic displays cohesiveness in a dream differs because the firmness of the underlying differentiating structures is very fragile and is disrupted with any significant increase in instinctual activity. Every dream is fueled by instinctual activity, but the boundary of the schizophrenic's dreaming self can only include instinctual activity that does not require defense. Higher degrees of intensity will threaten the structure of the dream and be symbolized as a dangerous presence outside the dreaming self.

The previously mentioned patient later reported a dream that is illustrative:

I was in a boarding school and needed to call my mother. I felt homesick and had to make contact with her. The head of the school was there and gave me permission to take all the time I needed. She stood watching. I couldn't find the money to put into the phone and she became more frightening and ominous as I struggled to make the call.

The manifest content symbolizes a search for the influences of an object that can offer safety and containment, reflecting the limited capacity to regulate instinctual activity. The existence of an obstacle was associated with a buildup in instinctual intensity, which was incorporated into the image of the head of the school. This benign figure then assumed dangerous properties that escalated as the dream progressed.

In order to construct a manifest dream, the representation of a self and object that are united and differentiated must be at least available to some extent. The schizophrenic in a waking state has not even the slightest vestige of this level of psychic organization. Although there is an advanced realm of psychological experience represented in a basic schizophrenic process, and it is united with a system of object impressions, the self system is depleted in its instinctual aspect and the representations of an object's influence are based entirely upon conformity. The unions established in this realm are not stable enough to support the construction of a dream, and it is split off from the infantile realm of instinctual experience that instigates the dreaming process. The split is maintained by a pathological defense containing the fused representations of bad self experience and a bad object's influence, creating distortions patterned after the attributes of a destructive symbiosis.

In going to sleep, the advanced realm is more closely allied with the pathological defensive structure to guard against the dangerous influx of external stimuli that continue to be registered. The schizophrenic moves from wakefulness to sleep with great difficulty and is awakened by minimal intensities of external stimulation. To the extent that such minor stimulation is successfully eliminated, a dream may be constructed. When cohesiveness and continuity of experience are well established in the personality, falling asleep entails a gradual suspension of more advanced psychic functions, a regressive pathway is well structured, and suspended functions can be easily reestablished. In the schizophrenic, the infantile realm of experience must remain split off in spite of a constant move toward attachment to an object, since it is the area most vulnerable to destruction. In sleep, the threat of effecting an attachment under the distorting influence of the internal saboteur is markedly diminished, and equally vulnerable islands of healthy functioning can serve as a foundation for a dream. The dream, however, will reflect the enormous instability, readily take on nightmare proportions, and when the dreamer awakes, the barely suspended functions of the advanced realm of psychological experience become dominant. The anxiety emanating from the dream often remains. The limitations in psychic content accessible for the dream work affect the process of symbolization, and the manifest dream will frequently mirror reality more accurately than is the case in a more structured personality.

## Distorting Influence of the Internal Saboteur and the Importance of the Manifest Dream

A basic schizophrenic process is equivalent to Winnicott's (1965) description of a true and false self carried to its ultimate extreme. The true self includes the infantile realm of good infantile instinctual experience and the fantasies of an adequate symbiosis. It is a true self because it is undistorted by defensive operations and is the core experience of integrity upon which identity is based. The false self

encompasses the instinctually depleted realm of advanced functioning. It is a false self because it is a compensatory development and is
based upon a submissive conformity to the expectations of need
supplying external objects. This extreme expression of a true and
false self depends upon the effectiveness of the defensive constellation organized to maintain them as separate from each other. The
representation of a pathological symbiosis, originally necessitating the
split in the self, operates as a nidus to consolidate fused self and object
images of impinging, depriving, and overstimulating experiences into
a defensive structure. With advancing steps in development it is
expanded to distort any potential influences of a good object, so as to
obviate against instinctual attachments. This defensive alignment
functions as an internal saboteur.

The internal saboteur has access to all the advanced functions of
the false self, its corrupting influence is never included within the
core of self identity, and it ensures that the true self remains split off
and preserved. Different patients, in referring to the internal saboteur, have personified it with various names reflecting the experience
of its effects as a powerful separate entity. It has been called "the black
mama," "the devil," "the corrupter," or "the quiet enemy," all capturing the essence of destructiveness and the aura of helplessness in its
presence. The internal saboteur is most active at those crucial
moments when a schizophrenic break is imminent. Excessive adaptational demands, changes in the intensity of the drives, the attraction
to a love relationship, and the stresses of separation are all examples.
Adolescence is an especially vulnerable period, since a combination of
all of these factors may be in operation. It is also the case when
confronted with the potential for an instinctual attachment within the
framework of a well-managed therapeutic relationship.

The internal saboteur works to provoke flaws in any external object
exhibiting the potential for offering good qualities in a relationship.
Weaknesses are exposed, defensiveness evoked, or pressure exerted
to elicit behavior that is resonant with the original pathological
symbiotic partner. The schizophrenic individual's sensitivity is selec-
tivity tuned in to an external object's unconscious responses, and
destructive interactions are recreated. The effect is to reenforce the
strength of this defensive structure and to protect and preserve the
split. The pressure is equally an appeal for an external object to
diminish the distorting influence of this defensive maneuver successfully and allow an infantile instinctual attachment that will not result
in damage or destruction.

Although the internal saboteur is a destructive entity, it has also
been and continues to be an ally. It motivates the transformation of

good influences into bad, but also motivates the search for an object who will be steady and not allow this to happen. It is the means by which a therapist can be informed as to what constitutes a pathological defense reenforcing intervention, provides a vehicle for diminishing distortions, and prepares the way for the profound regression necessary to establish a therapeutic symbiosis. When good instinctual experience is present in sufficient amounts, hope can be sustained in an unyielding search for the missing conditions of an adequate symbiosis. Under the domination of the internal saboteur, pressure is exerted to provoke pathological conditions, and if successful, the conditions are rejected and the person offering them distrusted. Such individuals have a greater capacity to guide a therapist into interpretive interventions that simultaneously lessen the distortions and resonate with fantasies of an adequate symbiosis. With lesser degrees of good instinctual experience, pathological defense reenforcing conditions are readily accepted.

The schizophrenic can only reveal the unique features of an adequate symbiosis with the greatest difficulty, since the act of communicating these vulnerable yearnings is so evocative of the regressive pull toward an infantile attachment. It is a frightening experience, accentuated by the annihilation anxiety engendered by the internal saboteur. Therefore, a schizophrenic patient must test a therapist's mode of understanding of what is unexpressed and hidden early in the therapeutic contact. The testing is subtle and often manifested in talking without meaning. A therapist who does not recognize the absence of meaning, or who has a tendency to attribute meaning to it, may be indicating the potential for projecting onto the patient. It informs a patient that when confronted with confusion, uncertainty, and not knowing, the therapist's adaptive response is to project. Developmentally, the original symbiotic partner was experienced as projecting psychic contents that were destructive in nature. Projections are thereby potentially dangerous or perceived as having annihilative intent, and there is a reactive awareness that they will be evoked by the internal saboteur. The schizophrenic is fearful that a therapist giving meaning to what has no meaning cannot be trusted with meaningful infantile communications. It is in this area that a manifest dream can be an aid in both revealing a patient's unconscious perception of the therapeutic relationship and in providing validation for the therapist's intuitive responses.

The psychic organization of a basic schizophrenic process enables the awareness of what is happening within, but with no ability to do anything about it. Only small glimpses of what is known to reside in the deeper layers of the personality can be exhibited and the individual is a helpless victim of the powerful influence of the internal saboteur. A totally regressed vulnerable state is necessary to express fully the contents of the infantile realm of experience, which cannot be allowed until a therapeutic symbiosis is reached. The individual has to be assured that the therapist possesses enough understanding of the attributes of an adequate symbiosis, and that the distortions produced by the internal saboteur can be eliminated, before this level of regression can transpire. The glimpses that are cautiously revealed tax a therapist's ability to see the implicit, and empathic interventions require a great deal of access to intuitive understanding.

Each time a therapist understands, pressure may be exerted to destroy or confuse that understanding. It is therefore essential to recognize when communications are straightforward and direct and when they are distorted. The pressure is designed to evoke responses resonant with the impressions of a pathological symbiosis; at the same time the patient hopes to be unsuccessful. When a therapist's interpretive interventions and management of the framework are not defensive but display an appreciation of the core of integrity at the foundation of this pathological defense, a regression accelerates the potential for an infantile attachment. Ultimately, a therapeutic symbiosis is established, allowing the body ego experience of an infantile instinctual attachment to be registered. It represents a new outcome to the developmental dilemma necessitating the original split. The associated merger of separate realms of psychological experience is fragmenting, but it is not of traumatic proportions, does not instigate a withdrawal, and is a step toward achieving a new integration. The experience will have to be repeated frequently, as it is initially tenuous and easily lost, until the balance shifts and the split in the self no longer has to be maintained.

A manifest dream can be an important and sometimes vital guidepost in signifying whether movement toward a therapeutic symbiosis is being realized.

> This was shown in the treatment of a young adult woman exhibiting evidence of all three stages of schizophrenic pathology. The case was discussed briefly in chapter 7 to show how the manifest dream is indispensable in determining what form of treatment is indicated in the schizophrenias. She had a number of schizophrenic breaks that required hospitalization, could only vaguely recall being out of contact, and was told she spoke "gibberish." A schizophrenic process of repair was manifested in a periodic upsurge of hallucinations emanating from a compelling background world where she felt alternately safe and in enormous danger. She had also split off and preserved sufficient quan-

tities of good infantile instinctual experience to maintain a basic schizophrenic process, was convinced she had to relive her infancy and be reparented in order to be complete, and was searching for a relationship that could provide the healing she knew was needed.

She had seen a number of therapists, was immediately sensitive to their weak spots, and put pressure upon them to behave defensively. With each one she had provoked a rejection and then withdrew. These efforts were interpreted to her as manipulative and controlling. She submitted to this perception, and after a time, repeated the same pattern. She was referred from a hospital, where she had been for several weeks, after a violent rupture in a therapeutic relationship had devastated her. She had been encouraged to express her hatred with assurances that it would only enhance the relationship, finally did so in a form that was intolerable to the therapist, and the relationship was ended.

After a short time she began to express her conviction that what she needed from this therapist could be offered only by a woman, and in proceeding to describe such a woman, she defined the conditions of an adequate symbiosis. This involved warmth and sensitivity against a firm background of a helpless, clinging, and dependent infant. In the process of talking about the need for a woman therapist, infantile yearnings were aroused that activated a "black mama" inside her. This compelling internal force drove her to demand comfort and reassurance, accompanied by intense pressure for the therapist to hold her lest she go crazy or kill herself. The therapist recognized that the motivation was coming from her internal saboteur, consistently interpreted her attempt to enlist his participation in the destruction of her autonomy, and also reflected that this was the only way she could test the trustworthiness of the relationship. The therapist was presenting his view of the autonomy-supporting responses characterizing an adequate symbiosis.

She became more adamant in insisting she could not find what was required with the therapist, felt she had to be touched by a woman who was a mother, and repeatedly expressed her belief that a man couldn't possibly fit such a role. She worked hard at convincing the therapist, adding that his efforts were admirable but ineffective, and yet there were brief moments when she felt something important was happening inside of her.

She then had a series of vague dreams in which she was lying on a couch but could not recall anything else about them. They made her think of why she couldn't use the couch. It was too distant. The therapist would be disconnected from her, she could get lost in an uncontrolled regression, become psychotic, and end up in a hospital. It seemed too frightening to have the therapist out of sight; she would lose all contact with the external world. Her words were reminiscent of similar statements as to why psychoanalysis was contraindictated in the schizophrenias, and the therapist commented that he had an entirely different view of the couch. It seemed to him it would bring him much closer to her internal experiences, more in touch with the deeper parts of her, and that her present position of face-to-face contact felt like it was holding him at a distance where he was often out of touch with what was transpiring inside.

In the following session she described feeling dizzy since she had left, as though she were spinning around, with no thoughts to explain it. The therapist remarked that he was reminded of how they had talked about the couch, which made him think she was spun around by his words toward looking at it in a different way. She then recalled a dream from the night before:

> I was on a couch and a woman was my analyst. I became smaller and smaller and was surprised I wasn't frightened and felt I was in the right hands.

The symbolic imagery pictured the evolution of a profound regression under conditions of safety and containment, providing important validation for the efficacy of the therapist's interventions. Her attempt to recreate a relationship based upon a pathological dependency had a two-pronged motivation: to preserve the realm of infantile experience by reenforcing the structure maintaining the split, and to test the therapist's ability to facilitate a growth-promoting infantile attachment. The therapist's interpretive stance lessened the distortions created by the internal saboteur, echoed with the conditions of an adequate symbiosis, and accelerated a regression. She had found the right "woman" and was preparing to move into the therapeutic symbiosis portrayed in the dream.

The distorting influence of the internal saboteur may arouse confusion in the day to day conduct of the treatment by making it difficult to read a patient's validating responses accurately. A dream, in utilizing the derivative of an unconscious perception as the anchoring point for its construction, can present clearer guidelines for directing a therapist's interventions.

This was exemplified in the following dream of a young adult schizophrenic woman who had numerous therapeutic contacts that had left her feeling in despair and hopeless at the prospect of finding help. She felt an infantile world of intense longing and hunger inside that seemed inaccessible, and she knew that longing had to enter a relationship for her life to be complete. She spent a number of sessions trying to communicate her fantasy life, which revealed the conditions she required to engage in a therapeutic symbiosis. She felt terrified at the regressive pull she experienced when struggling to articulate these infantile yearnings and would frequently be interrupted or distracted leaving huge gaps. She then reported a dream:

> I was in a glass observation tower that needed to be fixed. I went out and could only keep my balance if I was held by someone just right or I would fall into space. Another person was there trying to hold me, but it wasn't quite right. I went back inside thinking I'll have to try it again later.

The symbolic image of the damaged observation tower gave expression to her inability to perceive without distortion. The manifest content pointed to the great danger in attempting to repair it alone. It required another to hold her just right lest she fall into space, reflecting the need for a differentiating influence in order to safely negotiate a symbiotic regression. The dream suggested that she had unconsciously perceived the therapist's difficulty in fully grasping the significance of the fantasies she presented and his inability to have a clear view of what constituted an adequate symbiosis. It indicated the crucial importance of gaining a deeper understanding of her infantile world before a regression was either implicitly or explicitly encouraged. The dream also portrayed a willingness to try again, implying she saw some evidence for hope in the therapist's efforts to understand her internal world.

## The Manifest Dream as a Map of Therapeutic Progress in the Schizophrenias

The schizophrenic individual is capable of completely withdrawing from contact with the external world and becoming surrounded by a primitive self boundary, rigidly held to protect against the impact of any stimuli. This regressive movement is simultaneously extremely attractive and frightening, since it entails a loss of more advanced functions and of all attachments to the external world. The basic schizophrenic process evolved in a pathological symbiosis. The infant needed an attachment to live, but the nature of it was destructive to life. The infant's response was to glean whatever good self experience was available, and then split this aspect off from any attachment to preserve it from destruction.

The dilemma emerged with a pathological symbiosis in which the very ingredients necessary for growth and survival carried the seeds of total destruction. The major source of the pathology can rest in a faulty or defective background object of primary identification, in which case the experience of a symbiosis is distorted, and the likelihood of sustaining a basic schizophrenic process is minimal, often breaking down within the symbiotic period. In other situations a basic schizophrenic process may remain intact for extended periods of time. If an instinctual attachment is made under conditions of repeating the original trauma, the consequence is in a schizophrenic break and an ensuing process of repair.

The amount of damage depends upon the frequency and degree to which a schizophrenic break has taken place, and if the process of repair is extensive, a regressive healing therapeutic endeavor is rendered ineffective and disruptive. In such a situation the best and most helpful approach may be to offer support for the pathological structures formed to compensate for self damage. Dreams are enormously helpful in revealing the extent to which good self experience is latently available, in delineating the potential viability of a therapeutic symbiosis, and in portraying the way the treatment environment is unconsciously perceived.

The following sequence of dreams, reported by a young schizophrenic man, is presented to give an example of the information that can be obtained from the manifest content and the aid it gives in monitoring therapeutic progress.

The first dream was recalled at the the beginning of his treatment and was identified as a dream that had recurred over a span of several years:

I am in the basement of a house that has been bombed out. The basement is a shell and I am alone in the dark. The terrain outside is filled with bomb craters and bombs are exploding everywhere. Everything is desolate.

The aspect of self experience in contact with the external world in the schizophrenic individual is so empty, instinctually depleted, and false that a firm sense of a discrete self is simply nonexistent. Yet this first dream clearly depicts a nonfragmented, well-outlined self, and at first glance it would appear inconsistent with the structural organization of a schizophrenic personality.

In waking life a schizophrenic individual is acutely aware of the existence of splits in the self and that it is extremely difficult to establish a self boundary. When a schizophrenic individual moves into sleep, the advanced realm is allied with the internal saboteur to be occupied at the surface of the personality, guarding against any stimulus that could activate infantile yearnings. Highly vulnerable facets of good self experience can have enough safety to form the foundation upon which a dream is constructed, and the manifest content can represent a well-defined self but with a narrow boundary in an extremely precarious setting. Thus, the conditions of diminished perceptual contact with the external world, less accessibility to functions involving motility, and the circumstances inherent in sleep are such that this is one situation wherein the schizophrenic can represent a coalesced self entity.

A self boundary is determined by perceptual functions; a well-functioning boundary is characterized by the capacity to register incoming stimuli. Darkness or light symbolizes the degree of their effectiveness, and the dreamer is represented as alone and in the dark. The darkness implies that there is difficulty in this area and hints at a defect in the ability to perceive. Any tendency toward the disruption of a dream is often presaged by the emergence of darkness, since the integrity of the dreaming self is in jeopardy and involves invoking a new set of perceptual conditions as an emergency measure. Although this dream has not reached such a point, the setting is fraught with danger. It does appear to be approaching nightmare proportions with the dreamer barely able to maintain the structure of the dream.

The explosions are the only indication of movement, suggesting that instinctual activity carries with it an enormous overload of unneutralized aggression that is destructive in its effects. The house in which the dreamer is located seems to have symbolic reference to body ego experiences unable to be encompassed within a self boundary, and it is portrayed as having been bombed out. This picture implies that there has been a significant amount of damage. There is little in the dream discretely symbolizing the impressions of an object, although the destructive nature of an object's influence is intimated in the image of the craters. The desolate scenario hints at the lack of a viable and stable connection to an object, and captures the absence or unavailability of any resources for promoting growth. There is enough structuralization for the dream work to successfully build a manifest dream, but it only seems to depict the primitive, archaic, and destructive forces in his personality.

The derivative of an emotionally important unconscious perception is required to serve as the dream's nucleus. This repetitive dream had been recurrent over a span of years. It indicated that the day residue had been consistently the same; the symbolic imagery underscored explosiveness and destructiveness, presenting a picture of the unconscious truth he perceived as reality. The extent of self damage symbolized in the dream alluded to the possibility of a number of schizophrenic breaks, but his position in the basement still protected him from the onslaught and suggested that he had salvaged a considerable amount of good infantile instinctual experience. The dream thereby had both a negative prognostic implication in relation to the degree of self damage and a positive prognostic implication in relation to the extent to which good self experience had been preserved.

A second dream was reported after a long period of psychotherapeutic contact:

I am in my sister's house talking to my niece. As I talk with her the flesh begins to melt off her hands and face and a skeleton appears. I look and see that I have a deformed, twisted, ugly doll in my hands, which I try very hard to hide from my niece.

The first dream was constructed prior to the onset of therapeutic contact, and though its emergence had meaning in the treatment situation, it gave expression to the level of psychic organization previously predominant. The second dream presents a more penetrating view of the basic schizophrenic disturbance and of some of the effects the therapeutic relationship is having during this period of treatment. In the first dream the house, symbolizing the system of self representations, was almost completely destroyed. In the second dream the dreamer is in his sister's house. Although the unconscious significance of its being his sister's house cannot be understood without the appropriate associative connections, or at least knowledge of its unique meaning to the dreamer, some speculation can be offered. In order to symbolize self experience as belonging to someone else, it would have to be determined by external rather than internal forces. In this phase of the treatment the dreamer is apparently attempting to enhance a system of self representations by conforming to the expectations and wishes of a need-supplying object. In addition, he is no longer in the dark and the content of the dream, although troublesome, is more explicitly symbolic.

The image of the young female child possesses attributes symbolic of a week and poorly integrated object world. It immediately raises a question as to how effective these impressions of an object's influence can possibly be in providing the degree of regulation necessary to manage vast intensities of primitive unneutralized aggression. This is exemplified when the dreamer notes the flesh melting off his niece's hands and face until a skeleton appears. It gives a portrayal of an emerging object system that is vulnerable and unable to tolerate being perceived without losing its substance. Although there is a clearly defined connection between the self and object, the self system is represented in a way that suggests that a false self is being constructed and the object system is symbolized as young and ineffective.

The dreamer is aware of having a twisted deformed doll in his hands that must be hidden from his niece. It is possible to speculate about the meaning of the doll even without knowing its specific unconscious significance to the dreamer. It possesses the characteristics of a transitional object, representing a bridge between the self and object, and is the object impression counterpart of the background object of primary identification. In the dream it is depicted as deformed, twisted, ugly, and having to be hidden, implying that a child could not tolerate seeing such damage. It may reflect a defect in this basic mental representation, a frequent occurrence in schizophrenic pathology, which may be the primary cause of the disturbance.

The manifest content symbolized the dreamer's effort to develop and grow, but at this stage he had only succeeded in forming a false self and a weak, infantile object system. At the time the dream was reported, the therapist was unconsciously reacting defensively to the depth of the pathology and consciously focusing attention on the patient's strengths and assets. The image of the niece who had to be protected by keeping a deformed doll hidden from view was a derivative of the dreamer's unconscious perception of the therapist's attitude, and appeared to be the day residue that anchored the dream. It pointed to the presence of extensive self damage, which was unconsciously perceived as too frightening to the therapist to be acknowledged or addressed. The dream aided the therapist in recognizing this countertransference response, which had stood as an obstacle to the unfolding of a therapeutic regression.

The next two dreams were reported later with a short time span between. The first exhibited the impact of an empathic failure, and the second took place after the lapse in empathy had been rectified. A clearer picture of the underlying structural organization of the personality and the status of the treatment was then accessible.

> I am in my sister's house. I look outside and a nuclear war is going on. I know if I stay in the house I am safe. I expect an enormous effort is necessary to keep the door closed, since it is the only way I can prevent the devastation from destroying me.

The dreamer is holding the door closed to protect himself against a life-threatening stimulus, knows he is safe as long as he stays in the house, and is capable of keeping the door closed. The portrayal of a nuclear war raging outside emphasizes both the immediacy of the danger and that it refers to events outside the realm of self experience. This would have to involve either the unseen dimension on the continuum of instinctual demand, aspects of self experience that cannot be contained within the dreamer's self boundary, the impressions of an object, or the symbolic representation of the stimuli of the external world. Each of these possesses differing attributes, and were they discretely symbolized in accordance with their disparate qualities, the source of the threatening disturbance could be more readily identified. The image of a nuclear war only captures its intensity.

The symbolic act of holding the door closed, accompanied by a feeling of safety as long as he does, gives some indication of the primary source of the threat. The dreamer's effort clearly symbolizes a defensive response, and one in which contact with the impinging stimulus is continuously sustained. The particular defense being utilized in a dream delineates to some extent the nature of the danger and helps in identifying whether it is instinctual or the consequence of an unempathic interaction. Instinctual defenses include primal repression, which functions as an impenetrable wall, repression proper, which functions to direct perceptual attention away from the source of a threatening stimulus, and prohibitions, which offer restraint through threatening injury or disapproval. None of these is in evidence in the dream, so that the protective response does not have the features of a defense against instinctual activity. The attempt to hold a door closed appears to symbolize the use of all available ego functions to prevent an external stimulus from being internalized. There will always be some instinctual coloring to an external stimulus because of its evocative resonance with instinctual demands of impinging intensity, but were the threat to represent primarily an instinctual impingement, remaining in contact with it would be the greatest danger.

In the previous session the dreamer had hesitantly spoken of his feminine qualities, expressing thinly disguised concern about their homosexual implications. When he anxiously wondered if the therapist could understand these feelings or whether he would be repulsed by them, he seemed to be projecting an unwanted homosexual part of himself. The therapist had offered an interpretation underscoring the patient's concern over his homosexuality, and in exaggerating the intensity of the anxiety had a dim awareness of a defensive response. The patient's unconscious perception of this impinging interpretive attitude appeared to be symbolized in the image of the nuclear war, which in turn resonated with all the destructive forces in his personality. A source of danger thus resided in the external world, and was a product of a lapse in empathy in the therapeutic interaction. Nevertheless, there was a sense of confidence that the door could be held and that safety was attainable through his own efforts, suggesting that the lapse was perceived as transient.

The therapist became aware of the empathic failure, was able to recognize its internal determinants, acknowledged and rectified his role in the resulting impact, and interpreted its effects. The following dream was reported shortly afterward:

> I am walking through my house from one room to the next. My parents are in the other room. Between the two rooms is another room without a floor. It has a bottomless pit with a tiny passageway across it. I'm in the process of inching my way across in order to reach my parents' room.

This dream is more revealing of the changes that had transpired over the intervening period of treatment, since it did not display the disruptive effects of an unempathic stimulus. The dreamer is in his own house, signifying that a true self is consolidating. The manifest content symbolically represents the vital task a schizophrenic patient must accomplish in order to heal the split in the self. There is a picture of the need to reach an object, to effect an attachment, and to negotiate the narrow pathway through extremes of neediness, lack of differentiation, and potential destruction before the goal can be achieved. In the body of the dream, parental imagoes are located, the ground that must be traversed is identified, and the dreamer is anxiously engaged in crossing this dangerous space. The movement through fusion and merger is symbolized as a bottomless pit, which must be carefully negotiated to gain access to a separate good object's influence.

The dream gives expression to the considerable progress that has taken place toward enabling split-off representations of good infantile instinctual self experiences to be attached to the impressions of an object, and in such a manner that continuing advances in self differentiation can occur. There is a unified system of self representations no longer predominantly based upon conformity, a system of object impressions, and a bridge capable of establishing a linkage. The previous dream had clearly shown the degree of vulnerability continuing to be present, which was also reflected in the narrowness of the passage in this dream. Although there is access to effecting an instinctual attachment to an object, there is little room for absorbing narcissistic injury. The following dream was reported several months later:

> I am in a spaceship going to another planet to rescue some people, since the atmosphere there is becoming unlivable. The people look like humans except for the way they dress. Their color coordination is all messed up. I am helping load fish, which is their diet, onto the spaceship. I have to wash my hands and everyone is yelling at me to get on board but I don't care because I don't want the smell on my hands. I get on the spaceship and we get back and land in Florida.

The content of this manifest dream includes a well-defined self, a system of objects symbolically represented as being in danger of destruction on another planet, and a vehicle linking one to the other. Fantasies are the means by which the self and object systems of representation are structurally united, and the image of a spaceship traveling to a distant planet and back encompasses the pathway utilized in structuring the ego ideal. The focus of attention is upon rescuing objects in mortal danger, hinting that the foundation of object constancy is not firmly anchored and the dreamer's ability to maintain contact with a separate object's influence is in jeopardy.

It appears as though the object world has not been consistently available as a source of constructive identifications, but may have been valued largely due to idealizations. Idealizations, rather than being self-enhancing, are self-depleting, in that the object is made admirable at the expense of self awareness. The manifest dream implies that the object's deficiencies can now be seen, idealizations are thereby no longer possible, and the influences of an object must be positioned closer to self experience in order to survive.

The dreamer is occupied with the task of providing sustenance to keep the objects alive until they can be brought down to earth, but is concerned with the smell of fish on his hands and is compelled to be rid of it before embarking on the journey. This dream imagery appears to symbolize the use of masturbatory acts to maintain viable contact with an object, but they are so infused with conflict that all traces must be removed. In addition to the masturbatory implications, it also hints at anal attributes, suggested by the shape of the vehicle providing access to the object world. The combination of a focus upon feeding his objects, a concern over smelly hands, and the anal-phallic representation of a spaceship point to a conglomeration of inadequately blended instinctual activities, which is consonant with the object world's characteristic of having poor color coordination.

The dreamer has seemingly organized an obsessive-like character structure, but the resulting object world is too distant and he is seeking a new way to sustain contact with their influence. The atmosphere on the planet is no longer livable, intimating that idealizations are no longer effective. The dreamer seems ready to take a closer look at their meaning. The movement in the dream, of traveling a long distance over a short span of time, also implies a great speed that is apparently manageable. The underlying structural organization of this manifest dream tends to verify the achievement of healing the split in the self, but also emphasizes the great difficulty now present in sustaining a stable enough foundation for continuing progression to be realized. The influences of an object are available, and the dreamer seems to be searching for a way to bring them closer, but is confronted with the conflicts engendered in the resulting attachment.

The day residue was not explicitly apparent, but it could be inferred from a closer inspection of the dream imagery. A therapeutic relationship offers an opportunity for disturbing psychic contents to be projectively identified and placed within the container of a therapist's introjective attitude. The potential exists for them to be returned in a more integrated form through interpretations. The manifest content does possess a powerful image of the dreamer transporting himself to a distant planet, which is consonant with a symbolic representation of this aspect of the treatment. The need to bring food in order to be certain of the object's survival, with the dreamer's hands getting dirty as a result, then emerges as a strong statement of the patient's unconscious perception of the therapeutic relationship.

The dreamer's preoccupation with giving sustenance is an implicit statement of the objects' inability to care for themselves. Furthermore, the associated discomfort in providing for them, in addition to having veiled reference to unconscious instinctual drives, gives concrete expression to the difficulty in maintaining a free flow of projective identifications. Because a therapist's responsibility in caring for a patient is of primary importance, the patient's involvement in caring for a therapist is often overlooked. When this mutual undertaking is properly balanced, it is an essential ingredient for constructive growth. The dream, however, implies that it is out of balance and that the therapist is requiring more care than is comfortable for the patient.

In the previous session there had been some indirect references to the fee, which the therapist had seen as relatively insignificant until hearing the dream. Earlier in the treatment the fee had been markedly reduced to enable the patient to continue. At the time, it created a problem by arousing intense anxiety about the blurring of boundaries. It was clear that it would ultimately have to be rectified. In this sense the lowering of the fee was a mistake, although a necessary mistake if the treatment was to go on, and it now appeared important to correct the mistake and address its unconscious meaning. The dream had indicated the patient was too burdened with caring for the therapist's narcissism, making it essential to establish a more defined boundary through instituting an appropriate fee. The patient had needed a therapist who was willing to make a mistake, which in this situation involved a reduced fee, but also needed the therapist to know when it was time to correct it.

Individuals exhibiting the debilitating effects of splitting in the self have so many destructive, distorting influences and gaps in continuity of experience that at times the only way needed therapeutic intervention can be helpful is through a therapist's internal willingness to engage in a "leap." A leap refers to a paradoxical situation in which the only pathway to the truth is through an error. A therapist who is unwilling to take a leap into the darkness and make a mistake may be unable to offer certain primitive patients the experience they need to find enlightenment. Once a leap has been taken, and the underlying truth recognized, it must then be rectified and the reason for the necessity exposed. Dreams can be of enormous value in guiding a therapist in this complex task. A therapist guided by rules will never make these errors of *commission,* and in the process be unable to treat some patients for whom errors of *omission* can be devastating. Leaps always involve a mistake of some kind, which, if permitted, will work against constructive growth and, if perpetuated, will prevent it.

Effective therapeutic intervention leading to a more advanced level of self differentiation is a remarkable achievement for the schizophrenic. Once this occurs and intrapsychic conflict can be symbolically represented in a manifest dream, it is enormously reassuring to the dreamer, who has previously had no experience whatsoever with this different quality of frustration and anxiety. Within a schizophrenic's experience, frustration and anxiety have been life-threatening propositions.

This was shown in the dream of a young woman who had suffered a schizophrenic break in young adulthood and entered treatment at the behest of others concerned about her bizarre behavior, hallucinations, and paranoid ideation. Treatment began when she was irrational, delusional, had eaten only token amounts of food for two weeks, and would not communicate. Her childhood years were devoid of meaningful contact with others and she felt mechanical, had no joy, and was fearful of spontaneity. She based her life on what others expected of her, but felt like two separate people, as if she were living a lie. After graduating from college, she formed a love relationship and became confused and disoriented, and began to feel fused with everyone. Every conversation entered her, she was terrified, and felt as if she had no skin. She began to hear voices and had vivid fantasies that she could not differentiate from memories. She thought she was a criminal, feared the police were after her, and became increasingly terrified. Then she thought the only way she could hold onto herself was to stay totally immobilized in one position and not exercise any bodily function.

During the course of her treatment, there were long periods of time when she was totally unable to sleep and dreams were never reported. She was gradually able to allow the regression, vulnerability, and lack of differentiation embodied in a symbiotic attachment, and to represent a new solution enabling the split in the self to be healed. She became aware of the potential skills and abilities that had always been dormant, allowed herself to sleep, and dreams became accessible. At this point she reported a dream:

> I was in the court of a French king, was offered anything I wanted, but couldn't allow myself to have what was available.

Her reaction to the dream was one of enormous relief. It reflected a deepening recognition that the obstacles to her growth existed within, which was accompanied by a feeling of containment and of being in charge of her life. Dreams were now available to represent internal experience, added to her sense of possessing a self boundary and of being able to contain conflictual feelings, and were an aid in the process of gaining perspective. This was a marvelous feeling for her, since she had once felt as if she had no skin. She now felt like a whole person with troubles, conflicts, and problems, which was reflected in the manifest content of the dream.

# 9

# Dreams in the Borderline Personality

The borderline personality achieves enough differentiation for splits in the self not to be manifested, although splitting within the ego persists as the major defense. The urgent demand for reenforcement of pathological defenses is motivated by an active threat of losing differentiation or of fragmentation, whereas a search for a separate good object's influence gives expression to the thrust for developmental progression. Cohesiveness and continuity of experience is not structured. Any threads of advancement in that direction are readily disrupted and vulnerable to narcissistic injury, and regressive movements are consistently out of control. Invoking distorted pathological defensive structures is the only available means of shoring up differentiation.

An unconsciously empathic environment facilitates the expression of sparsely represented good self experience consolidated in the interior of the personality. It enables the discovery of the impressions of a separate good object and structuralizes cohesiveness, and a new, more advanced level of psychic organization is reached. A borderline condition is then no longer in evidence, and a benign therapeutic regression becomes possible.

A manifest dream with the borderline individual is not only helpful in giving a symbolic picture of how the therapeutic relationship is unconsciously perceived, but is also an invaluable source of interpretive material and useful in strengthening any strands of cohesiveness.

Encouraging associations to specific dream components aids in supporting what is usually a weak or deficient function of self observation by focusing attention on psychic contents relatively unaffected by the mechanism of splitting.

## The Nature of Pathology in the Borderline Personality

The earliest phases of psychological development are occupied with the vital task of building up a representational world capable of supporting self differentiation. Splitting within the ego is essential during the symbiotic period in order to enable differing qualities of self experience to coalesce into discrete good and bad entities. The primordial ego, in a primitive state of lack of differentiation, allows a stimulus to be registered at a site away from its source. It is a translocation of perception that is the basis for the mechanism of splitting.

The initial impression of the containing, physiological, metabolizing functions of the intrauterine environment is represented as the background object of primary identification and serves as the nidus around which good self experience is coalesced. Although the contact occurs at the periphery, it is registered at the interior where its containing influence is needed to buffer the impact of biophysiological demand. The massive impingement at birth is registered at the periphery, serving as the nidus around which bad self experience is coalesced. The continuum of biophysiological demand possesses a dimension with an intensity incapable of representation without defense and hence is an aspect of bad self experience. Although the stimulus is occurring at the interior, it is registered at the periphery where its protective, differentiating influence is most needed.

When sufficient quantities of good self experience have accumulated, they can be structuralized, and the intrapsychic events associated with separation and individuation are initiated. The ongoing consolidation of good self experience rises to the surface where empathic contact with an external object takes place, leaving structured remnants at the interior to offer stability and containment. Concomitantly, the consolidating representations of bad self experience recede into the interior, leaving structured remnants at the periphery to offer protection and foster differentiation.

The original translocation of perception is corrected as empathic resonance with an external object and instinctual overstimulation are registered at their source. The borderline individual has either not negotiated this developmental step or has done so inadequately because of a paucity of good self experience. Therefore, the mechanism of splitting persists, with good self experience remaining carefully protected in the deeper layers of the personality. Splitting within the ego assures a clear although divided sense of self but is debilitating to constructive growth. The major source of a good object's influence is embodied in the representation of symbiotic experiences of fusion and merger, which are actively viable and exert an inordinate regressive pull toward a lack of differentiation.

The impressions of a separate good object's influence are extremely sparse, poorly differentiated, uncoalesced, and localized at the point of perceptual contact with the external world. Splits in the ego have obviated against the internal search for and discovery of these good object impressions, preventing the full formation of the eye of consciousness and function of self observation. Observing the impressions of an object has an organizing influence, and the inability to coalesce its differing facets into a unified entity is thereby exaggerated. The impinging, overstimulating, and depriving impressions of a bad object are excessive, not well discriminated, and uncoalesced. They are utilized to bind poorly neutralized, orally determined aggression, accentuating their archaic qualities. They are located at the point of perceptual contact with the impact of biophysiological demand.

Biophysiological demands are on a continuum of intensity ranging from that which does not require defense and is represented as an aspect of good self experience, to that which necessitates defense and is represented as an aspect of bad self experience, to that which cannot be included within self experience, leaving the impression of a bad overstimulating object. The line of continuity is interrupted by the retention of split entities in self experience. The impression of an overstimulating instinctual object serves as the nidus around which all aspects of a bad object's influence are organized. The incomplete status of self differentiation, and the accompanying lack of continuity in self experience, contribute to the instability and absence of consolidation of the impressions of an object. Instinctual activity is very poorly regulated, since the influences of an object are both archaic and unstable. Although these mental impressions may represent each advancing stage in psychosexual development, they remain uncoalesced and are always colored by an overloading of oral aggression.

Transitional space is the psychological background upon which all differentiating mental structures are formed. It arises from two sources. One is the psychological space created with the boundary of the self is expanded with the recognition of a separate good object's influence. In the borderline personality, this developmental step has, at best, been managed in a tenuous fashion, is easily disrupted, and readily breaks down in the face of any defense-inducing stimulus. The resulting transitional space is unreliable as a stable background for anchoring mental contents. The second source involves the fantasies elaborated from the impressions of a transitional object. This facet of transitional space has evolved to a limited degree and provides the background support for whatever derivatives are available to express unconscious mental activity. It also provides for the construction of a manifest dream. The relative instability of this mental background is reflected in the nightmarish quality of most dreams of a borderline individual. The dreams usually contain a sense of impending danger with the threat of being disrupted. In the well-structured personality, transitional space functions as the stable background for systems of mental activity to operate with continuity at differing levels of consciousness.

When separation and individuation are successfully negotiated, object constancy is secured, the self and object systems of representation are united and differentiated, and cohesiveness is established. The wherewithal is then present for an oedipal constellation to evolve, enabling the shift from a narcissistic to an object-related orientation. The genital fantasies of an oedipal conflict structure a new boundary for the unconscious that maintains an evocative connection to all aspects of the personality, thereby ensuring continuity of experience. The borderline individual has not established cohesiveness, an oedipal constellation has not emerged, and the boundary of the unconscious system is narcissistically structured. This is a rigid boundary activated by any stimulus with impinging attributes. Its effect is to exaggerate interruptions in continuity of experience. Any continuous sense of personal identity is severely disturbed, and it operates as a serious obstacle to a free associative process. The ineffective regulation of instinctual activity in combination with the absence of a firm sense of self results in rapid, unstable mood fluctuations and a readiness for action-discharge modes of adaptation.

The borderline personality is structured to guard against the fragmenting, destructive impact of unneutralized oral aggression and to maintain differentiation in the presence of a regressive pull toward fusion and merger that threatens the loss of all functional capacities. The highly unstable pathological defenses that are constructed, in conjunction with an action-discharge mode of adaptation, motivates a need for prolific and intense engagements with external objects seeking reenforcement and discharge. The extent and nature of these internal dangers is reflected in the following dreams:

I am lying on a bed of words that will turn into knives and cut me to pieces if I move.

There is a figure in the background compelling me to come closer. I can feel that I will be totally absorbed and lose myself if I move.

The first dream represents the threat of fragmentation from the effects of unbridled, archaic oral aggression. The second dream represents the threat of losing differentiation by responding to the pull of fusion and merger.

The intrapsychic events accompanying separation and individuation structure cohesiveness and continuity of experience, so that a given stimulus has an interconnected conscious, preconscious, and unconscious component adding depth as it echoes throughout the personality. This makes any associative chain of thoughts and feelings useful in an introspective process of self exploration. The psychic functioning of the borderline individual, however, is so dominated by the persistence of splitting that one set of experiences can readily be replaced by another with no continuity or connection, an associative pathway is constantly interrupted, and determining the unconscious meaning of a particular internal or external stimulus is extremely difficult. The fantasy linkages necessary for a stable, continuous sense of identity are consistently disrupted, revealing the ongoing inability to successfully negotiate separation and individuation.

The borderline individual stands at the brink of establishing cohesiveness, repeatedly trying to master this developmental step. Characteristically, there are limited forays into this more advanced level of organization, which can only be manifested when the external conditions of an unconsciously empathic, well-contained therapeutic relationship are uniformly present. At these moments it is possible to perceive the impressions of a good object from a differentiated position, but it cannot be sustained and readily breaks down with any failure in empathy or increase in intensity of poorly regulated instinctual activity.

These advanced forays are embodied in the construction of a manifest dream, as was shown in the dream of a 15-year-old boy who had entered treatment after having had a psychotic episode in response to the loss of a loved object.

My conscience was arguing with God as to whether I really loved her or whether she represented a previous love I had lost and was trying to replace. Conscience and God went over a checklist. The final question was could I see her as herself? The answer was yes, and I was relieved.

The content of the dream reflected the functioning of self observation, as the dreamer was engaged in a symbolic act of self examination. This capacity is based on the recognition of a separate good object. It enabled the dreamer to attain some measure of perspective and alleviated the threat of loss of differentiation.

The borderline individual has gleaned sufficient quantities of good self experience for its varied aspects to consolidate into a whole, but they are not sufficiently represented to become structuralized at the interior. Phase-specific instinctual gratification, the activity of the autonomous ego functions, and the background object of primary identification are all part of good self experiences present with enough consistency to coalesce. Consequently, self differentiation is initiated and a symbiosis is negotiated relatively successfully, but there is a failure in the ongoing process of separation and individuation. Biophysiological demand requires the containing effects of good self experience to be available as a buffer against trauma at the interior of the personality. When it is in abundant supply and structuralized, separation and individuation can be negotiated. It is then possible for good self experience to continuously coalesce, expand, and rise to the surface to engage in a search for the mental impressions of a separate good object's influence. In the borderline personality the dearth of good self experience is such that the lines of cleavage defining the differing facets are under stress. It must remain represented in the deeper layers of the personality where it is overvalued, protected, and vulnerable to fragmentation. The mechanism of splitting persists beyond stage and phase specificity, and every movement toward the periphery is fraught with anxiety.

This difficulty was depicted in the manifest dream of an 11-year-old boy suffering from an inability to sustain relationships or to perform adequately in school.

My mother, father, and I were moving to Florida in a van. My mother didn't want to go and was fighting with my father in the front, while I tried to ignore it in the back. We got to Florida and it was beautiful. It didn't last long because it was time for school. I walked into the classroom, looked at everybody, and they were all strangers. They looked at me and turned away—like I was strange to them also. I felt all alone and uneasy, as if the slightest thing could shatter me.

The symbolic imagery of the dream portrayed hostile, destructive object imagoes that were both distant and separated from the dreamer. The trip to Florida appeared to represent the search for a separate good object's influence, and the brief moment of contact with this source of warmth and pleasure was quickly interrupted. A life-giving connection could not be sustained. The dreamer was then unable to buffer the impact of internal or external stimuli and the threat of impending fragmentation ensued.

With splitting within the ego operating as a major defense, bad self experiences of instinctual overstimulation, reactions to impingement, and sensory deprivation consolidate and remain at the surface of the personality. This is also the site where the uncoalesced impressions of a good object are located. In order to maintain differentiation, a distorted version of the grandiose self is formed that is highly unstable and requires external reenforcement to be sustained. The union is of instinctually overstimulating self experience with the optimally gratifying aspect of a good object, and the individual is impelled to seek interactions having the characteristics of a perversion to support differentiation.

Under conditions evoking a regression, the linkage is readily disengaged, and another distorted, unstable union is formed at the interior where good self experience and the uncoalesced impressions of a bad object are located. The resulting addictive and paranoid constellations must then be reenforced by parallel interactions with external objects. These unions of good and bad qualities are at the foundation of pathological defenses, frequently shift from one to the other, and create great difficulty in adaptive functioning. Uniting bad self experience with the sparse and uncoalesced impression of an optimally gratifying object intensifies the problem of instinctual regulation, whereas the linkage of already limited good self experience with the impression of an impinging or overstimulating object further diminishes its availability. In the absence of external support, or in the presence of excessive stimulation, a regression can get out of control. Fragmentation and a loss of differentiation are a constant threat and desperate efforts to retain an object's differentiating influence are manifested.

## The Pathological Grandiose Self in the Borderline Personality and its Effect upon the Manifest Dream

The mechanism of splitting is operative during the symbiotic period to facilitate the organization of self experience into unified good and bad entities as a preliminary step toward self differentiation. The borderline individual has successfully negotiated this step, but an insufficiency in good self experience has prevented its structuralization, and splits in the ego persist. Although there may be some forays into recognizing a separate good object's influence and initiating separation-individuation, these progressive advances in psychic organization cannot be sustained. They are not structured, exist only as a skeletal pathway toward achieving object constancy, and can be momentarily functional when the conditions of the external environment are unconsciously empathic. They are, however, involved in the construction of a dream, which depends upon these dormant connections to a separate good object's influence to support the process of symbolization and to retain the manifest content within consciousness.

The degree to which advanced forays are present is proportional to the degree of organization within the borderline personality. Borderline disturbances range from the most advanced, reflecting a partial negotiation of separation and individuation, to the most regressed, reflecting the barely adequate negotiation of a symbiosis. A given individual may fluctuate throughout this range depending upon the internal and external conditions. At either end of the spectrum the representational world is composed of good self experience, consolidated in the deeper layers of the personality along with the isolated impressions of a bad object, and bad self experience, consolidated at the surface along with the isolated impressions of a good object. Any movement toward the periphery to locate the internal impressions of a separate good object mobilizes the threat of fragmentation, and the influences of a good object embodied in fusion and merger threaten differentiation. A defensive alignment must then be structured to reenforce the split in the ego and provide an object's differentiating influence.

The borderline individual has not attained object constancy, splitting mechanisms persist as the ego's primary defense, and bad self experience remains localized at the periphery. Good self experience is deficient and buried deep within the personality; there is an inordinate vulnerability to narcissistic injury and insufficient stability for healthy structure formation. A symbiosis has been negotiated, but the regressive pull of fusion and merger is extremely active. The level of self differentiation is unstable and a healthy grandiose self cannot evolve. A differentiating influence is essential. Pathological variants of a grandiose self are structured to fullfill this defensive need.

The most advanced is formed at the periphery, where the consolidated representations of bad self experience and the isolated impressions of a good object are located. The bad instinctual experience in the ascendancy, colored by an overloading of oral aggression, unites with the uncoalesced impression of an optimally gratifying object to form a pathological structure possessing the characteristics of a perversion. The particular instinctual activity that is predominant determines the nature of the perversion; when orality is emphasized it is greed, with anality it is sadistic, with phallic activity it is voyeuristic, and genitally, it is incestuous. The resulting structure is distorted, since it combines good and bad qualities. It is highly unstable due to the diffuseness of an isolated object impression and requires reenforcement to be maintained.

The construction of a manifest dream cannot be adequately supported by this underlying organization, so that any dormant, more advanced forays must be utilized. Therefore, the dream is highly labile and ready to be disrupted by any increase in intensity of instinctual demand. The borderline features invade the symbolic imagery. This is a dream that has been used several times to illustrate the varied kinds of information contained within the body of the manifest content. It is true of every dream, although some tend to be more revealing than others of a particular element. The 12-year-old's dream of baby Godzilla is filled with movement and lends itself to a clearer exposition of its structural components.

> The following dream of a 12-year-old boy is representative. He was constantly engaged in seeking out sadistic interactions to reenforce an anally derived, perverse, and distorted grandiose self, and struggled against losing his sense of differentiation. While talking about episodes of feeling weird, disoriented, and out of contact he recalled a dream:
>
> > I was in a cafeteria, a table wiggled, and baby Godzilla came to life. I was terrified. A boy began to beat me up, and baby Godzilla pounded him to protect me. He carried me home in his arms like we were friends, and on the way we had to get bigger and smaller to cross through openings. He then set me down and chased me. I looked over my shoulder very frightened, ran into a pole, was stunned, and awoke.
>
> The manifest content mirrored the manner in which bad self experience was organized at the surface of the personality to protect highly vulnerable good self experience buried deep within. Baby Godzilla symbolized his bad self and gave expression to his constantly dangerous position because of this structural alignment.

A perverse organization is the most advanced borderline position, but this level of functioning can only be sustained by engaging in parallel relationships that provide continual reenforcement. When external resonance is unavailable, this attachment to an object's influence at the periphery is lost, regression begins to get out of control, and the threat of fragmentation and loss of differentiation escalates. An attachment is made to the influence of an object at the interior, and another pathological variant of the grandiose self is structured. The good instinctual aspect of self experience is linked to the impression of a bad instinctual object forming a pathological structure with the characteristics of an addiction. A chemical substance or overly dependent relationship having this attribute then operates as a source of external reenforcement.

The distorting effect on good self experience that has been overvalued and protected accentuates the search for a good object's influence. The impressions of a separate good object cannot be located in the internal world, and the manner in which it is sought in the external world is destined to failure. Good objects are invariably transformed into bad through projective identifications and the pressure exerted to reenforce pathological defenses. The manifest dream in a borderline personality will often symbolize the underlying pathological grandiose self designed to maintain differentiation, particularly when there has been a regression.

> This was shown in the dream of a 14-year-old girl presented before because of the questions it raises concerning her prognosis and to demonstrate the dream's borderline qualities. The manifest content reflected that her primary mode of functioning was based upon an addictive borderline organization:
>
> > I had a baby boy and my mother sedated me so she could take it over and control it. I screamed in anger that it was mine. The baby grew up and was becoming attached to her. I felt enraged because I was losing the bond.
>
> The symbolic representation of the baby and mother captured the essence of an addictive organization, uniting good self experience with the overpowering impression of a bad instinctual object. It gave expression to the erosion of these highly valued good qualities.

Any further regression leads to a highly unstable paranoid configuration, in which good self experience is linked to the impression of a bad impinging object. When a malignant regression cannot be curbed by the pathological variants of a grandiose self, it begins to assume ominous proportions, and mobilizes a desperate effort to hold on to the influences of an object. Hypochondriacal constellations are formed at the interior by incorporating the isolated impressions of a bad object within the loosening boundary of good self experience, representing the initial stages in the emergence of a borderline depression. The feeling is one of disturbing body sensations, identified as being invaded by a foreign bad object, often approaching delusional dimensions. A depression in the borderline personality represents a last-ditch effort to be connected to the differentiating influences of an object and is indicative of an impending psychotic episode. The impressions of a bad object are included within good self experience at the interior, and the impressions of a good object are included within bad self experience at the periphery. The individual fluctuates rapidly between feeling threatened with destruction by a bad object, to feeling a good object's vulnerability to destruction by the self. Transient psychotic episodes of fragmentation and loss of differentiation are a frequent occurrence, and last until a previously established pathological grandiose self can be evoked.

## Conditions Conducive to Constructive Growth in the Borderline Personality and the Importance of the Manifest Dream

The borderline individual is driven to attain reenforcement of a pathological grandiose self, is incapable of consistently utilizing the function of self observation, perceives the self primarily through observing the reactions of others, and is compelled to search for a good object's influence in the external world. The search for a good object is distorted by the need to use external objects as a source of support for unstable, pathological defenses, and as a container for primitive, projective identifications. The transference relationship becomes the arena in which the inability to negotiate separation and individuation is reenacted, repeating its specific components in an attempt to achieve mastery.

The contents of the deeper layers in the borderline personality consist of good self experience, and a free associative process is designed to facilitate their expression. Psychoanalytic treatment thus fosters a progressive rather than regressive movement, since splitting mechanisms prevail as the primary ego defense. The borderline patient is unique in that regard because splits in the ego must be healed before it is possible for a regression to be contained enough to be therapeutic. Healing splits within the ego involves the recognition of a separate good object's influence, and is associated with attaining a more advanced level of psychic organization by structuring cohesiveness and continuity of experience in the personality. A borderline disturbance is then no longer in evidence. There is a realignment of forces in the representational world, repression proper evolves into the primary ego defense, and a therapeutic regression becomes possible. This is in contrast to the schizophrenias, in which a split in the self necessitates a therapeutic symbiotic regression in order to gain continuity of experience. It also contrasts with those who have structured continuity of experience within the personality during the developmental years, for in that situation a therapeutic regression is necessary to integrate repressed infantile instinctual conflicts.

In the borderline personality there is a sequence of steps in a regressive pathway that, if unchecked, lead to a psychotic episode, with each step representing an attempt to guard against this terrifying eventuality. The individual may frantically seek therapeutic help, and the urgency may give a therapist little time to make an accurate assessment of constructive treatment needs. A dream, if available, can be a useful adjunct in achieving a diagnostic understanding, and can identify the inevitable lapses in empathy that are often a product of a beginning relationship.

The following dream reported by a young woman patient in the early stages of therapeutic contact is illustrative. (The dream was discussed earlier in regard to the relationship between the agencies of perception; here the underlying structural elements will be more closely examined.) She sought help because of her great distress at the loss of a relationship, attempted to minimize the seriousness of her disturbance, and on the eve of her third session awoke during the night from a bad dream. She entered the session appearing sad and distraught, as the feelings from the dream continued to stay with her.

I was in a totalitarian society and was facing a firing squad. I was shot a number of times and could feel myself dying. The dream shifted and I was in a place where I could see a light coming in through a window. As I was dying I said my boyfriend and parents were the most important things in my life. I died and awoke crying.

The dreamer is located in oppressive surroundings and portrayed in great danger, implying that she is at the mercy of need supplying objects with no freedom of movement. In that immobilized position she is confronted by a firing squad from which she cannot escape and is mortally wounded. The objects in this sector of the dream are symbolically represented as overpowering and destructive, appearing to encompass a combination of oral qualities of incorporation, anal qualities of sadistic control, and phallic-genital qualities of bodily injury. These harsh archaic impressions of a bad object's influence are represented as attached to a helpless and tacitly good self. This linkage of vulnerable good self experience to the impressions of a bad object is consistent with the structural organization of a borderline personality, and reflects the underlying presence of a regressed pathological variant of the grandiose self, possessing the characteristics of an addictive and paranoid constellation.

The eye of consciousness, which is almost totally suspended in sleep and suspended to a lesser extent in a benign therapeutic regression, may be totally nonfunctional in a malignant regression. The feelings within the dream have lingered, suggesting that the eye of consciousness is not in operation and that a regression is beginning to lose control. The linkage symbolized in this dream, of a vulnerable good self and an archaic bad object, hints that the dreamer has regressed from a previously structured perverse union and is probably anticipating that she will be unable to gain external reenforcement for these pathological defenses in the therapeutic relationship. She is therefore fearful of an ongoing malignant regression, and expecting it to go unchecked.

The persistence of splitting has resulted in a structural alignment in which the consolidated representations of bad self experience and isolated impressions of a good object are localized at the periphery, and the consolidated representations of good self experience and isolated impressions of a bad object are at the interior. The only union that can take place to maintain differentiation is of good and bad qualities, and the resulting structure is distorted, highly unstable, and requires external reenforcement to be sustained.

In the initial session, the patient's opening remarks were about feeling alone in the waiting room and fearing the therapist would not come out to get her. She then described how her decision to seek help was dependent upon the status of a relationship with her boyfriend. When it went well, she put off making therapeutic contact. Control and abuse characterized the relationship, which was consistent with an anal sadistic perverse grandiose self being in the forefront. Her anticipation that the therapist would not appear suggested the presence of an ineffective hold upon an object. Her delay until an attachment was lost hints that a pathological differentiating structure was being reenforced. They both implied that her primary motive for treatment involved the search for a replacement.

When the scene of the dream shifted, the dreamer was placed in a space where lights came in through a window, symbolizing the effects of perceptual activity, and the death of the self was noted. The perceptual agency of the superego eye is involved in registering a dream, and those aspects of self experience incorporated in the underlying structures cannot be represented as dying and still have the dream continue. The act of registering perceptions is a function of good self experience, yet a self has been shot, implying that the consolidated entity of good self experience remains viable. It suggests a loss of contact with the consolidated entity of bad self experience, and is indicative of the lack of continuity within her personality.

The dreamer's thought as she was dying, of her boyfriend and parents being the most important to her, pointed to the specific attachment that was destroyed. It tended to validate the inference that what was lost was the entity of bad self experience, probably because the connection to an optimally gratifying object had dissolved. The symbolic imagery encompassed the existence of separate entities of self experience, hinted at the dissolution of the structural organization of a borderline perversion, and gave expression to the subsequent regression to a paranoid configuration.

The day residue, in being founded upon the derivative of an unconscious perception of the therapeutic environment, symbolizes the attributes of the relationship. These include a contained psychological space in which attention is directed toward exposing the unconscious meaning of internal events. The totalitarian society in the dream appears to be a symbolic portrayal of the containing properties of the therapeutic framework, which is making her feel trapped. An unconscious perception of a good enough container might very well be pictured as a totalitarian society with the borderline individual, but it would be unlikely to result in destruction unless an empathic failure was involved. The light coming in the window seems to have symbolic reference to the therapist's interpretations, which are illuminating the loss of a connection to loved objects and the destruction of a self.

The gunfire directed at and killing the dreamer implies that she is either not feeling securely held, or that interpretive interventions are being experienced as destructive. The dream took place following a session in which a change in the next appointment time was requested and granted with no discussion concerning its meaning. Later in the same session, an interpretation was given about her expectation of being controlled and abused in the therapeutic relationship. These two factors apparently combined to trigger the subsequent malignant regression, remained in her preconscious to serve as the nidus around which the dream was constructed, and were symbolically represented to give a picture of the way they were unconsciously perceived.

This manifest dream calls attention to a crucial therapeutic dilemma with the borderline patient. It centers around the vital necessity for the ground rules and boundaries of the treatment to be firm and clearly defined, while at the same time these very conditions may be so frightening as to not be well tolerated. Developmental experience has been filled with ruptured interpersonal boundaries, the transference expectation is of these impositions being repeated, and pathological defenses work to recreate them. Consequently, attempts will be made to rupture firm boundaries, to gain gratification of regressive cravings, and to provoke a therapist into modifying well-managed ground rules. A contained therapeutic framework is required, but the borderline individual then feels trapped since adaptation has been based upon action discharge modes of functioning. The therapist's task is to create an environment providing the necessary containment, within which the feeling of being trapped can be tolerated and interpretive therapeutic work then ensue.

The young woman was ready to feel trapped in a contained relationship, and the therapist unconsciously perceiving this transference-based expectation was unwittingly trying to demonstrate flexibility by not having rigid ground rules. The appointment was changed without discussion, implying that other modifications could be granted, which had the paradoxical effect of evoking the influences of a bad object. Modifying the therapeutic framework with the intent of being humane had instead confronted her with the harsh, attacking impressions of an impinging object. This happened before the therapeutic alliance was on firm ground, making it difficult to recognize the empathic failure, and the dream helped to identify its origin. Any effort to offer a corrective experience or to exhibit good intentions only serves to intensify distrust, since it is based upon an isolated facet of a good object's attributes. A good object is a unified entity encompassing optimal gratification, optimal frustration, and the qualities of a transitional object. Gratification in the absence of a blend with these other attributes is not optimal, only introduces an interaction that, at best, reenforces a pathological defense, and consequently is resonant with destructive forces obviating against constructive growth.

An ideally functioning therapist presents the combined qualities of a good object, which vary in accordance with the patient's level of psychic structuralization. Optimal gratification for the borderline individual encompasses the experience of perceiving the influences of a separate good object, attained through receiving unconsciously empathic interpretive interventions in a well-managed framework. Optimal frustration encompasses the experience of a contained relationship in which pathological defenses are not reenforced. The qualities of a transitional object encourage a free flow of projective identifications, enabling the transference to unfold without interference from impositions or projections.

The therapist must create an environment with clearly defined ground rules and boundaries that are firm but not rigid. Within this context unconsciously empathic interpretations foster a progressive movement toward establishing cohesiveness, but in order to do so they must include the added dimension of perspective. The function of self observation is deficient in the borderline individual, and a therapist's perspective strengthens the recognition of thready, poorly differentiated impressions of a separate good object. The pressure exerted to provoke a therapist into unnecessary and even harmful modifications is based upon the particular pathological grandiose self maintaining differentiation. The relationship must have enough latitude to allow these relatively primitive projective identifications to be made, which must be welcomed by the therapist in order to garner the information required to accurately interpret the contents of the representational world and the purpose they serve. When a pathological defense is not reenforced, it instigates a malignant regression initiated by a gap. The gap is created by the effects of splitting, and unless it is breached by amplifying the influences of a separate good object, the regression will continue. A gap is therefore indicative of the need for an interpretation, which will be registered as unempathic and impinging if perspective is not added.

> Webster defines kindness as including natural, proper, and appropriate characteristics. The application of the basic psychoanalytic principles in accordance with the psychic structuralization of a patient is thereby an act of kindness. When a therapist's grasp of a patient's internal world is incomplete, kindness can only be determined by projection. It was this supposed offer of kindness in changing the appointment, in addition to the interpretation given without the added dimension of perspective, that was unconsciously perceived as controlling and attacking. It remained in this patient's preconscious system, served as the day residue around which the manifest dream was constructed, and became symbolically represented as the dreamer in a totalitarian society being shot by a firing squad.

In the borderline individual bad object impressions of instinctual overstimulation, impingement, and deprivation are excessive, whereas good object impressions of optimal gratification, optimal frustration, and of a transitional object are sparse. These object impressions are not adequately coalesced and differentiated. For this reason it is especially important for the therapeutic relationship to maintain steady ground rules and boundaries. In their absence, the impact of a bad object's influence is intensified, and in being poorly differentiated they are felt as an attack. Diminishing containment activates these bearers of poorly neutralized aggression, and interpretations not modulated by including perspective are readily experienced as having destructive intent.

In an initial session a therapist may not have achieved a diagnostic understanding of sufficient depth to offer what is most needed, and yet the need remains. It is often from early lapses in empathy that a more accurate diagnostic picture is formulated, and the therapeutic relationship can then gradually be shaped to fit the requirements for constructive growth. There may be a tendency to deal with this problem by establishing rigid ground rules and boundaries, which are disruptive in their own way. They either recreate the traumas of early development for the borderline individual, or operate to reenforce a pathological defense. The desperate need to feel contained is fueled by the transference compulsion to recreate unempathic impositions and impingements. The power of the transference is so great that a therapist may easily be caught up with trying to be humane, and in the process ignore the kindness associated with firm ground rules and boundaries.

> The constant pressure to rupture boundaries is partly a transference phenomenon and partly an attempt to feel more contained. The dilemma for the therapist is to balance the requirements of containment with ameliorating the terror of being trapped. Action discharge has been the primary mode of adaptation, narcissistic injuries are not well absorbed, and within a contained space the poorly differentiated impressions of a bad object are the source of a destructive attack. The totalitarian society and firing squad gave symbolic expression to the patient's helplessness in managing this vulnerable internal position. It pointed to the therapist's task of providing enough containment to soften the destructive effect of unneutralized aggression, so that the experience of entrapment can be the focus of effective interpretive work.

A major component of a growth-promoting interpretive intervention centers around the necessity of supplying the missing or deficient function of self observation. The mental representations required for self observation to be functional are available, but they are sparse. They are not aligned in a position where they are accessible and are thereby not structurally connected. To the extent that these tenuous linkages are present, it is possible for them to be amplified and strengthened, which leads to the healing of splits in the ego. A borderline organization is then no longer in the forefront, and the capacity for introspection and derivative formation is enabled and enhanced.

In this more advanced position good self experience rises to the periphery, bad self experience recedes into the interior, and the new intrapsychic realignment of forces makes it possible to structure cohesiveness by uniting and differentiating good qualities in the self and object. The emergence of self observation as a viable function has an organizing effect upon the impressions of an object and furthers their consolidation into recognizable good and bad entities, and the resulting awareness of a good object's bad qualities anchors object constancy. The object relationship formed in the transference shifts in accordance with these new developments. The therapeutic need is for active interpretive interventions to ease the heightened fear of dependency, to modulate archaic prohibitive responses, and ultimately to expose overstimulating instinctual demands to the integrative functions now available.

## Dormant Resources in the Borderline Personality and the Manifest Dream

A continuous period of empathic resonance with an external object is required at the outset of postnatal life before a symbiotic attachment can be made. The background object of primary identification, representing the physiologic, metabolizing functions of the intrauterine environment, must be amplified enough to enable the necessary lack of differentiation. The symbiotic phase represents a developmental advance and is essential for structure building. Varied qualities of self experience are registered and represented in an undifferentiated state, and then have to organize and coalesce into well-defined entities preparatory to initiating the process of individuation.

When good self experience is abundant it can be structuralized at the interior, where it continues to serve its buffering function and to operate as a foundation for unconscious perceptions. The process of consolidation gradually moves toward the periphery at the site of empathic resonance, while the organizing entities of bad self experience recede into the interior where the stimulus of instinctual overstimulation is taking place, leaving structured remnants behind to serve a differentiating and protective function. Once good self experience is localized at the periphery, it is possible to discover the impressions of a separate good object. The recognition goes hand in hand with the healing of ego splits. The first differentiated connection to the impressions of an object is established, and cohesiveness is initiated. It cannot be continuously sustained until there is a further awareness of the good object's bad prohibitive qualities and anchoring object constancy, and until the groundwork is prepared to form the structural precursors of the superego. This phase of development is particularly relevant for understanding a borderline disturbance, since the intermeshing of growth-promoting and pathologically distorting features is a consequence of the degree to which this step has been negotiated.

The basic difficulty of the borderline individual involves a relative insufficiency of good self experience. Although there has been enough for self differentiation to progress to a point of forming separate self entities, there has not been enough to structure good self experience at the foundation of the personality. It remains localized in the interior to buffer the disruptive impact of biophysiological demand, is extremely vulnerable to narcissistic injury, and is situated in close proximity to the influences of a bad object. Containment and stability are deficient, and splits in the ego must be retained as a defensive measure. Consequently, there is a deficit in the evolving capacity to discover the internal impressions of a separate good object's influence, the eye of consciousness and function of self observation is impaired, and cohesiveness and continuity of experience are not established.

The persistence of splitting contributes to the difficulty in clearly differentiating the influences of an object, and their lack of consolidation allows isolated object impressions to be utilized in structuring highly unstable pathological variants of a grandiose self. A perverse borderline structure is composed of bad instinctual self experience linked to the isolated impression of an optimally gratifying object, so that in a transference relationship the therapist is initially perceived as all good. Over time, the flow of projective identifications is directed into the relationship, the therapist becomes the receptacle of the contents of bad self experience and is then perceived as all bad. The change instigates a regressive shift to an addictive structure. An addictive grandiose self links good instinctual self experience to the isolated impression of a powerful, need-supplying, overstimulating object. The therapist is now the receptacle of good self experience and a source of envy, and the patient is left empty and depleted, feeling trapped and helpless.

Rapid fluctuations from one position to the other can sometimes occur, giving the appearance of what could be described as splits in the object world. This clinical observation is often presented as evidence of splits existing in the object, when it is in the realm of self experience that splits are active. The difference is significant for being able to identify the composition of pathological defenses, for determining what is required to amplify latent resources, and for facilitating structural change.

Borderline disorders range from those barely negotiating a symbiosis to those on the brink of negotiating separation and individuation, but there are almost always some thin threads of a more progressive position latently present. In an unconsciously empathic environment the most advanced position attained can be manifested, which may at times even include some limited forays into achieving cohesiveness. Although this union of good self experience with the impression of a separate good object is extremely tenuous and fragile, the construction of a manifest dream depends upon it, and when the connection becomes strong enough to be symbolically represented it is usually indicative of therapeutic progress.

> This was exemplified in the aforementioned dream of a 7-year-old-boy, discussed earlier in relation to its borderline characteristics. After initiating therapeutic contact in which it was possible to offer a measure of containment within an unconsciously empathic relationship, he reported a dream:
>
>> We were all on earth and it was freezing. My family was covered with ice and turning blue. My mother and I jumped to the sun, got all warm, and thawed out.
>
> The unconsciously empathic attributes of the therapeutic environment had amplified the thin strands representing an attachment to a separate good object's influence, and its constructive, life-giving properties were reflected in the symbolic imagery of being thawed out after jumping to the sun. The frozen figures on earth also symbolized the internal devastation accompanying the debilitating effects of splitting mechanisms, since the influences of a good object are unavailable for self enhancement and growth.

In the cohesive personality changes in the pattern of associations to a dream are extremely helpful, since they reveal the conflicting forces at work in differing sectors of varying levels of consciousness, all of which are interrelated and connected to one another. In the borderline personality, splitting persists as a primary defense. There is an absence of continuity of experience, and changes in the associations to a dream are hard to unravel, very confusing, and complicate the process of understanding the latent dream thoughts and dream work. The dream work must use the dormant resources in the deeper layers of the personality for the dream to be retained within consciousness. The manifest content may be the clearest route for understanding unconscious forces because it is less subject to the effects of splitting. In addition, it is a mental production symbolizing the derivative of an unconscious perception, and consequently guides a therapist in the application of the basic psychoanalytic principles.

A borderline individual may find it helpful to have attention directed to the various components of a dream, since they are founded upon a differentiated connection between the self and object and thereby have a tendency to call forth the most advanced levels of psychic organization available. This is often useful in fostering the degree of progression necessary to recognize the internal impression of a separate good object, and in conjunction with a therapist's unconsciously empathic interpretive interventions, it can aid in supporting and sustaining the function of self observation. Latent resources based on threads of cohesiveness are then evoked, a borderline organization is no longer manifested, and a therapeutic regression is possible.

The borderline individual is in an intermediary position where an unconsciously empathic environment fosters progression rather than regression, due to good self experience occupying the deeper layers of the personality. A transference neurosis cannot form because there is insufficient structuralization for this entity to evolve, although a new edition of an old illness can be elaborated in the transference relationship. When that occurs it is based upon the pathological defenses designed to maintain differentiation, and this transference repetition provides the interpretive material used to enable progress to a more advanced level of psychic organization. The manifest dream is a segment of psychic content not subject to splitting. Eliciting associations to specific dream elements can be a helpful adjunct to the grown-promoting properties of the relationship, and it is a useful guide in monitoring the treatment.

## The Manifest Dream as a Map of Therapeutic Progress in the Borderline Personality

When a borderline individual makes use of the therapeutic relationship to negotiate separation and individuation successfully, the subsequent state of cohesiveness is vulnerable, hard to sustain, and relatively unstable. The boundary of the unconscious system tends to be rigid, oral aggression is excessive, the ability to regulate instinctual demand is limited, and prohibitive forces are archaic and punitive. The individual is embroiled in intense intrapsychic conflict, which may trigger an effort to revert to a previous borderline configuration. The regressive return to an old pattern is no longer the same, however, since it is infused with the effects of perceiving a whole object. Dreams can be an effective means of monitoring therapeutic progress because they reflect the movement taking place in a treatment relationship, and at the same time give material especially relevant for discerning structural changes.

This was demonstrated in the following series of dreams, which revealed the initial disturbance, the growth that had evolved during the course of treatment, the residues of earlier borderline pathology, and the underlying instability that was still present. The dreamer was a woman who began psychotherapy displaying all the features of a borderline personality, and at the outset had repetitive dreams of being lost, wandering through abandoned streets devoid of any semblance of life. The dreams captured her internal sense of desolation, the unavailability of the influences of a good object, and the lack of direction and purpose she felt in moving through her life. A bad object's influence is a constant presence in the borderline individual, either in the form of internal attacks and overstimulation or in the form of deprivation, as was the case in these dreams.

She achieved a more advanced level of psychic organization after a period of several years, and a sequence of dreams reported over a relatively short interval of time gave evidence of the changes. The first dream:

My parents and you were there, approving of me, but it was not enough.

The manifest content symbolically represented objects with approving attitudes, included an undisguised image of the therapist and the self, though seeking approval was not represented with explicit goals or intentions. There was no indication within the body of the dream as to what was approved or as to why it was not enough. The specific instinctual experiences are thereby hidden, and can only be surmised by the way in which the objects are portrayed.

In approaching the task of delineating the underlying structural organization upon which a manifest dream is constructed, it is important to identify the particular stage of psychosexual development being symbolized. An orally derived object possesses nurturant or incorporative qualities, an anal object fosters mastery or exerts sadistic control, and it is a phallic object that is either approving or humiliating. Thus, in this dream the attributes being symbolized are of a good, phallically determined object. Although instinctual experience is obscure, by implication phallic exhibitionism is involved.

The statement that the object's approval was not enough appears to reflect the absence of a stage and phase specific match. This connection of self and object is reminiscent of the hysteric's character defenses based on an infantile attachment to a phallically derived object and overstimulating phallic instinctual experience. In this constellation there is a readiness for phallic exhibitionism to escalate in intensity and become overstimulating and voyeuristic. The approval and admiration of an object contains little of the much needed restraints, in part since the act of admiration requires that more be exhibited. When instinctual regulation is already unreliable, this movement initiates a state of overstimulation.

The therapist's undisguised image seems to be the day residue, serving as the derivative of an unconscious perception around which the dream was built, and would not contain the good quality of approval were it to concern a failure in empathy. The portrayal of a good phallic object's influence not being enough suggests an internal change has taken place unknown to the therapist, so that an earlier unconsciously empathic stance is no longer effective, most likely due to an intervening regression. The consequence is in a lack of synchrony, with the right ingredients being available but at the wrong time.

Shortly thereafter she had another dream:

There was a funeral. A bunch of people were standing in a circle holding hands. I was going to say I was the victim, but I felt I had done something wrong.

The elements symbolically represented in this manifest dream include a funeral, a group of people holding hands, and a statement about being a victim amended to the feeling of having done something wrong. The objects are connected to one another, symbolizing a line of continuity in the object system that is neither interfered with nor interrupted. The funeral implies that there has been a loss with no overt indication as to its nature.

Once again the dreamer's characteristic style in presenting self experience is manifested, and there continues to be an aura of motives remaining somewhat secretive and obscure. Were the loss to represent an attachment to an object at the foundation of a stabilizing fixation point, object constancy would be threatened. Were it to involve the underlying structure of the grandiose self and ego ideal, the dream could not be continued. Were it to symbolize an oedipal attachment, it would probably be associated with an expression of movement or at least some opposition to movement. None of these situations is in evidence.

Instinctual activity is the motivating force fueling the dreaming process and therefore must be present in some form, although this dream gives no clear indication of impulsion. There is only a group of objects linked to one another, and by implication, involved with a death. Instinctual drives that are successfully repressed are readily symbolized as being dead or buried. The lack of observable movement and the absence of clearly defined motives confirm that the loss has to do with this facet of self experience. So much energy is invested in assuring that instinctual demands are repressed, nothing is available to give shape, substance, motivation, and intent to the dreaming self.

The words, "I was going to say I was the victim," give expression to the idea of having been the recipient of an attack. They imply that there was an earlier time when she experienced the influences of an object as being directed against her, and of being in a subservient position. The further statement, "But I felt I had done something wrong," is indicative that a new level of psychic organization has been structured in which guilt is a predominant feature. The dreamer does not portray what has been done wrong, which would convey the essence of what had been buried, but only this superego response to instinctual activity is accessible.

The varied impressions of an object are organized into defined entities possessing good and bad qualities, and the line of continuity of prohibitive experience maintains a connection from one to the other. This is the perceptual pathway by which the prohibitive influences of a bad object are available to be included within self experience, creating reaction formations to ensure the repression of instinctual activity. The objects in the dream are depicted as being linked, appearing to symbolize this relationship, suggesting that the process of identification with an aggressor is particularly active and that the resulting reaction formations are a prominent feature in the dreamer's psychic functioning at the moment. The emphasis upon reaction formations, the superego response of guilt, and the aura of over control in the body of the dream all point to an obsessive constellation. In isolation the dream could reflect either an underlying cohesive narcissistic personality disorder highlighting obsessive mechanisms, or an obsessive with character pathology. Either way it leads to the speculation that the instinctual activity pushing for expression involves anal sadistic impulses.

The reference to having been a victim hints that the dreamer had been in a narcissistically vulnerable position and has responded to the therapeutic relationship by solidifying cohesiveness and attaining consolidation of a functional superego. The statement, "I was going to say I was the victim, but I felt I had done something wrong," then emerges as highly significant when considered as a comment upon the intrapsychic changes that have been achieved after several years of treatment. The previously existing splits in the ego have apparently been healed, and an unstable but cohesive personality has been structured.

The combination of these two dreams presents a picture similar to what is observed in the cohesive narcissistic personality disorders, in which there can be a fluid shift from a hysteric to an obsessive constellation over a short span of time. The statement may thereby emanate from the residual effect of a borderline organization, and be replaced by a more advanced level of psychic structuralization.

One week later a third dream was reported:

I was on the couch and I fell off onto the floor. I fell off and you patted and hugged me.

This manifest dream portrayed a great deal of movement for the first time, signifying that instinctual drives have gained access to expression. There is also a clear picture of the self engaged in an action, which depends upon the availability of instinctual activity. In this dream, movement is clearly in evidence, and the self is pictured as falling, suggestive of an instinctual regression.

The undisguised images of the therapist and the couch represent the objects in the dream, with the therapist accomplishing what the couch could not by patting and hugging. This symbolizes the attributes of a good orally derived nurturant object. The manifest content can aid in determining whether an empathic lapse has entered the therapeutic relationship, because a dream is built around the day residue of an emotionally important unconscious perception, and the image of a good object again implies that an empathic lapse has not been the instigating factor. The couch's function is primarily one of holding and containment, and the dreamer falling off onto the floor seems to symbolize a failure in this containing function. The missing containment was then successfully provided in a more regressive position by the undistorted figure of the therapist. It was indicative that interpretive interventions and the management of the framework were offering containment in the presence of an instinctual regression.

The background object of primary identification is the original representation having this containing property. It is formed through contact with an empathically responsive object, and the therapeutic relationship appears to be amplifying this basic mental representation. In the previous two dreams the patient shifted from a phallically determined character defense to an anally determined character defense in a short segment of time, showing signs of initiating a regressive movement. This third dream gives more direct expression to instinctual activity, but with an emphasis upon orality. The sequence hints that the therapeutic interaction facilitated the expression of unconscious instinctual wishes, and the nature of the ensuing transference attachment could not be contained in a position symbolically represented by the couch. A defensive instinctual regression to an orally derived position created the necessary conditions to enable an attachment to be represented, and allowed the dreamer to feel held.

The relatively orderly pattern in the regression represented in this sequence of dreams was indicative of the cohesiveness now structured in her personality. There was a firm enough attachment to a separate good object's influence for the feeling of containment to be viable, and this new level of psychic organization was making it possible for the regression to be therapeutic. The difficulties in its management were probably the consequence of the residuals from the earlier period of borderline functioning.

A fourth dream was reported a few weeks later:

I was on a road, which turned into a waterway. I was driving a boat, it was choppy, and the spray came up and hit me. There was a man on land waving at me.

Movement is a prominent feature of this dream, reflecting the increasing mobility of instinctual drives. The dream is initiated upon a stable foundation symbolically represented as a road, and shifts to the more fluid underpinnings of water. It was significant because there was enough leeway to navigate in spite of the underlying instability, and the dreamer was at the wheel, capable of controlling the direction. The fluid environment of the water, with attention called to the spray touching her, was indicative of her reactive awareness of the regression taking place in the transference relationship. This was especially important for this patient, since the regressive waters of her early development were of a different order than those present when cohesiveness is established in childhood. Her regressive waters, in being more primitive and archaic, are potentially dangerous. Therefore, it was particularly meaningful that the spray could touch her with no ill effects. The choppiness of the water probably referred to this greater degree of difficulty, and it gave validation to the appropriate conduct of the treatment.

The only object in the dream was symbolized as a man waving his hands, the movement hinting at an instinctual attachment, and the connection existed at a distance. The dream imagery was suggestive of a girl's developmental task of navigating the choppy waters of a negative oedipal conflict, preliminary to effecting a displacement to the male, which shed light upon the previous regression. In the third dream the dreamer was held by orally nurturant qualities, and this portrayal of an instinctual regression could now be seen as a response to the inordinate conflict engendered by a genital attachment. The fourth dream began on the solid ground of a road, moved on to the less stable foundation of water, and placed the dreamer in a position where she could visualize an instinctual attachment to a man off in the distance. It appeared to give expression to what was unsuccessfully contained on the couch in the third dream. She had apparently found a regressive solution and was now attempting to move progressively forward.

The fluctuations from one level to another were a product of the instability in the structures maintaining cohesiveness, and though extreme anxiety was not overtly evident, it could be inferred from the rapidity with which the changes occurred. In the first dream there was concern with an object's approval indicative of the anxiety accompanying a phallic organization; in the second dream there was concern with having done something wrong indicative of a shift to an anal level; and in the third dream there was concern with a loss of control eased by being held in a regressive oral position. The fourth dream symbolically represented a progressive move toward a genital organization, and the nature of the associated anxiety could only be determined by implication. The distance of the man waving on land hinted that a positive genital, oedipal attachment was too far from her immediate experience for the anxiety accompanying it to be in the foreground. The choppy waters on which the dreamer traveled, however, symbolized the presence of anxiety, but in a form that was ill defined. In addition to the anxiety of a negative oedipal attachment, it may have included the extent to which oral aggression continued to color all instinctual experience.

Taken together, the dreams documented the structural changes that had been effected during several years of treatment, and illustrated the differences from those in which cohesiveness is established developmentally. When good qualities in the self and object are united and differentiated in the course of a therapeutic relationship, any of the influences of a separate good object are utilized. In addition, oral aggression continues to be excessive, though it is now contained within an evolving id of the dynamic unconscious and no longer has a destructive impact.

# 10

# Dreams in the Narcissistically Determined Phobic Disorders

The phobias have established cohesiveness and continuity of experience, but they rest on an unstable foundation. The fixation points and self integrity are alternately threatened by the prohibitive influences of a bad object and self experiences of instinctual overstimulation, which are then phobically avoided. The capacity to express instinctual drive derivatives and the derivatives of unconscious perceptions are present, but they tend to lead to trauma without active interpretive help. Consequently, there is a readiness to seek reenforcement of defensive idealizing and mirroring narcissistic transferences to attain some measure of stability.

The manifest dream is a valuable adjunct within the flow of associations, since it provides much needed information concerning the specific instinctual activities that are overstimulating or the archaic prohibitive responses that require modulation. In addition, the phobic individual is exquisitely sensitive to even the slightest lapse in empathy, eliciting a phobic attitude toward the therapeutic situation, and the source of an empathic failure may be difficult to ascertain. The dream is constructed around the derivative of an unconscious perception, gives a symbolic image of how the therapeutic relationship is received, alerts a therapist to the presence of an empathic lapse, and offers some direction toward its correction.

## The Nature of Pathology
## in the Phobic Disorders

The phobic disorders are a consequence of the inability to negotiate the transition from narcissism to object relatedness. They represent a fixation in the beginning stages of cohesiveness, and are the equivalent of what are frequently described as cohesive narcissistic personality disorders. Early development has been characterized by an empathic symbiotic period, abruptly interrupted precisely at the point that self individuation is initiated. Good self experience is structured sufficiently to respond to the progressive thrust for separateness, but the conditions of empathic resonance with an external object are no longer present. A dramatic change has occurred and an influx of narcissistic injuries gives impetus to a precocious search for the mental impressions of a separate good object's influence.

Although perceptual functions are immature and the helplessness and vulnerability associated with separateness are exaggerated, the intrapsychic wherewithal has been represented to engage in a premature process of separation and individuation. Fusion and merger continue to exert a strong regressive pull, threatening advances in self differentiation, and an ongoing lack of empathic resonance does not offer the buffering necessary for absorbing narcissistic injury. The differentiated mental impressions of earlier empathic contact are orally determined, have coalesced and consolidated rapidly under stress, and are sought and located as a defensive measure. The recognition of a good object's bad qualities, through the line of continuity of prohibitive experience, forms a fixation point anchoring object constancy. The bad prohibitive qualities of an orally determined object, however, are engulfing in nature, and incorporation by a bad object and loss of function through fusion and merger are difficult nuances to distinguish. The similarities, in conjunction with a diminished capacity to make the distinction, create an overwhelming threat that must be avoided. The fixation point is thereby established on the basic of a phobic attitude toward the influence of a bad, orally derived prohibitive object. It is highly unstable, and cohesiveness is constantly in jeopardy.

This initial point of fixation functions to maintain differentiation and to provide the stability required to structure the linkages forming the grandiose self and ego ideal. In health it is established in the anal period based upon prohibitions having a much more stabilizing effect, and the grandiose self is structured at the height of anality when mastery and control are in the ascendancy. Good instinctual self experiences of mastery are linked to the omnipotent fantasy of an optimally gratifying anal object to structure the grandiose self, and a stage and phase specific match is present that perfectly balances the vulnerability of separateness. In the developing phobic the instinctual bond structuring the grandiose self is orally derived, composed of good instinctual self experiences of nurturance linked to the orally determined fantasy of an all-giving object. The underlying instability is behind a compelling urge for nurturant interactions to shore up the sense of self, thereby easing the threat to cohesiveness from the impressions of a bad object.

Good instinctual experience in being bound to a fantasy is unavailable for adaptive functions, and the ego ideal is structured to strengthen self experience by including the qualities of an object that are most needed and admired. In this situation, where the sudden loss of a source of empathic supplies has altered the subsequent course of development, it is the optimally gratifying impression of an orally derived object that is selected for identification. This is the same facet of an object's influence embodied in the grandiose self, and as a consequence, these structural precursors of the superego are contiguous to each other so that their functions are interwoven and overlap.

In health the ego ideal is primarily based upon the optimally frustrating qualities of a good object, which amplifies latent resources and strengthens gender identity. The resulting structural pathway to the influences of an object can also enable the prohibitive, impinging aspect of a bad object to be included within self experience, and it is especially needed at those moments when instinctual overstimulation requires additional restraint. This process of identification with an aggressor is at the foundation of reaction formations, and is an essential step in consolidating superego precursors into an independently functioning agency. The phobic's attitude of avoidance toward the prohibitive influence of a bad object closes off this avenue of identification with an aggressor, and its absence intensifies the continued dependence upon external objects for regulation. The ego ideal is constructed with the mental impression of an optimally gratifying object, the grandiose self with its fantasy elaboration. These structures, rather than functioning as defined entities, operate in harmony with little to distinguish between them.

The structuralization of the grandiose self and ego ideal is affected by the existing degree of stability, the extent of the vulnerability associated with separateness, and the phase of psychosexual development in the ascendancy when they are formed. Although interrelated with each other they are designed to accomplish discrete and separate functions. Embedded in fantasy, the grandiose self is suited to regulate mental activity in the preconscious realm, whereas the ego ideal firmly tied to external reality regulates mental activity in the conscious realm. In the neurotic the qualities of an object utilized in fantasy to form the grandiose self and those selected for identification to form the ego ideal differ, and there is a clear-cut distinction in their functioning. The obsessive forms the grandiose self with the anally derived fantasy of an omnipotent object, and the ego ideal with sadistic prohibitive object impressions. The hysteric uses the fantasy of a phallically derived admiring object to form the grandiose self, and seeks humiliating or castrative prohibitions in forming the ego ideal. Identifications with an aggressor create reaction formations in the self system that stabilize and entrench fixed character attitudes. Thus the object's bad impinging qualities in the neurotic are either sadistic, humiliating, or castrating, and are available as a source of prohibition and restraint.

In the phobic the grandiose self and ego ideal are orally derived, utilize the same optimally gratifying aspect of an object's influence, and blur the distinction between the two structures. In addition, the object's bad impinging qualities are orally incorporative, arouse anxiety of panic proportions, threaten self integrity, and are avoided. Therefore, the phobic is incapable of identifications with an aggressor, reaction formations are unavailable, and fixed neurotic character attitudes cannot evolve. One manifestation of this combination of factors is the readiness with which the eye of consciousness and the superego eye can blend and flow into each other. A phobic individual's manifest dreams will frequently depict two distinct images of the dreamer, reflecting the lack of any significant opposition to intermeshing the activity of these separate perceptual agencies.

The formation of the ego ideal directs perceptual attention into the self system, and with it there is an awareness of the good self's bad qualities through the line of continuity of instinctual experience. In health the resulting fixation point operates as a spur to the organization of the superego, while eliciting a call for prohibitive forces to be focused in that locale. The subsequent regulation of instinctual activity has a stabilizing effect, which is essential for the further expansion of the component instincts and their consolidation into a genital drive. Establishing a fixation point in the self system prepares the way for castration anxiety to be structuralized, which is accomplished by uniting the lines of continuity of instinctual and prohibitive experience. All aspects of the self and object are thereby encompassed within the aegis of this genitally determined structure, enabling its function in signaling the need to institute defense and furthering the amount of self regulation. It is a necessary precondition for the transition from narcissism to object relatedness, in order to monitor the increase in instinctual activity accompanying the full flowering of an oedipal conflict.

Castration anxiety is the manifestation of a specific structure, wherein the genital instinctual facet of self experience is opposed by the prohibitive influences of a genitally derived object. It is uniquely adapted to serve a signaling function by virtue of incorporating both good and bad aspects of the self and object. In health it does not always invoke the institution of excessive defense, since there are elements of genital instinctual experience that are regulated by the gently restraining influence of an optimally frustrating object. It is only when the intensity of instinctual demand increases that greater increments of prohibition are required. In the developing phobic individual a recognition of instinctual overstimulation elicits a potential threat to self integrity and must be avoided. Consequently, the fixation point is highly unstable, castration anxiety is not adequately structured, and an oedipal conflict cannot flourish.

Developmentally, the transition from narcissism to object relatedness is motivated by a phobic situation. The expansion of the component instincts through the advancing stages of psychosexual development can be represented within a narcissistically structured personality to the point of a genital consolidation. The necessary increase in instinctual demand is then potentially traumatic, and acts as a catalyst to instigate the formation of new object related structures capable of enlarging the capacity for instinctual representation. The movement from a narcissistic to an object related orientation is achieved by elaborating the genital fantasies comprising an oedipal conflict. The ensuing linkages between the self and object are structured to create an uninterrupted pathway for instinctual integration and a new, more flexible boundary for the unconscious system of mental activity.

The resolution of the oedipal conflict through selective identifications strengthens good self experience, and the extent to which instinctual drives previously requiring defense can be included is vastly enlarged. Concomitantly, the superego is organized into an independently functioning agency, operating in harmony with the interests of the ego, and repression proper evolves into an effective regulatory force facilitating ongoing instinctual integration. The neurotic individual has formed stable fixation points that remain bound to their infantile origins, consolidated an excessively harsh structure of castration anxiety, and elaborated an inordinately conflicted oedipal configuration that is largely unresolved. The narcissistically determined, object related phobic disorders are fixated in a phobic situation, which in health and in neurosis have initiated an oedipal constellation.

The phobic individual has an extremely limited capacity for instinctual regulation. Expansion into anal, phallic, and genital positions is unsteady and potentially traumatic, and a state of overstimulation can reach proportions that threaten cohesiveness. The fixation point in the self system is very unstable, since a phobic avoidance of instinctual overstimulation is easily invoked, and castration anxiety has not evolved sufficiently to serve a signaling and regulatory function. The union of genital instinctual demands and prohibitions has a traumatic impact requiring defense, in place of operating to signal for defense. There may be movement in the direction of a genital consolidation, but when oedipal fantasies are initiated, regulatory functions are insufficient to manage the mounting instinctual intensity and a state of trauma results. Although cohesiveness and continuity of experience have been established, self integrity is threatened by the influences of an orally derived prohibitive object and by instinctual overstimulation. The superego has remained at a very early stage in its development and is incapable of independent functioning, and narcissistic enhancement by external objects is sought to regulate self esteem. Repression proper, which has emerged as the primary ego defense, is rooted in its beginning phases. It works in opposition to instinctual integration by directing perceptual attention away from what is most threatening toward that which is least threatening.

## The Interrelationship of the Continuum of Phobic Symptoms and the Use of the Manifest Dream

The initial and primary threat to cohesiveness in the phobic disorders emanates from the influences of a bad, orally incorporative, prohibitive object, placing the fixation point that maintains differentiation in jeopardy of being dissolved. The threat resonates throughout the entire system of object representations, and any stimulus evocative of the impressions of a bad object increases the vulnerability to a loss of cohesiveness. The unsteadiness inhibits mental activities involving the impressions of an object, and is adapted to by elaborating the threat within the system of self representations. The ensuing symbolization of an object posing a danger to self integrity has a regulatory effect, the phobic object is avoided, and some measure of continuing instinctual expansion can then take place. This is the underlying interplay of forces behind an object phobia. It reflects the progressive movement toward object relatedness and a budding capacity to effect the complex compromises involved in the construction of a psychological symptom.

The increase in instinctual activity evokes a heightened level of anxiety that shifts the threat to cohesiveness into the self system. A defensive, regressive retreat to a narcissistic fixation is activated, and a self phobia or combined self and object phobia is manifested. With the regression, the stress upon the fixation point in the object system is temporarily alleviated, allowing some latitude for representing the new threat to cohesiveness from the effects of instinctual overstimulation. The self is then symbolized as in danger of losing its integrity from overstimulation within a confined space, and claustrophobic situations are avoided. This self phobia is usually a transient step on a regressive pathway to a narcissistic fixation, in which a threat to cohesiveness is actively present from both the influences of a bad prohibitive object and from instinctual overstimulation. These combined self and object phobias are manifested as vague, ill-defined phobic responses to environmental stimuli, since there is little capacity for representing the threats in either the self or object system.

In a given individual there is a readiness to fluctuate from one phobic position to another, depending upon the internal and external circumstances. This fluidity in psychic functioning is a product of the difficulty in negotiating the transition from narcissism to object relatedness, and can only occur because of the particular makeup of the grandiose self and ego ideal. The threat to cohesiveness is easily transferred from the object system to the self system and back, because the structures uniting and differentiating the two systems tend to function as a unit. The psychic activity involved in constructing an object phobia takes place in the self system of representations, accompanies each move toward a genital consolidation and elaboration of oedipal fantasies, makes use of adaptive mechanisms that are hysterical in nature, and is associated with severe limitation in the psychic activity of the object system. When the anxiety reaches panic proportions and threatens cohesiveness, a regressive retreat is invoked. The psychic activity involved in the construction of a self phobia takes place in the object system, makes use of obsessive mechanisms, and is associated with severe limitations in the psychic activity of the self system. Finally, under stress, a total narcissistic fixation is exhibited, with a paucity of activity in both systems.

The phobic individual often shows this mixed picture of hysteric, obsessive, and narcissistic features, whereas the clearly hysteric and the obsessive neurotic do not. The matrix upon which the neurotic character is structured possesses much greater stability, and such a mixture of adaptive modes is not in evidence. The neurotic hysteric has an abundance of varied representations in the self system, and a relative sparsity in the object system. Mental activity is dominated by imagery, body sensations, and affective responses, with a diminished capacity for intellectualization. The neurotic obsessive is dominated by intellectual activity reflecting the hypertrophy of the varied impressions of an object, while displaying a marked inhibition in the accessibility of imagery, body sensations, and affective responses. The firmness of the fixation points, the stability and discreteness of the grandiose self and ego ideal, and the effectiveness of repression in the neurotic obviate against the fluctuation from one position to another.

In an unconsciously empathic environment, an individual with a phobically structured personality will exhibit the advanced position of an object phobia, and will move toward a genital consolidation as greater dimensions of instinctual activity are able to be represented without undue trauma.

This was portrayed in the dream of the 5-year-old boy, mentioned in earlier chapters to illuminate perceptual functions and to show the structural organization in a phobic personality:

I was lying in my bed and my nightmares jumped right out of my head and into the closet. The first was a big monster. I got my sword, attacked him, and he began to cry. I was surprised, put him in my bed, and he became my friend. Just then a second nightmare jumped out of my head. This one scared me. He was a big angry tiger, and ate up all my toys:

The unconsciously empathic properties of the therapeutic relationship had enabled him to represent symbolically the threats to self integrity in the manifest dream, rather than having to avoid them phobically. The first nightmare initially appeared to be menacing, was actively confronted, was not seen as a threat, and then became a friend. This symbolic image of a previously avoided prohibitive object was now available for much needed instinctual regulation, was perceived as a source of supply, and could then be placed alongside the dreamer's self. At this point the second nightmare emerged, with attributes characteristic of orally derived instinctual overstimulation. This symbolic image of oral greed continued to be frightening, but was no longer phobically avoided. The manifest dream gave expression to his ability to represent instinctual activity of increasing dimensions, and was the initial step to lead ultimately to a genital consolidation.

The individual manifesting a self phobia has managed to represent the threat to self integrity posed by instinctual overstimulation, temporarily alleviating the danger associated with the influences of a prohibitive object. Prohibitions are not available to aid in regulation, however, which emphasizes the importance of modulating their archaic, incorporative qualities.

> This was symbolized in the dream of an adolescent boy who was unable to attend school because of a claustrophobic reaction to a classroom setting.

> I was trying to see my enemy and face him once and for all. I did face him. He was so monstrous and terrifying I awoke in fright.

> The dream graphically depicted the enormous anxiety aroused by a prohibitive object, displaying how unavailable this much needed influence is. The therapeutic task was to interpret the source of his extreme anxiety, thereby ameliorating the harshness of the attack and facilitating the use of prohibitions in defending against instinctual overstimulation. The therapist responded to the dream by stating that he had taken a courageous stance in deciding to face this internal presence, but did not have a clear enough view, and was so frightened that it appeared monstrous, just as an angry parent must look to a frightened young child. The interpretation was designed to show the dreamer what he could not see, and in this way modify the prohibitions so they could be utilized as a source of internal regulation.

The combined self and object phobias, or narcissistic personality disorders, are stuck in an unmoveable position. Instinctual activity and prohibitions are both a threat to cohesiveness, and the attempt at self regulation is manifested in a search for external support of idealizing and mirroring narcissistic transferences. These pathological defenses are invoked to shore up cohesiveness and occupy the center of perceptual attention. This leaves little room for growth-promoting interventions. A manifest dream can give important information for interpretive help and guide a therapist toward creating the unconsciously empathic conditions necessary to foster progressive movement.

> This was shown in the following dream of a 10-year-old boy:

> I was on a high wire and couldn't move. If I moved in any direction I would fall and I was terrified. It was over a battlefield and I could see explosions and fighting out of the corner of my eye. I had to be very careful for if I looked too closely I would fall.

The manifest dream was built upon the structural foundation of a combined self and object phobia, reflected the extreme instability, and portrayed the danger associated with internal exploration. Nevertheless, the dreamer was trying to observe, suggesting that he could use interpretive help if it did not require that he move from his precarious position. The content of the dream gave some limited expression to powerful destructive forces, which he could not see very well, pointing to an area that might be more fully illuminated.

In previous sessions he had sat in silence, finding it very difficult to talk. The therapist, in turn, had also become silent, somewhat at a loss at finding effective interpretive words. When the dream was reported, it presented substantive material as to what it meant to him for the therapist to remain silent. The therapist began by acknowledging how helpful the dream was in giving a deeper view of how the relationship was experienced. The therapist went on to elaborate that the patient had been unable to move or talk, and the therapist was similarly immobilized. There was little to work with, but the dream opened an avenue for exploration. The explosions and fighting implied that he could only anticipate finding hostility in the therapist's silence, and though he was trying to look at this aspect of himself, he could not allow a full enough picture without being in danger. The therapist could now add to his vision by interpreting the aggression he feared both inside and outside of himself. The consequence of this intervention was in eliciting a stronger feeling of containment, steadying the underlying instability, and enabling the expression of instinctual drive derivatives.

Unconscious forces are given expression in a manifest dream by virtue of the dream work, which consists of condensations, displacement, symbolic representation, and secondary revision. Affects, though displaced, possess the most direct line to the latent dream thoughts; symbolizations reflect the implied meanings that unconscious impulses or perceptions convey. Secondary revision makes use of advanced ego functions to fill in gaps and render the dream relatively comprehensible; associations shed light upon the condensations that have taken place. The manifest dream is a valuable adjunct for individuals who are unable to provide associative material but need interpretive help. This is often the case in the phobic disorders, particularly when the patient is under stress.

Combining a delineation of the structural organization of the personality with a view of how the therapeutic relationship is unconsciously perceived, and adding to it the therapist's ability to read the implicit significance of symbolizations, makes an immense source of interpretive material available. It can augment a patient's feeling of containment through being unconsciously understood, enlarge the capacity to represent greater intensities of instinctual demand, and enable associative derivatives to be forthcoming.

The phobic disorders are narcissistically determined, display advances toward object relatedness, attain cohesiveness against a background of instability, and consequently shift from one phobic position to another. A helpful therapeutic response to a manifest dream depends upon whether the threat to self integrity emanates from the influences of a bad, prohibitive object, from instinctual overstimulation, or from both sources. It must also take into consideration the dream content being portrayed and the context in which it appears. In an object phobic position, a dream symbolically represents movement toward a genital consolidation and the mounting level of anxiety with the emergence of an oedipal conflict. It is indicative of a need for active interpretive assistance, which may or may not require asking for associations to dream content. When a dream reflects a traumatic situation that cannot be faced, and a therapist requests associations, it displays an unempathic lack of appreciation of the dreamer's predicament. This may happen often if a phobia is seen as symbolizing a specific instinctual danger instead of representing a threat to self integrity.

An object phobia is in a transitional phase between representing a threat to the self and representing an instinctual danger. The ability to form symptomatic compromises is incomplete. The phobia itself symbolizes the threat of self integrity, whereas a psychological symptom incorporates an instinctual impulse, its defensive accompaniment, and a superego response. A self phobia is in a transient, more regressive position, and the threat to self integrity emanates from instinctual overstimulation. In most situations, encouraging associations to various dream components would not be indicated, as it would tend to foster the expression of instinctual derivatives and further threaten fragmentation. A combined self and object phobia is in a narcissistically fixated position, and both prohibitive responses and instinctual activity are a threat to cohesiveness. In this situation no additional associations are called for, and the manifest dream is especially helpful for discerning what is required to facilitate growth.

Although it is true that the manifest dream cannot directly reveal the unconscious forces at work, and it requires associative linkages to expose the latent dream thoughts, the manifest content can give implicit directions to aid in the conduct of a therapeutic relationship. Requesting associations under conditions where they cannot be safely produced introduces an empathic lapse, which in the phobic is evocative of early trauma. The lack of firmness in the fixation points maintaining object constancy and stabilizing self experience is a product of the phobic attitudes upon which they are based, arising from the effects of excessive narcissistic injury. They create an inordinate dependency on external objects for regulation, an empathic failure echoes with the traumatic events of early development, and a phobic perception of the therapist is elicited. When such lapses can be identified, acknowledged, rectified, and their unconscious significance interpreted, phobically avoided experiences can become integrated, leading to a constructive outcome.

## The Composition of Pathological Defenses in Phobias, the Significance of Empathic Failures, and the Importance of the Manifest Dream

In the phobic individual what is most and least threatening fluctuates somewhat depending upon whether an object phobia, a self phobia, or a combined self and object phobia is manifested. Compensatory measures are instituted to allay the anxiety of fragmentation; they are designed to draw perceptual attention away from the particular internal experiences endangering cohesiveness and are at the foundation of pathological defenses. The source of the most crucial and primary threat is from the impressions of a bad, prohibitive object. Cohesiveness, differentiation, and object constancy are anchored by an awareness of a good object's bad qualities, which in this situation must be phobically avoided due to their orally incorporative properties. The danger is then symbolized as an object phobia, and the subsequent regulatory effect enables some progression toward a genital consolidation. The inhibition in any psychic activity requiring the impressions of an object is not eased until idealizations are elaborated enough to shore up the valuable influences of a good object. Instinctual experience reaches traumatic intensities quickly, however, and the threat to cohesiveness shifts into the self system. Mirroring is then sought from external objects, by gaining support and admiration of good self qualities, in order to alleviate the threat. Idealizations and mirroring are resonant with the pretraumatic empathic infantile experiences that have been utilized in structuring cohesiveness, and thereby they serve well in constructing defenses to guard against a loss of self integrity, though at the expense of reenforcing a narcissistic orientation.

The initial object relationship formed in the transference is determined by the particular pathological defense most in need of support. When the threat to cohesiveness from the prohibitive influences of a bad object is active, as in the object phobias, idealizations shore up the object system and occupy perceptual attention. When the threat to cohesiveness from instinctual overstimulation is active, as in the self phobias, mirroring shores up the self system to occupy perceptual attention. These idealizing and mirroring narcissistic transferences reenforce a pathological defense, stabilize the sense of self, and alleviate the immediate threat to cohesiveness. They represent a compensatory attempt at self cure, and reflect the continuing inability to negotiate the transition from narcissism to object relatedness. Dependency upon an external object for regulation is exaggerated by a therapist's participation in fostering idealizations and providing mirroring.

Kohut (1977) described these narcissistic transferences as the product of a developmental arrest and advocated their encouragement. This approach was based on the observation that it strengthened the sense of self and alleviated the anxiety of fragmentation. Although it does steady the background of instability, and in this way structures a firmer narcissistic position, it does not lead to the changes required to gain an object related orientation. Conceptualizing a therapeutic alliance as a bond between the therapist's analyzing functions and the patient's more advanced observing ego functions has particular relevance for these cohesive narcissistic personality disorders. This concept of an alliance has a tendency to place emphasis upon conscious empathy, which increases the likelihood of reenforcing a pathological defense. The initial narcissistic transferences confront a therapist with being idealized or sought as a source of mirroring responses. The former may gratify any lingering narcissistic aspirations, and the latter any residual need to be seen as a good parental object. A therapeutic alliance consisting of a bond between the patient's unconscious perceptions and the therapist's unconsciously interpretive communications and management of the framework places unconscious empathy in the forefront, and pathological defenses are then either silently noted or interpreted but not reenforced.

The prohibitive influences of a bad object and self experiences of instinctual overstimulation are held in abeyance by repression proper, as perceptual attention is directed to the idealizing and mirroring narcissistic transference.

> The effect of interpreting their defensive function was symbolically represented in the dream of a 15-year-old boy, after a session in which he talked about his fear of never overcoming his internal opposition toward reaching out to find a girl friend. In the course of the session he consistently attempted either to idealize the therapist or to seek praise

for his accomplishments, which the therapist interpreted as an effort to avoid the anxiety of an instinctual attachment. That night he had a dream:

> I was with a girl friend and we were talking and laughing. I was having a good time and she gave me her phone number. I dialed it, and as I got to the last number I hung up. I felt uneasy but decided to try again. This time I got her father, who accused me of having sexual intentions. I became horribly embarrassed and hung up.

The manifest dream was based on mental structures that could not allow genitally derived, unconscious instinctual wishes to gain full access to representation. The therapist's interpretive intervention had enabled the instinctual strivings and their accompanying prohibitive response, existing behind the narcissistic transferences, to be openly manifested. They stopped short, however, of moving into an oedipal constellation. This was consistent with his having sufficient structure to respond to the thrust for developmental progression and attaining a genital consolidation of the component instincts, but the beginning elaboration of oedipal fantasies was unable to form the genitally determined structures at the foundation of object relatedness. The therapist, in desisting from reenforcing his narcissistic transferences and, instead, interpreting the underlying instinctual danger, had facilitated the expression of unconscious wishes to the extent that they could be managed. The therapist's words were symbolized into the accusatory voice of the father, indicating a direction for further interpretive help in enabling oedipal fantasies to flourish.

In the phobic disorders, regression possesses two opposing functions, making it essential to distinguish between them and to identify the way in which they are manifested. A benign regression is necessary to discover and integrate psychic contents that have been repressed and rendered inaccessible. It is facilitated by an unconsciously empathic environment, and results in the expression of instinctual derivatives. A malignant regression is utilized in the service of defense, is encouraged by an emphasis upon conscious empathy, and results in derivatives expressing the unconscious perception of an empathic failure.

> The signs of a malignant regression after an empathic lapse was symbolized in the following two dreams of a 15-year-old boy. The therapist had consciously empathized with his acute pain in being rejected by a loved girl friend, rather than interpreting the feeling of rejection as a derivative expressing a lack of recognition of his transference longings.

I was in a train surrounded by war refugees. Everything was desolate. We came through a tunnel into the glitter of a modern remodeled train station. It was all a sham, like we were headed for the gas chamber. The other refugees cried out in happiness and excitement, fooled by the glitter. I wandered off.

Immediately after reporting the dream he recalled another from the past:

I went to the freezer and it was filled with quick and awful fast foods dressed up to look great. I angrily threw them out looking for good food. Another part of me was off to the side amused.

The despair in watching the destructive consequences of being fooled by glitter in the first dream, and the anger at finding awful food dressed up to look great in the second dream, gave symbolic expression to his unconscious perception of the unempathic attributes of the therapist's intervention. The use of conscious empathy in the therapeutic interaction had echoed with the unempathic traumas of early development, demonstrated its ineffectiveness, and was indicative of his readiness to engage in a benign regression.

A malignant regression makes use of pathological defenses manifested by a demand for the gratification of regressive cravings. For some, the need to maintain narcissistic transferences may be so great that they are clung to tenaciously, and any attempt to interpret their meaning is only consciously received as a rejection. An aura of uncertainty about the unconsciously empathic properties of the relationship is introduced, which may be difficult to ascertain from communications motivated so strongly by pathological defenses.

At these moments the more reliable symbolic imagery of a manifest dream can be an invaluable aid, which was the case in the treatment of a 30-year-old man demanding a prescription for medication to ease his anxiety and inability to fall asleep. The pressure arose after he expressed derivatives indicating that a harsh, punitive, prohibitive view of the therapist was disrupting an idealizing narcissistic transference, and he appeared to be seeking this form of gratification to restore the idealized image. The therapist's persistence in holding to a listening, interpretive posture made him feel defeated, and that night he had a dream: (This was the dream described in Chapter 3 to show how readily the impressions of an object can be placed in the service of defense.):

Some men were robbing a bank. I got a chain to try and help stop them. Suddenly I was one of them and the woman bank teller was a hostage with her hands chained. I knew I had to get away. I ducked into a pipe system with no way out, and I tried to get over a fence but it was endless and had barbed wire. I kept looking for a way out and knew I would eventually find one.

The men robbing the bank symbolized his efforts toward attaining reenforcement of a pathological defense, and implied an unconscious awareness of it working against his constructive growth. Although initially he was in opposition to this activity, he quickly became immersed in it and was cognizant of his involvement; the rest of the dream was occupied with his struggle to escape detection.

His lack of success in gaining the therapist's participation in supporting a narcissistic transference had triggered a conscious feeling of defeat, but the dream exposed its pathological defensive function. His conviction that he would ultimately find a way out acquainted him with the tenacity of his defensive posture, and led to a broader recognition of the injurious consequences. In an unconsciously empathic environment, instinctual demands emerge from the effects of repression, and the transference relationship undergoes a change. The therapist, who initially has either been idealized or is seen to be a source of narcissistic supplies, becomes a potentially overwhelming instinctual or profoundly dangerous prohibitive object.

The effects of trauma during the oral period have extended into all of the advancing stages of psychosexual development, and with a genital consolidation, the ensuing attachment to an object poses an inordinate instinctual or prohibitive threat. Empathic lapses tend to evoke the representation of the original trauma, which involved an alteration in the qualities of empathy at the point individuation was becoming viable. The phobic possesses an intense reactive sensitivity to empathic and unempathic stimuli, since unconscious perceptions are not muted by the presence of well-structured character defenses. A narcissistic perspective is solidified with even the slightest lapse in empathy, while the farthest reaches toward object relatedness are displayed in an unconsciously empathic environment.

When an empathic lapse becomes a part of the therapeutic interaction, it must be identified, rectified, and its unconscious meaning exposed and interpreted. In this way the phobic elements of the pathology are engaged in the transference relationship, and unconscious empathy is restored. The movement toward object relatedness is reasserted, and the therapist is unconsciously experienced as an instinctual or prohibitive object with the attendant dangers expressed through derivatives. Efforts to enlist the therapist's participation in reenforcing idealizing and mirroring narcissistic transferences are then more readily revealed as a regressive, defensive retreat from the anxiety associated with an evolving oedipal conflict.

Unconsciously, empathic interpretive interventions amplify the containing forces in the personality, provide an effective therapeutic hold, and enable the fuller expression of instinctual derivatives. The dependency upon an external object for regulation and for support of pathological defenses is diminished, and the anxiety accompanying inevitable separations is of manageable proportions. The perception of a therapist as a phobic object is indicative of an empathic lapse, whereas intense anxiety in response to the end of a session or weekend separation suggests that a pathological defense is being reenforced.

## Effects of the Phobic's Unstable Fixation Points on Mental Structuralization and Its Appearance in the Manifest Dream

The phobic has accomplished the developmental milestone of establishing cohesiveness with a great deal of difficulty, reflected in the instability of the fixation points and in the effect they have on the structural unions necessary for progress to continue.

The memory trace of a good object's bad qualities at the foundation of the fixation point anchoring object constancy was symbolized in dramatic fashion in the aforementioned dream of the 15-year-old boy who was preoccupied with what he described as an enemy within working against him.

I was trying to see my enemy and face him once and for all. I did face him. He was so monstrous and terrifying I awoke in fright.

The prohibitive influence of a bad object was not only dangerous but threatened self integrity, creating a nightmare situation, and the dream had to be interrupted. Cohesiveness was maintained on the basis of a phobic attitude toward a prohibitive object, placing continuity of experience on an unsteady foundation.

The makeup and functioning of the mental structures utilized in building a dream are often reflected in the symbolic imagery portrayed, and the following dream of a young phobic woman illuminates the particular disturbance encountered in structuring the grandiose self and ego ideal.

I was on my way to an airplane. I had left the terminal and was in a train that went from the terminal to the plane. I thought the plane was going to be blown up, but instead terrorists blew up the terminal. I was relieved that I had left the terminal. The train I was in started to get out of control, I pulled the emergency brakes, the train stopped, and I woke up.

The symbolic images included an airplane, a terminal, and a vehicle transporting the dreamer from one to the other. The terminal possesses the characteristic of a stationary structure where things begin and end, which is consonant with the self representational system. The representations of an object result from the mental impressions of independent stimuli, making them more distant, less under control, and more susceptible to fantasy distortion. The airplane appears to symbolize the functional activity of this system. A major attribute of instinctual activity is impulsion, and the train connecting the terminal to the airplane is in motion.

The manifest content thereby depicts an instinctual movement from the self system (the terminal) to the object system (the airplane), consistent with the pathway by which the grandiose self is structured. The composition of the dream seems to be focused upon the trouble encountered with the establishment of this unifying and differentiating structure. The motivation for forming the grandiose self is the vulnerability and helplessness associated with the recognition of separateness. The purpose is to provide balance by participating in the fantasied omnipotence of an object. It functions to regulate the dreaming process. The high level of its instability is suggested by the inadequate regulation exemplified in the body of the dream.

The dreamer's movement was accompanied by an explosion in the terminal, after the dream first had the idea that it would take place on the airplane. This symbolic representation implies that the object world was fantasied as being filled with aggression, hinting that the powerful restraints of a counter aggressive force were needed from the influences of an object. The dream also presented a symbolic picture of the unavailability of the process of identification with an aggressor, so necessary for effecting restraint through prohibitions, and of the superego not as yet consolidating its precursors into a functional agency.

The explosion intimated that instinctual experience contained an overloading of aggression; libido is binding when phase specific and overstimulating when excessive, whereas aggression is differentiating when phase specific and destructive when excessive. The train getting out of control referred to the need for more adequate defensive opposition, but the only defensive functions available were those offered by the structured remnants of reactions to impingement and those instituting a more inclusive self boundary. This was symbolized by putting on the emergency brakes to stop the train, and then invoking the

advanced functions associated with the eye of consciousness by awakening. These structural underpinnings of the manifest dream revealed
the narcissistic organization of the personality, and the absence of any
progress toward an object related perspective.

On those occasions when an object phobia can be symbolically
represented, there is an advance toward a genital consolidation and an
object related orientation. The ability to symbolize the phobia allows
progressive movement, but the lack of regulatory forces makes the
resulting instinctual activity overwhelming.

The unsteady foundation upon which cohesiveness is structured
enables a shift to a self phobia, an internal state that was symbolically
represented in the following dream of a 38-year-old claustrophobic man:
(This dream was initially presented in Chapter 3 to illuminate the
significance of how the self system is represented.):

> I was driving in a bus very high up in the driver's seat. It was extremely
> precarious. I felt that I would topple if I moved. From the outside
> everything was in proportion, but inside I was too high up.

Although the unconscious drives fueling the dream are not specifically revealed, any movement jeopardized the entire functioning of the
dreaming self. The symbolic imagery captured the lack of a firm background for instinctual representation and the subsequent fear of sexual
excitement.

Conceptualizing a phobia as representing a specific instinctual
danger leads to an interpretive attitude that addresses genital instinctual strivings prematurely. It interferes with any movement toward
structuring an oedipal conflict, and in this sense introduces a lack of
unconscious empathy into the relationship.

This was shown in the previously discussed dream reported by a
young phobic man:

> I was with a girl who I knew was going to die. It had something to do
> with the X-ray machines in an airport terminal. The dream changed. I
> was with the same girl, only this time I knew she was going to die in
> three weeks. I made plans to be with her and she died. At the same
> time that I was dreaming I was watching the dream from above and
> trying to figure out what it meant.

Psychoanalytic psychotherapy is devoted to a process of internal
exploration, to encouraging a free flow of projective identifications,
and to expanding self awareness through the vehicle of a regressive

transference relationship. Generally, the derivative of a patient's unconscious perception of the therapeutic interaction operates as a nidus for attracting the unconscious instinctual drives that give impetus to the construction of a dream. It is included as the day residue and can be identified from the symbolization of the particular properties of the treatment. The one feature in the dream containing this symbolic element involved the X-ray machine, which was deemed to be the cause of a love object's death. By implication, a penetrating view of the significance of this attachment was responsible for the loss, and the dreamer could not tolerate what was being exposed in the treatment.

A system of represented objects is multidimensional in nature, with a variety of differing qualities, but in this dream the only object portrayed is a girl in the process of dying. It seems to reflect the absence of depth and richness in the world of objects, and suggests that the structural connection symbolized by this figure is readily dissolved. The perceptual agency engaged in registering the dream continues to be functional, and the dream is neither interrupted nor does it assume nightmare qualities to awaken the dreamer. The integrity of the dreaming self is not in jeopardy, therefore the structural linkages to the influences of an object required to maintain object constancy and cohesiveness remain intact.

Although the death is related to the effects of an X-ray machine, giving expression to an unconscious perception of the therapeutic relationship, it also refers to the way in which the self and object systems of representation are united at the interior of the personality. The genital fantasy linkages of an oedipal constellation are structured in this locale to enable the shift from a narcissistic to an object related orientation. Primal scene fantasies are linked to bad self experience to structure a pathway of integration. Incestuous fantasies are linked to the impressions of an overstimulating instinctual object to structure a boundary for the unconscious system. Primal scene fantasies are accompanied by a proliferation of instinctual derivatives and by movement toward increased integration. Incestuous fantasies are accompanied by prohibitions and by an ascendancy of repressive and defensive forces. This dream encompassed a visualized object, identifying it as the derivative of an incestuous fantasy. The object was so easily lost it indicated an inability to firmly structure an oedipal conflict.

The need to carry advanced functions into the regressive state of dreaming was consistent with the dreamer's defensive posture, and is characteristic of the phobic disorders. The engagement with an object having an oedipal cast signifies that there has been movement into forming an object related perspective, but the therapist's interpretive interventions appear to be interfering with the difficult task of structuring an oedipal constellation. The absence of any evidence of fixed character defenses, the ease with which contact with an incestuous object was lost, and the excessive defensiveness embodied in the dreamer's awareness of dreaming all point to the internal changes still needing to occur in order to achieve this more advanced level of psychic organization.

## The Transition from a Threat to Self Integrity to Representing an Instinctual Danger Reflected in the Manifest Dream

Once the crucial step of separation and individuation has been negotiated, cohesiveness and continuity of experience are structured in the personality. The mental capacity is present to advance from narcissism to object relatedness, which is manifested in the movement toward a genital consolidation and the evolution of an oedipal conflict. In the narcissistically determined, object related phobic disorders, the anxiety engendered by an unfolding oedipal constellation instigates a regressive retreat to narcissistic defenses organized to support cohesiveness. These disturbances may or may not display overt phobic symptomatology, but when symptoms are present they reflect the transition from representing a threat to self integrity to effecting the complex compromises embodied in representing a specific instinctual danger. The composition of a manifest dream will be founded upon this underlying transitional position, and will symbolically represent the experiences threatening self integrity.

The dream of a 5-year-old phobic boy is an example. He had been raised by his single mother, and was struggling with a conflicted desire to gain independence and distance from her. Whenever he tried to be on his own he was drawn to his mother by powerful infantile longings, which accentuated his search for male figures as a source of identification. He had requested therapeutic contact because of his concern about fights with his mother and an overwhelming fear of the dark when going to bed at night. Shortly after his initial session he reported a dream:

I was enveloped by a huge spider and was afraid I'd suffocate. I slipped away and ran to my grandfather's house. He had a big shotgun and shot the spider. I yelled, "He's a dead duck."

The manifest content symbolized the enormous threat to self integrity posed by the impressions of an orally determined incorporative object and by the loss of self functions encompassed in the regressive pull toward fusion and merger associated with his infantile longings. His ability to represent the danger alleviated the threat to self integrity, symbolized in the dream by his slipping away from an enveloping spider. The figure of the grandfather with a powerful shotgun gave expression to his attempt to identify with masculine attitudes, which apparently had been elicited in response to engaging in the therapeutic relationship. The dream signified that he was preparing the way for an emerging capacity to represent specific instinctual dangers at advancing levels of psychosexual development. It indicated a beginning movement toward a genital consolidation of the component instincts, which ultimately could lead to the evolution of an oedipal conflict.

The initial stages of cohesiveness can only be attained when sufficient quantities of good self experience have been structuralized at the foundation of the personality, since there is then enough stability and containment to support advances in self differentiation. The impressions of an object are coalesced, consolidated into clearly defined entities, and well differentiated, but they continue to retain their narcissistically determined qualities. The ability to perceive an object as having independent objects of its own is an integral facet of an oedipal conflict and an indication that the transition from a narcissistic to an object related orientation has taken place. This ability is accompanied by and interrelated with the capacity to register and represent the unseen dimension on the continuum of instinctual demand.

An oedipal configuration requires that unseen objects can be represented, and the resulting genital fantasies are structured to ensure cohesiveness at the interior of the personality. Although the phobic individual may exhibit some movement in the direction of developing an oedipal conflict and object related perceptions, the associated increase in instinctual demand is too overwhelming for it to flourish fully and be structured.

This was depicted in the following dream of a 10-year-old girl: (described before as an example of the phobic's problem with instinctual regulation).

I was in love with a rock star, which made me feel extremely excited and alive. I went to a concert, he announced he had just gotten married, and I felt heartbroken. He introduced his wife. I killed her, and felt relief.

The manifest content represented the initiation of an oedipal constellation and the subsequent inability to tolerate the perception of an object having independent objects of its own. It also captured the narcissistic attributes of the object world. The evolving genital instinctual wishes and the conflicts they engendered were aborted by an aggressive act of destruction, alleviating the overwhelming threat.

The conditions of psychoanalytic treatment support a benign regression, eventuating in a frightening genital instinctual transference relationship. An effort may then be exerted to focus attention upon idealizations or to seek mirroring responses, revealing the defensive intent of these narcissistic transferences. It is then incumbent upon a therapist to actively participate with unconsciously empathic interpretive interventions in order to facilitate the full elaboration of an oedipal conflict. The phobic individual has not developed a structuralized oedipal constellation, and it is only under the special circumstances accompanying a well-managed psychoanalytic framework that the necessary flourishing of genital fantasies can unfold.

The transitional position between narcissism and object relatedness was clearly portrayed in the symbolic imagery of the following dream reported by a young woman, who referred to it as a nightmare:

> I was in France in a hotel built inside of a cliff. There was a very steep path down although it was full of foliage and flowers. I was in the hotel and they wouldn't let me go. I kept trying to leave, but was held captive. Then there was something about John Lennon. He let me know he was sexually available to me, and I awoke in panic.

The content of the dream (referred to briefly in Chapter 6, explored in more detail here) represents the dreamer as being severely restricted on one side by the presence of prohibitive objects, and on the other side by a precipitous drop-off. The setting of the dream, well-entrenched inside of a cliff and in a foreign country, was significant because it implied that unconscious drives were involved and that there was a measure of safety and protection in her position.

The most direct access for leaving this enclosed space was blocked by imposing, prohibitive guards, although a steep pathway fraught with danger also represented a way out. The foliage and flowers along the path appeared to symbolize features often attributed to genital exploration through masturbatory activities and the danger of instinctual overstimulation. It implied that in order to gain freedom of movement she either had to modulate prohibitions or attain a larger capacity for instinctual integration. The objects in the dream are particularly noteworthy, and their relationship to the dreamer captures the attachments that are an integral part of these narcissistically determined and object related disorders. They include the poorly distinguished guards, possessing phobically avoided, prohibitive attributes, entrapping the dreamer, and later there is a vague sense of an attachment to John Lennon that immediately elicits an anxiety of panic proportions, which interrupts the dream.

In the first part of the dream the symbolic representation of a phobic attitude toward a prohibitive object and toward instinctual overstimulation reflected the functioning of narcissistically determined character defenses, and the repeated efforts to escape these confines led to the entrance of John Lennon as a genital sexual object. The dreamer had been encased within a narcissistic fixation, struggling to move forward; genital sexual innuendos arose, and the abrupt increase in anxiety became unmanageable because of the overwhelming threat of an oedipal attachment. The figure of John Lennon clearly had idiosyncratic meaning; nevertheless, it contained the property of being a star and of arising from the dead out of the past. The dreamer's father had died late in her childhood, making the choice comprehensible.

The transition from narcissism to object relatedness led to a sudden confrontation with the potential for a genital instinctual attachment. It was represented by symbolizing a resurrected figure from the past, was found to be too overstimulating, threatened the integrity of the dreaming self, and created a nightmare situation. It was indicative of advanced forays into an oedipal constellation having been latently present, suggesting that the treatment had facilitated this progressive step. The nightmare ending, however, also implied that the emerging object related transference had not been adequately interpreted, making it necessary for the dreamer to utilize a symbolized figure from the past as a center of instinctual interest. The setting of the dream appears to symbolize the fixed narcissistic position the dreamer has had to maintain, with the therapeutic relationship giving impetus to the emergence of early steps toward elaborating an oedipal constellation. The absence of interpretive aid in addressing the evolving genital instinctual transference attachment left the dreamer unable to manage the increased demand for regulation, and the only option available was to invoke a new set of perceptual functions by awakening.

The day residue of the dream is not immediately noticeable, but since the central theme focuses upon the idea of being held captive, in all likelihood it includes an unconscious perception of the treatment. The depiction of a way out through instinctual activity, symbolized as a steep pathway covered with foliage, is a dangerous alternative. This implies that it has been traveled before, has been found inordinately threatening, and is too risky to be traversed. The vague figures blocking her way to a safe exit at the front of the hotel appear to be symbolizing an unconscious view of the therapeutic relationship, probably in response to narcissistic transferences not being reenforced. Idealizing and mirroring narcissistic transferences are a manifestation of the pathological defenses designed to shore up an unsteady sense of self. A therapist participating in their support does aid in alleviating fragmentation anxiety, and were this occurring, the dreamer would not likely feel trapped. In abstaining, the dreamer is confronted with the unmanageable instinctual overstimulation accompanying an oedipal constellation. This would make it essential for a therapist to offer active interpretive help in integrating instinctual dangers as they arise, in order to modulate the threat to self integrity.

Strengthening narcissistic transferences allays the threat to cohesiveness, but does not allow the full flowering of oedipal fantasies necessary to structure an object related perspective. The manifest content reflects the transitional position maintained in the phobic disorders, pictures the traumatic impact of a genital instinctual attachment to an object, and indicates the consequences of blocking off one avenue by not reenforcing narcissistic transferences and another by not providing enough interpretive help.

Under favorable conditions, the earliest forays into a genital consolidation and oedipal constellation may evolve, and when they do, the deficiencies preventing continuing progression are revealed.

The dream of an 18-year-old girl, fixated in the transition between narcissism and object relatedness, is illustrative. It was reported after a session in which she felt the strength of an attachment to her mother and the pain of a rejection.

You were with me. My mother and father were arguing. My father disappeared and my mother tried to take my makeup. I fought to hold onto it and she hit me. She screamed at me and was jealous of my materials, wanting them for herself.

The symbolic imagery pictured an emerging oedipal rivalry projected onto the figure of the mother, with the father fading into the background. Instinctual activity and a prohibitive response were both condensed into the maternal imago, and then portrayed as a source of attack and injury necessitating defense. In this way the manifest dream reflects the ineffectiveness of castration anxiety in serving as a signaling and regulatory function, and the inability to utilize prohibitions in managing the intensity of genital instinctual drives. The genital fantasies of an oedipal conflict were unable to flourish fully, which obviates against the formation of a new interior structure that ensures cohesiveness and the evolution of object related perceptions.

The effects of psychoanalytic treatment upon movement in the direction of structuring an oedipal conflict were exemplified in a sequence of two dreams reported by a young girl who was initially referred because of a variety of phobic reactions. The first dream was presented in her first session at the age of 9, having taken place the night before in anticipation of the therapeutic encounter:

> I was being chased by a gorilla in the hall outside of your office, and I ran into your office to be safe.

The symbolization of an object threatening self integrity and a haven of safety suggested that under the proper conditions, ongoing instinctual representation was possible. A second dream two years later showed the oedipal constellation that had evolved during the intervening period of treatment:

> I was in the produce department of a grocery store with a man who looked like you and with whom I felt safe. A woman drove up with a 2-year-old baby. I held the baby, became aware it was mine and had been produced by my father in another life, and I couldn't let it go.

The age of the baby matched the passage of time from the initial contact and gave expression to her newfound ability to confront an oedipal attachment in the containing arms of the therapeutic relationship: her hold on the baby was indicative of its structuralization. At the time of the first dream, genital instinctual wishes were totally overwhelming and traumatic, but now they could be symbolically represented within the context of a manifest dream.

Primal scene fantasies unite the unseen dimension of instinctual demand to the representation of an instinctually overstimulated self, forming a structured pathway of instinctual integration that ultimately gains access to sublimation and secondary autonomy. Incestuous fantasies unite overstimulating genital instinctual self experiences to the impressions of a forbidden instinctual object, invoking defensive responses designed to strengthen repression proper and forming a new structured boundary for the unconscious system. This organizing function of an oedipal conflict is unavailable to the phobic, making sublimations more difficult, leaving a rigid, inflexible, narcissistically structured boundary for the unconscious system, and allowing little leeway for instinctual expansion.

# 11

# Dreams in the Neuroses: The Obsessive and the Hysteric

In the neurotic individual, a dream is built on a more stable foundation, and genital instinctual drives are the primary source of intrapsychic conflict symbolized in the manifest content. The various dream components are more revealing of their infantile origins, illuminating the associative context in which it is reported. Character defenses are an important part of the neurotic's defensive organization, and they must be intervened with successfully for a benign therapeutic regression to unfold. The effect is to enable the emergence of defense transference and transference constellations, leading to the full flowering of a transference neurosis.

Character defenses are based upon a pregenital attachment to an object and pregenital instinctual experience, and underlie the defenses against the transference. Defense transference and transference configurations are determined by genital instinctual experience, and are expressed through incestuous and primal scene fantasy derivatives. This continuum of transference experience is symbolically represented in the dream imagery, shedding light on the status of the treatment. The manifest dream is a valuable indicator of the movement taking place in a therapeutic regression, and an enormously important vehicle for exposing latent dream thoughts. The process of unraveling the dream work to gain access to the unconscious forces embodied in the manifest content is equally a process of instinctual integration.

## Underlying Stability in the Neurotically Structured Personality

Neurotic disorders are pathological entities occurring on a developmental foundation in which an object related perspective has been established. The oedipal conflict is structured but is unresolved, and the final step on a pathway of instinctual integration has not been adequately negotiated. The fixation points remain tenaciously bound to the memory traces of an infantile attachment to an object and to infantile instinctual experience, which is behind the pregenitally determined character defenses standing in readiness to aid in repressing genital oedipal fantasies and their accompanying instinctual and prohibitive dangers. The superego is not fully consolidated, as a consequence of which its functions are polarized, and opposed to the interests of the ego.

Neurotic disturbances, in contrast to all others, have established a firm, stable background of cohesiveness, continuity of experience, and object constancy. Good self experience has been fully structured at the foundation of the personality, and although an advanced level of psychic organization has been achieved, it has not prevented serious, and at times debilitating, psychological difficulties. Pregenital experience has shaped the oedipal configuration, and is embodied in the fixed character attitudes expressive of defenses against the transference. These pathological defenses are operative at the surface of the personality in opposition to the defense transference and transference fantasies held in repression in the deeper layers. Incestuous fantasy derivatives are expressive of the defense transference, reflecting the activity of the boundary of the unconscious system, while primal scene fantasy derivatives express the transference, reflecting movement along a structured pathway of instinctual integration. These genital fantasies engender an inordinate degree of conflict, and the lack of a successful solution does not allow a free flow of instinctual activity.

Incestuous fantasies are overdeveloped, and primal scene fantasies pose a threat that is heavily defended against. The demands of a genital object related orientation have resulted in the persistence of a highly conflicted infantile oedipal constellation. All stimuli are distorted to some extent by the memory traces of pregenital experience at the foundation of the fixation points.

Neurotic features in the personality can remain latent for extended periods of time, since the advanced level of psychic structuralization

required to organize an oedipal configuration enables healthy functions to be utilized under optimal conditions. When the particular
requirements of a given internal or external situation exceed the
ability to sustain a healthy adaptation, the dormant underlying
neurotic disturbance becomes dominant. This is not the case in all
other forms of pathology, because a narcissistic orientation cannot
support independent functioning. Thus any available strands of
healthy mental structure are too tenuously organized and unadapt-
able to stress or excessive stimulation. Neurotic disorders center
around the intrapsychic conflicts mobilized by an oedipal situation
and reflect the difficulties encountered in achieving a solution.

   Character makeup is determined by the nature of pregenital
experience, affects the way internal and external stimuli are perceived, shapes the genital consolidation from which oedipal fantasies
are elaborated, and directs the defensive alignments that maintain
unconscious instinctual drives under repression. The specific oedipal
wishes that evolve are colored by the manner in which earlier
pregenital tasks have been negotiated, and the formation of symptomatic compromises or the defensive distortions created by character
pathology carry the imprint of the individual's developmental history.
The new mental structures necessary to sustain an object related
perspective are well established, but they function inefficiently and
remain fixated in a conflicted infantile state. A mixed neurotic picture
is no longer possible, due to the advanced level of self differentiation,
the clear demarcation between the grandiose self and ego ideal, and
the stability of the fixation points.

   The manner in which stimuli are registered and represented forms
a background that is instrumental in determining the amount of self
expansion that can be realized during an individual's life cycle. Body
ego experiences are the basis for a system of self representations, and
their object impression counterparts are the nucleus for building a
system of object representations. Initially, the mental impressions of
independent stimuli are either split off from self experience or so
primitively differentiated as to be indistinguishable. These object
impressions provide the wherewithal for promoting psychological
growth by making the varied influences of an object available to
regulate, contain, and enhance ever-widening dimensions of self
experience. The mental foundation necessary for the unfolding of
self potentials is expanded when their good and bad attributes are in
balanced proportions; it is restrictive and unsteady when they are not.

   The influences of an object are an integral part of restraint,
prohibition, and defense. In addition, they provide constructive
identifications, aid in absorbing narcissistic injuries, abet the regula-

tion of self esteem, and sustain advances in self differentiation. In the earliest phases of development, the mechanism of splitting operates to foster the coalescence of defined entities of self experience, which are not connected to the impressions of an object. These superego nuclei exist in a form that must be gradually coordinated, then organized and structured into superego precursors, and ultimately consolidated into an independently functioning agency. During the crucial period of separation and individuation the two systems of mental representation are structurally united and differentiated for the first time, furthering self differentiation, strengthening adaptive capacities, enlarging the ability to represent increasing quantities of instinctual activity through the formation of derivatives, and fostering the process of symbolization.

Cohesiveness is initiated by the formation of a fixation point based upon the recognition of a separate good object's bad prohibitive qualities. It serves a differentiating function, anchors object constancy, and provides the stability required to structurally unite and differentiate the self and object systems of representation. This fixation point has an effect upon all ensuing advances in psychic organization, and its particular composition operates as the basis for character defenses. The degree of flexibility in this fixation point is proportional to the need for defense, which either limits or enlarges its expansion along the lines of psychosexual development.

The grandiose self is structured to balance the vulnerability associated with separateness by participating in the fantasy of an optimally gratifying object, and the ego ideal is structured to strengthen adaptive functions by including admired qualities of an object within self experience. These unifying and differentiating mental structures incorporate perceptual functions within their boundaries, solidifying the bond of cohesiveness at the surface of the personality. They also lay the groundwork for consolidating varied superego functions into an independent regulatory and guiding agency. Cohesiveness is initiated within a narcissistically organized state and is not truly steadfast and durable until an object related orientation has been attained. A number of preparatory steps must take place in order to gain the stability and regulation required to structure the transition.

The formation of the ego ideal structures a pathway for selective identifications, and at the same time highlights an awareness of the good self's bad instinctual qualities. This recognition forms a second fixation point based upon the instinctual experiences in the forefront, produces the stability necessary for new structures to evolve, and along with the first fixation point, anchors the foundation of character defenses. The first fixation point joined the good and bad qualities of an object into a functional entity by uniting the line of continuity of prohibitive experience; the second fixation point joins the good and bad qualities of the self into a functional entity by uniting the line of continuity of instinctual experience. In conjunction with the consolidation of the component instincts into a genital drive, these lines of continuity of instinctual and prohibitive experience can then be structurally connected to serve a regulatory and signaling function. Castration anxiety is the manifestation of this underlying structure, which is capable of instituting an appropriate defensive response by virtue of incorporating all facets of the self and object under its aegis. When gentle restraint is required, the optimally frustrating influences of a good object are sufficient, whereas the castrative threat of a genitally impinging object can be invoked when more extreme prohibitions are necessary.

The stage is then set for incestuous and primal scene fantasies to be elaborated, providing the structural linkages that unite the self and object systems in the realm of bad qualities of experience at the interior of the personality. These unions ensure cohesiveness and enable the unseen dimension on the continuum of instinctual demand to gain access to representation for the first time. Along with it, the independent qualities of an object can be perceived. This facet of internal stimulation created the necessity for splitting to be operative in the earliest stages of development, due to the inability of the immature psyche to represent the enormous impact of biophysiology. The intrapsychic conflict engendered by the genitally derived oedipal fantasies is based upon an object related perspective, and a successful solution results in the emergence of the superego as a regulatory and guiding agency freed of its infantile attachments. The neurotic individual has not successfully negotiated this step, and the pathological consequences are revealed in a manifest dream since the makeup of the underlying structures are reflected in the symbolic imagery.

Structuring the genital fantasies of an oedipal conflict solidifies cohesiveness, an object related orientation becomes functional, an abundance of defenses are available, the individual is no longer fixated in a narcissistic position, and a phobic avoidance is unnecessary. This characterizes and distinguishes the more advanced psychic organization of the neurotic disorders. Consequently, perceptions, projective identifications, adaptive responses, and object relationships all carry with them the ability to recognize the multidimensional qualities of an object. These object related experiences, however, activate intense intrapsychic conflict, are fraught with anxiety, and mobilize defensive distortions determined by the particular neurotic disturbance. The manifest content of a dream, by its very nature, is based upon linkages between the self and object. The mental representational world and especially its infantile origins are portrayed in the symbolic imagery; a view of the specific forces embodied in the connections is presented, and the neurotically structured developmental substrate is exposed. A developmental perspective is a valuable adjunct for attaining a deeper grasp of unconscious communications, and a manifest dream illuminates this aspect most clearly.

In the neurotic individual, mental structuralization is relatively firm and secure, unconscious instinctual conflicts are primarily genitally derived, pregenital conflicts serve a defensive function, and defensive alignments are tenaciously bound to infantile attachments. The inadequate regulation of genital instinctual drives often elicits extreme prohibitions from the function of castration anxiety, but they do not place self integrity in jeopardy as is the case in the narcissistically structured personality.

This was strikingly portrayed in the dream of a 30-year-old woman who had been preoccupied with the idea of becoming pregnant:

I was in the baby's room with my husband, and there were others present whom I could not see. I knew we were going to be beheaded and accepted it. I wanted us to be together but couldn't stand the idea of seeing his head cut off with all the blood. I decided to hold hands and not look.

The manifest content symbolized a castrative, prohibitive response indicative of the strength of the unconscious infantile instinctual wish pushing for expression, and the degree of conflict it engendered. The functions of castration anxiety and the fixation points are intermeshed, making character defenses more effective in reenforcing the repression of genital instinctual drives. It suggested that the latent dream thoughts consisted of the genital fantasies of an oedipal constellation.

Intrapsychic changes elicited by successful therapeutic intervention are gradual rather than abrupt, and when internal prohibitions are modulated the underlying stability is more in evidence.

This was exhibited in the dream of a 40-year-old woman, originally seeking help for episodes of seemingly unprovoked and extreme embarrassment, causing her a great deal of distress. She slowly became aware of the infantile instinctual wishes behind her symptom, leading to the dissolution of a firmly held conviction that she would never want children. It was followed by the revival of a repressed wished-for pregnancy before she became too old. In the session prior to the dream, the therapist commented upon the infantile wishes that had been warded off by her fixed belief.

> I was in a forest preserve with my husband and a friend. We had looked at everything, were satisfied, and about to leave. The friend pointed out that we had missed a beautiful flower that was extremely exotic. We looked, knew it was there somewhere, but were unable to find it. It was getting late and I had the feeling I would come back to see it at another time.

The therapist's interpretation had served as the day residue around which the dream was shaped. It was symbolically represented in the image of a friend pointing out a potentially beautiful flower but at a still-hidden site, and reflected her unconscious perception of its empathic attributes. The unseen presence appeared to refer to the unseen dimension on the continuum of instinctual demand, which was currently held under repression. Nevertheless, she anticipated that she would one day see it without the need for defense. This derivative of a primal scene fantasy was encompassed in the symbolic idea of an exotic flower, and showed the change that had taken place since its original impact. Although it still aroused conflict and could not traverse along a regulated pathway toward instinctual integration, it no longer possessed ominous properties.

The mental background for building the dream was neurotically structured, but firm and steady. The dreaming self was pictured with purpose and direction, and there was a vast array of regulatory forces available to enable instinctual representation and internal exploration. The connections to the impressions of an object, embodied in the figures of her husband and a friend, consisted of an abundance of good qualities and were well differentiated. There was no evidence of a need for extreme prohibitions, the implied frustration of being unable to gain immediate access to an instinctual wish was well tolerated, and there was a sense of confidence in her ultimate ability to attain this desired goal.

Each category of pathology is based upon a crucial developmental step that has not been negotiated, and with the neuroses, it is the lack of a successful resolution to an oedipal conflict. Object constancy, cohesiveness, and continuity of experience are well established. Repression proper functions as the major ego defense, and when neurotic symptoms are in evidence they are formed on a stable characterological substrate. Obsessive symptoms occur on an anally derived background of character, and hysterical symptoms on one that is orally influenced and phallically derived. Character makeup is a product of the individual's developmental history, and is not pathological until or unless it has the effect of creating significant distortions in the perception of internal and external stimuli.

Neurotic character pathology is manifested by fixed attitudes in response to a variety of differing stimuli, based on memory traces of infantile pregenital experience. The fixation point anchoring object constancy has not been depersonified or replaced, and the fixation point stabilizing self experience has been defensively retained beyond its stage and phase specific function. The status and composition of these fixation points are a crucial determining factor as to whether symptomatic compromises or character pathology is in evidence.

Although the neurotic continues to base object constancy on an infantile attachment to a prohibitive object, a pathological disturbance in character depends upon the defensive alignment of the fixation point in the self system. This fixation point is based upon a memory trace of pregenital overstimulation and is either transiently relinquished in conjunction with some partial resolution of the oedipal conflict as in the hysteric, or it may undergo a regressive breakdown when its defensive function is ineffective, as in the obsessive. The influx of new stimuli, without the modulating and defensively distorting influence of pregenital memory traces, resonates throughout the personality, evoking a state of genital overstimulation in the deeper layers that cannot be managed. Regulation is then accomplished through effecting the compromises included in a neurotic symptom. Symptoms are only present when the fixation point stabilizing self experience is either relinquished or no longer functional, and character pathology is only present when it is intact and effective. The mechanisms involved in effecting symptomatic compromises are bound into maintaining the fixations of character, and when successful, symptoms are not necessary.

All defensive functioning evolves upon the background of a self and object system of representations and their interrelationship with each other. The infantile origins will be most clearly brought out in a manifest dream because of the nature of symbolization and of the proximity to more regressive experiences during sleep. In the neurotic disorders, the interrelationship is maintained by mental structures uniting and differentiating the two systems, both at the periphery and at the interior of the personality. The initial connections are made during the process of separation and individuation, when a stabilizing fixation point in the object system leads to the formation of the structural precursors of the superego. Later, another stabilizing fixation point is established in the self system, leading to the formation of new object related structures.

Fixation points function to provide stability, which is essential for new structure building, but they also narrow the range of perception and must change to facilitate growth. The fixation point in the object system must be retained to anchor the differentiating influences of an object required for independent functioning, but it must expand and be freed of its infantile attachments. It is gradually depersonified and eventually replaced by the impressions of new and independent objects. The fixation point in the self system stands as an obstacle to registering new object related experiences without distortion, is relinquished in conjunction with a successful resolution of the oedipal conflict, and its stabilizing function is taken over by a well-consolidated superego. With neurotic character pathology, the fixation points are tenaciously bound and defensively maintained beyond stage and phase specificity. They continue to distort the way internal and external stimuli are registered, and are behind the pathological defenses manifested in a transference relationship. Character defenses are designed to monitor, regulate, and determine the individual meaning of stimuli, and it is only when they function to distort perceptions that it is indicative of their pathology.

## The Nature of Pathology in the Obsessive Neurosis

The obsessive's early development has involved a relative deficiency in libidinally gratifying experiences, excessive sensory stimulation in other areas, an overloading of frustration and aggression, and a hypertrophied use of autonomous ego functions. The excessive frustration during the oral period, in conjunction with an overemphasis on autonomous functioning, leads to separation and individuation being initiated somewhat prematurely with entry into the anal phase. The obsessive locates the impressions of a separate good object's influence very early in the anal period, with the carry-over of oral aggression exaggerating the intensity of anal sadistic drives. Aggression, which in balanced proportions is differentiating in its effects, in this situation is more disruptive to the unification and stability of evolving mental structures.

The recognition of a good object's bad prohibitive qualities forms a fixation point based on an infantile attachment to an anally sadistic object. The degree of fusion of the libidinal and aggressive drives is diminished, the impressions of a bad impinging object are not well modulated, and the vulnerability associated with the recognition of separateness is extreme. The grandiose self is structured by linking instinctual experiences of mastery and control to the impression of an optimally gratifying anal object through a fantasy of the object's omnipotence. The composition of the grandiose self is similar to what has occurred in health, but the fantasied omnipotence of the object is greater, the underlying foundation for structure formation is less stable, and the balance of the drives is more disturbed. It is at this stage that the obsessive's development is seriously affected by the distorting influence of defensive maneuvers.

In structuring the grandiose self, instinctual experience not requiring defense is engaged with a fantasy of the object's omnipotence. The already existing difficulty with managing an overloading of aggression is intensified, since good instinctual self experience is additionally depleted and unavailable for adaptive functions. Aggression is increasingly dominant and threatens to become overwhelming. A prohibitive force powerful enough to regulate this buildup of anal sadistic drives is needed, motivating the formation of the ego ideal. This takes place during the height of anality under urgent conditions, and the prohibitive influences of an impinging anal sadistic object are selected for identification. The optimally frustrating influences of a good object, which are ideally suited for structuring the ego ideal in health, offer little to the incipient obsessive. Although some elements of a good object's influence may be included, it is the anally sadistic qualities that are most needed and admired. These identifications with an anally sadistic aggressor are the means by which reaction formations are developed within the self system. The arousal of anal sadistic impulses immediately instigates a prohibitive response guarding against their expression, enabling perceptual attention to be focused upon overdeveloped and overvalued aspects of good self experience.

The concomitant recognition of the good self's bad instinctual qualities occurs prematurely during the anal period, and the resulting fixation point based upon anally determined sadistic instinctual experience is inextricably bound to the evolving reaction formations. Together they are at the foundation of emerging attitudes of orderliness, cleanliness, and overconscientiousness designed to prevent any expression of sadistic aggression. The resulting character pathology is defensively maintained through all the succeeding development stages, giving a profound anal coloration to continuing instinctual expansion. There is sufficient structuralization for a genital consolidation to take place, but phallic and genital experiences are distorted by the memory traces of anality embodied in the fixation points. The lines of continuity of instinctual and prohibitive experience incorporated into the structure of castration anxiety display this strong anal influence, and its regulatory functions are harshly punitive in nature.

The developing obsessive enters into an oedipal situation still struggling with poorly managed anal sadistic drives, and as a consequence, the unfolding genital fantasies are infused with their effects and generate an inordinate degree of conflict.

Genital instinctual attachments are perceived in anal terms. Incestuous fantasies and their derivatives reflect the boundary of the unconscious system, are accompanied by a heightened, defensive attitude, and are at the foundation of defense transferences. The male obsessive's incestuous fantasies are elaborated into a negative oedipal constellation. The strong anal influence has diminished the importance of the genital as the symbolic organ of attachment to an object, so it is readily relinquished under the harsh prohibitive threat of castration. In addition, the frustrating relationship with the primary nurturing maternal figure has left a hunger for mothering, and to the extent that an identification is made, the strength of the attachment is lessened. This makes feminine identifications both desirable and easy to effect. The male is then perceived as an anal-genital instinctual object, with anal penetration the route of attachment. The female obsessive's incestuous fantasies are elaborated into a defensively constructed positive anal-genital oedipal configuration. The development step of a negative oedipal conflict is avoided, since it is too filled with disappointment fed by an already existing overload of frustration and anal sadistic aggression. The displacement of anal-genital interest to the male occurs abruptly, and is possible because of the overdevelopment of the mechanism of isolation and the wide range of intellectualizing defenses available to protect against instinctual dangers.

Primal scene fantasies and their derivatives reflect a movement toward instinctual integration, and are at the foundation of the transference. In both male and female, primal scene fantasies involve a genital instinctual attachment to an unseen positive oedipal object, and are a source of enormous danger. The interrelationship between the new object related structures is out of proportion, with the boundary of the unconscious system being overdeveloped, indicative of the excessive need for defense. Instinctual activity elicits prohibitive responses that are harsh and punitive, having retained their anal sadistic properties. An anal fixation has shaped the configuration of incestuous and primal scene fantasies, there is a lack of resolution of the oedipal conflict; the fixation point in the object system is only minimally depersonified, and the fixation point in the self system is defensively retained.

The unseen dimension on the continuum of biophysiological demand is the source of the greatest instinctual danger, and requires the most active defense. The obsessive has represented the impact of this internal stimulus, and through primal scene fantasies has structured a pathway for its inclusion within the realm of self experience. Instinctual movement along this pathway is expressive of the transference, mobilizes the powerful opposition of repression proper to contain its effects within the id of the dynamic unconscious, and activates the harsh prohibitions of an immature superego. The newly structured boundary of the unconscious system, reflected in incestuous fantasies, is expressive of the defense transference and highly overdeveloped. Anally derived character defenses, expressive of defenses against the transference, serve to reenforce the effectiveness of repression proper, and are associated with a wide variety of ancillary defensive measures.

Although the traumatic intensity of instinctual demand centers around the impressions of a bad instinctual object, it is not experienced in that locale by the obsessive. The object system is so hypertrophied, with an abundance of defensive responses readily available, that the danger is not perceived as emanating from this area. The mechanisms of intellectualization, overideation, rumination, and doing and undoing are all based upon an overdeveloped system of object representations, and the obsessive's style of thinking is predominated by an overemphasis on these projective processes. The oedipal conflict has structured a heavily defended connection linking the impressions of an overstimulating object to the self system. The system representing self experiences is already infused with aggression and inadequately regulated, the impact of the stimulus echoes throughout, and the threat is then experienced in that sector. Repression proper operates either to direct perceptual attention to mental activities involving the object system, or to focus forcibly upon autonomous ego functions. The mechanism of isolation, necessary for functional tasks requiring concentration, is overused, conscious mental content is overcathected, and there is a preoccupation with logic and order.

Interpretive interventions that are confrontational or tinged with frustration are readily perceived as sadistic, and they solidify anally derived fixed attitudes, reenforcing defenses against the transference. With the obsessive, it is important not to be too silent and for interpretations to be framed in the language of feeling rather than intellect. Silence is often seen as a sadistic attack, intellectual communications tend to emphasize conscious mental activity, and affective language amplifies the experiences most vigorously defended. Management of the framework, silences, and interpretations all have potential sadistic meaning, and it is not until the distortions created by character defenses are diminished, recognized as dystonic, or rendered ineffective, that the underlying derivatives of an anal-genital oedipal conflict can be expressed in the transference relationship.

## Obsessive Character Pathology, Obsessive Symptoms, and the Manifest Dream

The neuroses, in comparison with all other pathological entities, possess a vast array of ego functions that are available to respond to the demands accompanying a therapeutic regression. This makes the regression less turbulent, and the exposure of unconscious strivings is generally an impetus to integration, self expansion, and growth. The obsessive exhibits a style of thinking that is inundated by intellectualizations, the mechanism of isolation is used to excess, and the ability to sustain contact with affective responses is interfered with defensively. When the pregenitally determined defenses embodied in character pathology are rendered ineffective, the anal sadistic impulses they are meant to contain can be extremely disruptive as they enter the field of awareness.

This was revealed in a dream reported by an obsessive young man, following a session in which he had been able to talk about the intense hostility he felt toward an older brother:

I'm with my brother. Suddenly I have a gun in my hand and shoot him in the head. I wake up screaming as I try to take it back, but it is too late.

The breakthrough of anal sadistic aggression was symbolically represented in the manifest content, capturing his reaction to coming in contact with these powerful emotions. He was most comfortable when ruminating and intellectualizing about his internal state.

The destructive effects of poorly managed aggression are a significant factor during the obsessive's pregenital phases of development, creating an exaggerated need for the stabilizing function of the anally derived fixation points. The tenacity with which they are retained from the time of their inception colors all further instinctual expansion, giving an anal cast to the unfolding incestuous and primal scene fantasies of the oedipal conflict. The obsessive represents the ultimate in character pathology. Reaction formations against anal sadistic impulses solidify fixed character traits, which often receive a great deal of external support. The subsequent preoccupation with logic and order presents a surface appearance of being totally in control, on a background of instability and vulnerability to a loss of control.

The following dream of a 45-year-old man, displaying the neurotically structured features of obsessive character pathology, gave symbolic expression to this difficulty:

I was out walking the dog. He ran into the street, and it was a busy street with lots of fast cars. I screamed and yelled at him. He froze and this put him in more danger. I got to him and then he did it again. I got so furious I kicked him hard, and he ran down the street yelping. I was in the house calling the vet and shaking with fear. I woke up trembling at the loss of control of my anger.

The dog symbolized the unconscious forces the dreamer was struggling to keep under control. When faced with the inability to do so, attention is focused on the loss of control of his sadistic aggression. He had utilized reaction formations to protect himself against expressing the anal sadistic aggression at the foundation of his character defenses. Their tenacious defensive function had been loosened from the effects of the therapeutic relationship, and the instability and absence of control in the deeper layers of his personality were clearly depicted in the body of the dream. Repression proper was at work in directing perceptual attention away from the unconscious meaning of the animal that had broken loose and toward the loss of control of his aggression.

The obsessive develops symptoms when the intensity of anal sadistic drives cannot be contained by reaction formations, causing a regressive breakdown in the fixation point in the self system and rendering the defensive function of a characterological fixation ineffective. The symptoms range in a descending hierarchy from the intrusive thoughts and ideational rituals incorporating the psychic contents of the object system to those involving the body ego experiences represented in the self system. At the lowest end of the hierarchy, the threat of fragmentation begins to emerge, bearing a close resemblance to the cohesive, narcissistic personality disorders.

This was manifested in the dream of a 9-year-old encopretic boy discussed in prior chapters:

I was looking for my penny in the grass. Just as I found it a car came toward me with its lights on. It was like a devil trying to hit me, but skidded out of control. Just before it hit me I shook and woke up.

The car, on the verge of losing control, symbolized the impact of unconscious instinctual drives when the oppositional counterforce of well-structured character defenses was not available. He had the same feeling when his bowel movements could not be stopped, indicative of the attempt at regulation through this symptomatic compromise. The use of a body ego experience was suggestive of the limited extent to which instinctual activity could be represented without posing a threat to self integrity, which was also implied in his body shaking.

## The Effect of the Therapeutic Relationship on the Obsessive as Revealed in the Manifest Dream

The neurotic individual has successfully negotiated the pregenital stages of development, but in a manner that is out of tune with stage and phase specificity. The obsessive has had a relatively frustrating period of orality and initiated the separation–individuation process somewhat prematurely. The fixation point anchoring object constancy is formed early in anality. The grandiose self and ego ideal are anally derived structures, and the fixation point stabilizing the self system is based upon anal sadistic instinctual experience. All further instinctual expansion is colored by this strong anal influence, which extends into the structure of castration anxiety and the genital fantasies comprising an oedipal conflict.

The following dream, reported by a young man who had entered treatment due to his frustration in his work, is illustrative of the obsessive's response to a therapeutic regression. It was presented as an example of the day residue, representing the derivative of an unconscious perception in chapter 6 and is now looked at in more detail:

> I am in a dormitory area at work. Someone points out that the wall dividing the bathroom from the sleeping area is leaking. I go to inspect it and water is seeping down the bricks. I go into the bathroom, notice a hole in the roof, and can see the sky. I think I can patch it from the inside, but would need a roofer to patch the outside.

The manifest content reveals the underlying structural organization of the personality, and gives a symbolic picture of the intrapsychic difficulties in the forefront. The dreamer was represented as moving to look at a leak between the bathroom and bedroom, discovering a hole in the bathroom roof, and searching for a way to cover it over.

Anally determined character defenses function to aid in repressing dangerous genital oedipal wishes. The leak in the wall separating bathroom and bedroom hints at their ineffectiveness, and the hole in the roof suggests that the connection, which had previously been closed off, was now exposed. This dynamic interplay of conflictual forces is characteristic of the obsessive neurotic when the protective wall of pathological defenses is successfully penetrated. Genital activity in the obsessive is perceived as a bathroom affair, since anally derived differentiating structures and stabilizing fixation points color all instinctual expansion. In addition, the dormitory in the dream may have some distant symbolic reference to an emerging negative oedipal constellation, and historically, his stay in a boarding school during adolescence carried homosexual innuendoes. It would, however, require a fuller exposition of the dreamer's associations to validate this component more clearly. The manifest dream is a starting place for unraveling the dream work to expose unconscious drives, and considering the obsessive makeup of the dreamer's personality, a negative oedipal transference would be expected.

Although there is evidence of a breakdown in defensive functions, symbolized by the leaking wall and hole in the roof, it is not particularly disturbing and there is complete confidence that they can be repaired. The dream implies that character defenses can be readily reinstituted, and the idea of hiring a roofer to complete the job suggests that external support is required. It seems to anticipate the dreamer's engaging the therapist in the relationship by reenforcing a pathological defense. With the obsessive this can transpire in a number of ways. Encouraging the evolution of an observing and experiencing ego is especially defense reenforcing, because it tends to strengthen reaction formations and fixed character attitudes. Seeking intellectual interpretations to enlist support in fostering overideational explanations directs attention to conscious mental activity, allowing character defenses to remain unaffected by therapeutic influence. Confrontations or silences emanating from frustration resonate with the prohibitive impressions of an anally sadistic object, more firmly entrenching already fixed character attitudes. Interpretations for the obsessive are most effective when they are simple and framed in affectively toned language.

Identifying the qualities of an object highlights the nature of the attachment it is meant to symbolize and helps in determining the function it serves. In this dream the primary object is pointing out a deficiency in need of repair, and mobilizes activity that, while performing a defensive purpose, is in the direction of accomplishing what is needed to attain mastery and control. The object thereby possesses good anal attributes, which are resonant with a therapist's interpretive function. It reflects an attachment consisting of potential autonomous ego functions linked to the impression of a good anal object, reminiscent of the composition of the ego ideal. There is a surprising absence of any overt evidence of anal prohibitions, however, which would be expected in a dream symbolizing repressed instinctual strivings in danger of being exposed. The lack of infantile prohibitions in a situation where they are much in need, in conjunction with the good qualities of an object being used defensively, suggests that a combination of two intrapsychic events may be taking place. First, it appears that the dreamer is replacing the infantile attachments at the foundation of the ego ideal with a new replica based upon the impressions of the therapeutic interaction. Second, it hints that the prohibitions associated with infantile instinctual drives may have been eliminated through the defensive process of idealization.

Idealization, which is the antithesis of identification and depleting to adaptive capacities, enables the destructive qualities of a bad object to be transformed into the needed qualities of a good object. The movement of the water along the bricks appears to symbolize infantile instinctual activity, and aside from the presence of the wall, there does not seem to be any noticeable opposition. The leaking wall and hole in the roof may also have reference to the missing feature of prohibitions. Assuming the dormitory is a distant echo of a homosexual transference that is as yet ill defined, it intimates that the danger of an emerging negative oedipal constellation has triggered the necessity to idealize the therapist in order to avoid inordinate prohibitions, since in the obsessive the harshness of prohibitions is extreme.

The setting of the dream is at the dreamer's workplace, reminiscent of his original complaint on entering treatment. At the time it was not clear whether he was referring to an inability to realize his potential, or whether intrapsychic conflicts aroused by work were interfering with his success. The obsessive consistently attempts to master instinctual conflicts by the overdevelopment of autonomous ego functions, projective mechanisms embodied in thinking are used excessively, and all available potentials are hypertrophied in the service of adaptation. Consequently, the obsessive is an overachiever, and generally highly successful in work endeavors that are an extension of overdeveloped ego functions and reenforce reaction formations. At the same time, the obsessive is hampered when a specific adaptive task is resonant with infantile instinctual conflicts. The locale of the dream, with its displacement from the work area to the bathroom, implies that work for the dreamer is evocative of repressed instinctual drives and is embroiled in conflict.

The figure in the dream pointing out the leak in the wall was also indirectly calling attention to the connection between bathroom and bedroom, which was consonant with the therapist's interpretive efforts to unveil the defensive function of his patient's fixed character attitudes. It would thereby appear that the dreamer's anally derived character defenses had been rendered temporarily nonfunctional by a combination of the therapist's interpretations and the discovery of personal information about the therapist. The unconscious perception of this inadvertent leak seemed to be resonating with latent negative oedipal wishes.

The following sequence of dreams was originally used in chapter 7 to demonstrate the effect of character defenses on the mode of functioning of the eye of consciousness and superego eye. They are repeated now to shed light on the mental representational world and infantile experiences characteristic of the obsessive neurotic and reveal the changes that had taken place in the treatment situation. The first dream was presented at the beginning of therapeutic contact:

I walked into a store looking for a shirt, saw a TV set, and a wall of dirt appeared with gun barrels buried in it. A zombie emerged covered with mud as though unburied, and I felt I was responsible for its coming into existence. It had a bright red opening in its chest. A woman connected to the zombie agreed it was my fault, and it came after me and frightened me. It seemed like I was afraid I would be connected to it in a way that scared me.

The wall of dirt with gun barrels buried in it symbolized the anal influence on phallic and genital instinctual experience, as did the zombie emerging from a hidden place all covered with mud. Anal-genital instinctual wishes, which had been held under repression by fixed, anally derived character defenses, were aroused and pushing for expression with the onset of a therapeutic regression.

Later he reported a second dream, symbolizing the continuing dissolution of his character defenses, but on this occasion with a greater readiness for integrating the unconscious genital instinctual drives that had been repressed.

I was living inside a huge dam that was holding back an enormous river. The house was at the top of the dam and was awesome. I discovered a government plot to destroy the dam so the water could surge through. I was excited at the prospect, not frightened, since it seemed like the water could rush through and cleanse the house. I looked up, saw yellow stains as though it was beginning, and the dream shifted. I was on an airplane on a special mission to Washington. The plane landed, but the brakes didn't work, and it looked as though it would go off the runway. I was excited, not scared, and it stopped right at the edge.

Although the dream imagery reflected concern about a loss of control, which is characteristic of the obsessive, the anticipation of a breakdown in controlling oppositional forces was accompanied by a feeling of excitement. It showed an increasing openness for integrating previously repressed genital instinctual drives, and was indicative of an enlarged capacity for managing the powerful impulses demanding expression.

A third dream was reported several months afterward, which symbolically represented the negative oedipal strivings appearing in the transference relationship in a more direct, less distorted fashion:

I was in the bathroom looking at a naked boyfriend in the bathtub and felt sexually aroused. I smiled with recognition and had the thought that this was what I'd been fighting against for so long.

The manifest dream displayed a negative oedipal defense transference impulse, based upon the derivative of an incestuous fantasy, and its expression was the consequence of a dissolution of previously effective anally derived character defenses. The negative oedipal constellation was consistent with the anal influence on a genital consolidation that is an integral part of the obsessive's developmental experience.

## The Nature of Pathology
## in the Hysteric Neurosis

The hysteric's early development includes an extended period of libidinal overinvolvement, diminished sensory stimulation in other areas, and an underdevelopment of autonomous ego functions. Consequently, there is an imbalance in instinctual representation with the oral components hypertrophied, and the process of separation-individuation is delayed until early in the phallic phase. The delay has some compensatory value in that an abundance of good self experience is structured at the foundation of the personality, creating a background of internal stability and a large capacity to manage a regression.

The hysteric locates the impression of a separate good, phallically determined object's influence, when instinctual experiences of phallic exhibitionism are in the forefront. The recognition of the good object's bad qualities, maintaining differentiation and anchoring object constancy, forms a fixation point based upon an infantile attachment to a phallically humiliating, prohibitive object. The grandiose self is not structured until movement into the phallic phase has evolved, when the vulnerability of separateness is centered around phallic exhibitionism. The grandiose self utilizes the fantasy of an optimally gratifying phallic object's admiration as a structural linkage. It is then that a stage and phase specific balance is lacking, and the susceptibility to humiliation is accentuated.

In health, and in the obsessive, the vulnerability associated with separateness occurs with anal experiences of mastery and control in the ascendancy and the anally derived fantasy of an optimally gratifying object's omnipotence offers a better match. Phallic instinctual experience is inadequately regulated, exhibitionistic impulses not requiring defense readily become overstimulating and voyeuristic, and the ego ideal is structured in the presence of a heightened need for the restraining influences of an object. The phallically derived prohibitive impressions of a humiliating object are included within self experience. The resulting identification with an aggressor establishes a reaction formation against phallic overstimulation. The concomitant recognition of the good self's bad instinctual qualities forms a stabilizing fixation point based upon voyeuristic experience.

The developing hysteric, in having delayed separation and individuation, is confronted with a complex sequence of intrapsychic events that are accomplished over a short span of time. Excessive oral libidinal involvement has infused the phallic overstimulation preceding a genital consolidation, and continues to color the elaboration of genital fantasies. Pregenital developmental tasks have been successfully negotiated, but the fixation points and structural precursors of the superego have all been formed rapidly during the phallic period. Phallic exhibitionism quickly escalates in intensity, reaction formations of humiliation are invoked as voyeuristic impulses threaten to emerge, and the dominant impressions of an object easily change from admiring to humiliating.

A constant state of either anticipating or experiencing humiliation is a manifestation of the hysteric's character defenses, which prepare the way for an oedipal conflict to unfold. The increase in intensity accompanying the consolidation of the component instincts into a genital drive exaggerates the already existent phallic overstimulation, and the lines of continuity of instinctual and prohibitive experience are united into the structure of castration anxiety under conditions requiring extremes in restraint. This signaling and regulatory structure overemphasizes the impinging influences of a genitally castrating object, and the contiguity of pregenital developments with the organization of an oedipal conflict has a profound effect upon how it is shaped and contributes to the lack of a resolution.

Genital primal scene fantasies, elaborated from the impressions of an overstimulating instinctual object, and incestuous fantasies, elaborated from the representation of overstimulating genital instinctual self experiences, comprise the oedipal conflict. They organize new structures at the interior of the personality to enable object related perceptions and ensure cohesiveness. The instinctual aspect of a bad object is the mental impression of the most threatening dimension on the continuum of biophysiological demand. During the oedipal period it is elaborated into a genital primal scene fantasy and structurally linked to the representation of bad instinctual self experience. The image is of the self being aroused by an unseen overstimulating sexual object, allowing the unseen dimension of biophysiological demand to have access to representation within the self system for the first time. The structuralization of genital primal scene fantasies enables the capacity to register the unseen aspects of an object in both the internal and external world, making it possible to evoke representable body ego experiences in response to the idea of an object having independent objects of its own.

During the narcissistic phases of development, the extension of the line of continuity of instinctual experience to the impression of an overstimulating instinctual object was interfered with by defensive reactions. The newly structured pathway of instinctual integration, manifested by primal scene fantasies, requires defensive regulation. The structuralization of incestuous fantasies forms a new boundary for the unconscious system, which performs a defensive function that can regulate the expanding influx of instinctual demand. The image is of the self being aroused by a visible and forbidden overstimulating sexual object, and it operates as a focus for prohibitive and regulatory responses.

In health the pathway of instinctual integration and the boundary of the unconscious system operate in a balanced interrelationship. Instinctual demand moves through the id of the dynamic unconscious and is linked by primal scene fantasies to be included as a fact of overstimulating instinctual self experience. Concurrently, the conflict engendered by oedipal fantasies motivates selective identifications, strengthening the realm of good self experience, and instinctual activity that was previously overstimulating no longer requires defense. This process of instinctual integration goes hand in hand with the dissolution of the fixation point stabilizing the self system, and instinctual demands are available for organizing isolated areas of conflict-free functioning into a well-defined system. With the hysteric, the degree of conflict engendered by genital oedipal fantasies is inordinate, the new boundary for the unconscious system is excessively active, and the structured pathway of instinctual integration is especially threatening.

The oedipal configuration differs in the male and female hysteric. Both have had an overdetermined emphasis on phallic instinctual activity, strongly affected by the overindulgence of orality. In the male, the enormous investment in phallic experience, in conjunction with a tenacious attachment to the maternal figure, does not allow a negative oedipal solution. This would require relinquishing the overvalued genital and displacing a genital instinctual attachment to the male. The male hysteric elaborates a highly conflicted positive oedipal attachment fraught with anxiety, which elicits the powerful prohibitive impression of a genitally impinging, castrative object.

The female hysteric is also tenaciously attached to the maternal figure and has anticipated libidinal gratification throughout the pregenital phases of development. With the consolidation of the component instincts into a genital drive, the primary maternal love object is a source of profound disappointment. A precocious, premature, and abrupt displacement of instinctual interest to the male is initiated, which adds a dimension of rivalry to the original disappointment in the mother and obviates against the developmental step of a negative oedipal attachment. The flight into heterosexual involvement is too infused with defensive distortions and regressive cravings to be considered a positive genital attachment, which can only transpire after a negative oedipal constellation has been fully elaborated.

The hysteric is an underachiever with many unrealized potentials, a product of libidinal overinvolvement, sensory deprivation in other areas, and a dearth of the optimally frustrating influences of a good object. Sensory deprivations and reactions to impingement are utilized in constructing defensive alignments designed to manage instinctual overstimulation, thinking is dominated by body sensations, imagery, and intuitive affective responses, the ability to articulate internal experience is imprecise, and adaptation is not oriented toward the use of intellectual functions.

## Hysterical Symptoms, Hysterical Character Pathology, and the Manifest Dream

The hysteric with symptoms manifests a level of psychic organization that is the most advanced of the neurotic disorders. Although separation and individuation has been delayed due to early libidinal overinvolvement, which in turn produces an orally influenced, phallic derivation to psychic structuralization, pathological distortions do not arise until the demands of an oedipal situation are encountered. A limited capacity for achieving a partial resolution of the oedipal conflict enables the fixation point based on phallic voyeuristic experience to be periodically relinquished. The resulting influx of new, object related stimuli invokes a state of genital overstimulation, mobilizing the ego to instigate symptomatic compromises in an attempt at regulation.

This all takes place on a solid foundation with many unused potentials for integrative functioning, which was revealed in the dream of a 30-year-old female hysteric. She had entered treatment because she developed severe stomach cramps when in an overstimulating social situation.

I discovered that Barbie dolls were now worth a thousand dollars. When my father died, we had moved and left drawers full of Barbie dolls behind. I knew I had a Skipper doll. Fewer of them were made, and they must be worth much more.

In addition to the implied infantile genital wishes encompassed in the symbolic imagery, the manifest content portrayed the internal resources latently present.

Hysterical symptoms evolve out of the substrate of a hysterical character, and when they do not effectively regulate instinctual activity, an underlying character disturbance becomes manifest. Hysterical symptoms and character pathology are intimately intertwined, with the differences centering around the narrow extent to which an oedipal conflict is resolved. The hysteric, exhibiting only the fixed defensive attitudes of character pathology, has been less successful in integrating instinctual demands, whereas the presence of symptoms is indicative that some measure of conflict resolution has been attained.

The differences between hysterical symptoms and character pathology, and in what is required of a therapist with each, was demonstrated in two previously discussed dreams. The first dream was reported by a young woman displaying the presence of hysterical symptoms:

I was trying to reach my parents to get some important information and every effort I made was interfered with by David Green. It was never clear who or where he was, but his presence was always in the way when I tried to make a phone call or to find my way there.

The dreamer exhibited the symptom of *globus hystericus* in social situations and had achieved a partial resolution of an oedipal conflict; the therapist's presence was primarily needed as a silent background of containment. The dream was the result of the therapist's question, unconsciously perceived as intrusive, which interfered with her regressive search for repressed infantile wishes. The question had interrupted her flow of associations and focused attention upon mental content that reenforced the repression of genital instinctual drives. The symbolic portrayal of her attempt to gain information reflected the capacity for representing larger quantities of instinctual activity.

The second dream was reported by another young woman manifesting the fixed, phallically derived attitudes of hysterical character pathology:

I was alone in a beach house. Teenagers were having a party on the beach and suddenly they threatened to invade the house. As they tried to enter, a man corraled them and talked to them, and I felt safe.

The dreamer perceived all stimuli as having phallic voyeuristic meaning, and constantly anticipated being humiliated. This fixed attitude operated to reenforce the repression of an inordinately conflicted underlying oedipal configuration, and the therapist's interpretive interventions were necessary to aid in integrating genital instinctual drive derivatives as they threatened to reach traumatic levels of intensity. The house symbolized the status of the self system, putting emphasis on its being constructed to exclude genital instinctual strivings. It was not able to prevent the invasion of threatening instinctual activities, embodied in the images of the teenagers, but with the containment offered by the therapist's interventions they could enter and be safely included.

The hysteric has had a libidinally overstimulating period of orality, which gives an oral cast to all mental representations. Separation and individuation have been delayed until early in the phallic phase, so that the fixation point anchoring object constancy is phallically determined. The grandiose self and ego ideal are phallically derived, and the fixation point stabilizing the self system is based upon phallic voyeuristic experience. The genital consolidation of the component instincts, structuralization of castration anxiety, and elaboration of oedipal fantasies all take place within a short span of time and display these orally influenced, phallically determined properties.

The following dream, reported by a 14-year-old boy, symbolically represents the phallically determined nature of the underlying structures characteristic of the hysteric, the oral influence that is always a significant factor, and the greater leeway in projecting self contents when they are not bound by the limitations imposed by character pathology. It was touched on before, but is now presented to give a more comprehensive picture of the information it contains.

I had gone away to camp. I got mosquito bites on the inner side of my thigh and was going to the doctor. A lot of other children in the camp had poison ivy and the doctor was giving them shots. I was on a conveyor belt with three other children, moving toward the doctor. The doctor said that if the first three children had poison ivy, the fourth did, too. The first three had poison ivy. I didn't want to have a shot. I started to scream, and my mother came to hold me.

The intrapsychic conflict, given emphasis in the manifest content, centers upon phallic and genital body ego experiences, symbolized by the mosquito bites on the inner side of the dreamer's thigh. Salvation is found, however, in the orally derived attributes of nurturance and comfort embodied in the image of the rescuing mother. Although the uncontrolled movement toward an implied penetration is associated with a high level of anxiety, it occurs on a solid structural footing of stability. The dominance of phallic and genital instinctual conflicts evoking an orally regressive defensive response, on the background of an advanced level of psychic organization, is diagnostic of the hysterical neuroses.

The symbolic image of the doctor is of an active, penetrating, genital figure, whereas the dreaming self is passive, immobilized, and at the mercy of the conveyor belt until saved by the mother. It would seem to indicate that the dreamer had projected all his masculine, genital strivings into the representation of the doctor, so as to sustain an attachment to the nurturing qualities of the mother. The dreamer's self boundary had apparently been narrowed to enable this particularly conflicted facet of self experience to be projected and symbolized. This signifies that the fixation point in the self system is not tenaciously anchored, and can, at least temporarily, be relinquished. In a waking state these genital instinctual impulses would either be repressed or be given disguised expression in a symptomatic compromise.

The hysteric's character defenses are either tightly bound to their infantile origins, in which case they create distortions and are pathological, or they are partially modified by some measure of conflict resolution, and regulation is achieved through the formation of symptoms. At those moments when the fixation point that stabilizes self experience is relinquished, the introjective arm of perception is open to register new object related experiences without undue distortion. They are received, however, by a psychic organization that is in a state of phallic and genital overstimulation. Regulation is accomplished by granting genital instinctual drives disguised expression in a symptom. This would encompass a disturbance in body sensations or bodily processes, and also incorporate a defensive, superego, and adaptive component.

Character pathology is manifested when there has been no conflict resolution, or when symptoms are not effective in their regulatory function. The fixation point anchoring object constancy is only minimally depersonified, as the influence of a phallically determined prohibitive object predominates. The fixation point stabilizing the self system continues to be defensively maintained, coloring all stimuli with the effects of phallic voyeurism. The functioning of pathological character defenses gives the hysteric the surface appearance of being overwhelmed by phallic overstimulation, while drawing perceptual attention away from the underlying derivatives of incestuous and primal scene fantasies. Although the impression is one of being out of control, these intrapsychic events take place on the solid foundation of a firmly structured personality. There is a strong underpinning of stability, and latent resources are available for managing a regression.

This was evidenced in a dream reported by a 40-year-old female hysteric, after talking about her constant fear of being humiliated by the therapist:

I was kissing my neighbor and felt sexually aroused, which seemed curious to me.

The manifest content gave symbolic expression to the derivative of an incestuous fantasy, which was behind her pregenitally determined character defenses and indicative of the defense transference that was moving into the ascendancy. The variety of defensive maneuvers accessible was implied by the absence of observable anxiety and the firm framework of the dream. It also showed the hysteric's style of thinking, in that attention was focused almost entirely upon body sensations and affective responses to the exclusion of intellectualizations and abstractions.

The function of hysterical character defenses was exemplified in the following dream reported by a young woman after an incident in which she had become aroused after observing a sexual scene:

I was shopping with my uncle and a salesman was helping us. I found a wonderful bright blue coat and decided to get a pair of boots to go with it. The salesman kept bringing them and none were exactly right. All of a sudden he brought a skirt, a shirt, and so many other things I got confused and walked out without anything.

The manifest content contained a clearly delineated image of the dreamer's self occupied with a discrete goal. It was not in jeopardy, faced with dissolution, or otherwise unsteady. It was indicative of a cohesive self, narrowed by the boundary established by the perceptual functions of the superego eye, registering the psychic contents of the preconscious system in symbolic form.

The self system incorporates a gamut of good and bad body ego experiences, with each facet possessing a particular function. Perception, memory, and motility are a product of the autonomous ego functions, containment is associated with the background object of primary identification, and phase specific instinctual gratification is embodied in structuring the grandiose self. Instinctual overstimulation, sensory deprivation, and reactions to impingement perform differentiating and defensive functions. The coat possesses the properties of covering the dreamer and at the same time of exhibiting the self in an attractive manner. These characteristics are suggestive of functions attributable to self experience, and seem to symbolize her phallic exhibitionism.

The dreamer then decided to add another item. The salesman brought more and more and when they became overwhelming she left. The dream intimates that phallic overstimulating voyeuristic impulses have not been included within the narrowed boundary of a dreaming self, and they have been symbolically represented as an object. The salesman would then be expected to display voyeuristic tendencies, which were not apparent in the initial dream report. In the course of associating to the dream, however, the salesman was described as making sexual innuendoes about her relationship to the uncle. It was this aspect of the dream that reminded her of an incident in which she had been aroused while observing a sexual scene.

The dream picture of a solid, cohesive self dealing with phallic overstimulation is characteristic of the hysteric when defending against oedipal wishes, and the silent accompanying figure of the uncle probably represented an underlying positive oedipal attachment. It hints that the transference relationship was mobilizing the activity of pregenitally determined, phallically derived character defenses, and the dreamer, in looking for a match to the blue coat, was seeking reenforcement of this posture. The dream also gave some indication that the therapeutic interaction had been successful in intervening with these pathological defenses, as evidenced by the ability to project voyeuristic experience into the symbolic image of the salesman and the beginning emergence of a genital oedipal transference.

## Effect of the Therapeutic Relationship on the Hysteric, Revealed in the Manifest Dream

Stage and phase specificity is a vital factor for the full realization of self potentials. The hysteric's early development has not been synchronous, and the entire manner of thinking, feeling, and adapting is profoundly affected. Libidinal overstimulation has led to the organization of a wide variety of defensive responses utilizing suitable aspects of self experience. Consequently, the self system of representations is enormously overdeveloped in some areas, with sensory deprivations and reactions to impingement being particularly useful for this purpose. At the same time, a lack of optimal frustration has led to the underdevelopment of autonomous ego functions, leaving latent potential unrealized.

Although the impression of an overstimulating instinctual object is structurally linked to the self system through primal scene fantasies, the self system is so well defended that the threat is not experienced in that locale. In the object system, the optimally gratifying impressions of a good object are abundant, but the restraining influences of an optimally frustrating object are diminished. The prohibitive impressions of an impinging object are incorporated in the ego ideal, and the impressions of an overstimulating instinctual object resonates throughout with little defensive opposition. The hysteric thus directs perceptual attention to the hypertrophied system of self representations to avoid the instinctual dangers associated with the influences of an object.

In the presence of symptoms, character defenses are operative, but without creating undue distortion. Under stress, excessive stimulation, or when there has been no oedipal conflict resolution, character pathology is manifested. Meaning is then attributed to every stimulus in accordance with the composition of the fixation points and the fixed attitudes emanating from them. Until these pathological defenses are made dystonic or rendered ineffective by exposing their infantile origins and defensive function, interpretations alone will do little toward facilitating a benign therapeutic regression. Only then will the repressed genital instinctual drives be able to enter the transference relationship. Meanwhile, the tendency will be to receive all interventions as an extension of a firmly held character trait.

> This was shown in a dream reported by a 7-year-old boy, after his questions about objects in the room were interpreted as an expression of his sexual interest:
>
> > My sister and I were in Mexico and a lady was showing us jewelry. The lady said mommies have babies and money.
>
> The dreamer placed special emphasis on the setting of the dream by locating it in Mexico, and it would be important to know the specific associations to the choice of that country in order to better understand the reason for its use. Nevertheless, even in their absence, some universal properties lend themselves to speculation. Mexico is geographically situated below the dreamer's land of origin, has a clearly defined boundary, and is a foreign land with a different language. In addition, illegal immigrants are known to cross the border, find their way into this country, and become involved in ways that prevent their discovery. All of these features lend themselves to representing symbolically the effects of unconscious mental activity.
>
> The dreaming self is discrete, related to and differentiated from others, and engaged with a sister and a woman showing jewelry. The sister's presence seems to be in the shadow of the dreamer, and probably reflects some feminine aspect that is difficult to incorporate. The attachment to the woman encompasses qualities having a good oral

component, in that she is a source of supplies, and a genital component, suggested by the idea of jewelry and babies. Again it would be helpful to know the significance of jewelry to the dreamer, but its universal properties can be an aid in postulating about its appearance. In the regressed state of dreaming, the concrete attributes of a given symbol are the most powerful, and the dreamer is showing interest in a valuable item, frequently worn to attract attention, kept in protected places, and that is hard and firm. It hints that the dreamer is being shown genital instinctual qualities possessed by a woman, in a form indicative of the effectiveness of his defensive responses.

The manifest content is thus constructed upon the background of an orally influenced, phallically determined hysterical character organization, with symbolic reference to hidden genital instinctual wishes. Movement in the dream is very subdued with no indication of active impulsion, nor is there open evidence of restraint, prohibition, or threat. Movement is implicit rather than explicit, insinuating that unconscious instinctual drives are held in check by effectively functioning character defenses. This was also exemplified in the portrayal of his attachment to the woman. The relationship was not adversarial. There was no expression of conflict. The dreamer, expecting one kind of information, was given another, and the connection between looking at jewelry and being told mothers have babies and money was left unclear. The woman possessed a valuable article and was the source of new and, by implication, surprising statements. Yet the dreamer's reaction was of quiet composure reflecting the defensive function provided by a fixed attitude. The therapist's interpretation of the dreamer's sexual interest seemed to be the day residue around which the dream was constructed, and the symbolic imagery hinted that the effort to enlarge his view was revealing more than he wanted to know.

With the hysteric, a therapist's silent presence is of the utmost importance in facilitating the emergence of unconscious genital instinctual strivings. The outward appearance of being out of control rests on a solid foundation capable of supporting a therapeutic regression, but it may stir a therapist into becoming too active in offering interpretations. Relative silence is desirable because it provides optimal frustration, encourages the use of untapped resources, and is not overstimulating. Interpretations are only indicated when distortions are dystonic enough to be recognizable, otherwise they tend to elicit infantile experiences of phallic overstimulation and strengthen defenses against the transference.

The unconscious perception of a therapeutic interaction is revealed in the content of a manifest dream, so that inadvertent breaches in the management of the therapeutic framework stand out in bold relief. This makes the dream helpful in identifying the source of a break in the containing properties of the treatment relationship, and in highlighting the infantile experiences behind the defenses that are mobilized.

This was a factor in a dream presented by a young man who had begun treatment due to his discomfort, fear of humiliation, and inadequate performance in group situations:

I am in a big cavernous building. Suddenly I am on the roof and I look across to see my female boss and another woman through a window. They are working and I get worried that I'll be seen there looking in instead of working. I go down inside the building and find a bunch of other workers.

The dream content includes a discrete self image contained within a large cavernous building, an object world consisting of two women seen at a distance, and a connection between them based upon the act of observing their behavior. The large cavernous space, symbolic of the self system, is filled with workers (reflecting upon the vast array of defensive responses available in this sector). In moving to the roof to observe his boss, the dreamer implies he is engaging in a forbidden act with a tacit threat of discovery. The location at the farthest possible distance from the foundation of the building suggests a defensive stance is in the ascendancy. The dream imagery appears to capture the underlying composition of the mental structures at the surface of the personality, whose function is to unite and differentiate the self and object systems of representation. These structures at the periphery are based upon pregenital developmental experience, whereas the structures uniting the two systems at the interior are based upon the genital fantasies of an oedipal constellation.

Neurotic forms of pathology are elaborated on the background of a relatively stable, cohesive personality, and center around the demands of an oedipal conflict. The manifest dream of a neurotic individual should give evidence of the recognition of an object's good and bad qualities, of an object having independent objects of its own, of the self having good and bad qualities, and some, at least implied, indication of incestuous or primal scene fantasies. This dream portrays an object working and being a source of potential disapproval showing its good and bad qualities, the object is involved with another woman, and the self is engaged with activities that have good qualities in the building and bad qualities on the roof. Although the structural components are present, there is no visible sign of an oedipal conflict. The setting of the dream, however, indicates that an oedipal constellation would not be openly manifested, since the symbolic imagery is determined by the mental structures at the surface of the personality and a defensive stance is emphasized.

The way in which a relationship is symbolized in a dream depends upon the particular level of psychosexual experience being stressed, and in this dream the relationship is one of implied approval for working, along with the threat of being discovered in a forbidden act of observation. The dream imagery places emphasis on the potential for the humiliating disapproval of an object, and the forbidden act of looking hints at voyeuristic components. A phallically derived union is thereby depicted, with the underlying structure of an ego ideal that has required an identification with an aggressor to achieve regulation. The linkage of phallic exhibitionism with the fantasy of an admiring audience, comprising the structure of the grandiose self, is vaguely implied in the background. This is not surprising because of this structure's instinctual makeup, and defenses against instinctual activity are highlighted.

The manifest content also suggests that a masculine presence has been largely absent or unavailable, and that feminine identifications have been utilized to strengthen the self system. This fits with the symbolic representation of a large cavernous building. The dream configuration of a young man displaying a strong feminine influence and struggling with phallic voyeuristic impulses is characteristic of the hysteric neurotic representing pregenital defenses against an underlying oedipal conflict. Character defenses are built around pregenital conflicts. The unconscious genital instinctual drives giving impetus to the dream work are thereby not directly expressed, and an oedipal configuration is not visible as a consequence of their effectiveness. Movement in the dream symbolic of unconscious instinctual activity is never overt, although it is implied by the abrupt changes in locale.

There was no direct reference to the day residue, and with no further information, one could speculate that the dreamer had seen the therapist outside the office. The identifying features of a treatment situation include maintaining a contained space within which a regression can take place, along with an attempt to shed light on what is hidden. The manifest content conveys the idea of looking at an authority figure from a position outside the working area, with the implication of its being forbidden and of anticipating discovery. In this way the dream implies that the dreamer has been avoiding analytic work in order to engage in observing the therapist secretly, and the therapist felt defensive about the idea of being observed by the patient. Upon hearing the dream, the therapist recalled having seen the patient driving on a highway, had wondered if the patient noticed, and had briefly felt defensive about being observed. The incident was promptly forgotten, and had never been mentioned. It hinted that in this moment of contact outside of the office a powerful unconscious communication had taken place, evoking voyeuristic impulses in the patient and a defensive countertransference response in the therapist. The episode apparently served as the derivative of an unconscious perception of the therapist's as yet unspoken knowledge, became the nidus utilized for the dream work, and gave

symbolic representation to the pregenital defenses constructed to protect against unconscious transference wishes.

When there is a firm, stable, cohesive personality in the background, there is little necessity to encourage associations to specific
elements in the content of a manifest dream. The obsessive's already
overdeveloped pathological defenses would only be reenforced, and
the hysteric's spontaneous style of thinking does not require a
therapist's direction. Participating in this manner would tend to be
overstimulating or infantilizing.

## Significance of Incestuous and Primal Scene Fantasies and Their Appearance in the Manifest Dream

The genital fantasies of an oedipal conflict form two major
structures at the interior of the personality, which establish the basis
for an object related perspective, ensure cohesiveness, and provide
the foundation necessary for advances in psychic organization to be
realized. The tripartite structures of id, ego, and superego are then
clearly defined, and continuity of experience is maintained throughout varying systems of consciousness.

In health an unobstructed pathway of instinctual integration
operates in harmony with a structured pathway for selective identifications, eliminating the need for a fixation point in the self system.
That fixation point had to be anchored during the period of oedipal
organization, and until it is relinquished, all new experiences are
colored and distorted by the memory traces embodied in its composition. With the resolution of the oedipal conflict, instinctual drives
requiring defense are integrated, the function of the self stabilizing
fixation point is replaced by the rising effectiveness of a conflict-free
sphere, and new experiences from an object related perspective can
be registered without opposition. Concomitantly, the fixation point
anchoring object constancy, which must be retained, undergoes
alterations to loosen the tenacity of the attachment to an infantile
object. The greater accessibility of conflict-free functions and expanded capacity for symbolization allows a gradual process of depersonification, which is essential to reduce the distortions it creates and
to prepare the way for its replacement by an attachment to new and
independent objects.

The mental impression of an overstimulating instinctual object is
the nidus around which the combined influences of a bad object have

coalesced, and it represents the potentially traumatic dimension on the continuum of instinctual demand. Genital primal scene fantasies are elaborated during the oedipal period and structurally linked to the bad instinctual aspect of self experience, expressing genital overstimulation by an unseen instinctual object. Instinctual demands previously incapable of being registered are thereby given structured access into the self system. Simultaneously, bad genital instinctual self experience is elaborated into incestuous fantasies that are structurally linked to the impression of a genitally overstimulating object, expressing an instinctual attachment to a visible, prohibited object.

Primal scene fantasies are the manifestation of a structured pathway toward instinctual integration, and are most in evidence when a successful solution to the oedipal conflict is taking place through the vehicle of selective identifications. A given instinctual demand can then move from what has been unseen and unrepresentable to being represented as an overstimulating object, and through the linkage of primal scene fantasies to inclusion within the realm of self experience requiring defense. The attendant conflict motivates a solution by selecting those influences of an object that strengthen the self system and including them within good self experience. These identifications enhance the capacity for integration and expand the range of instinctual activities that can be encompassed without a need for defense. In no longer requiring defense, they have attained secondary autonomy and are available for sublimatory activities and conflict-free functions. Incestuous fantasies are the manifestation of a new object related boundary for the unconscious system, and are most in evidence when the intensity of genital instinctual demands cannot be managed effectively. They are accompanied by the mobilization of defenses designed to reenforce repression, and activate pregenitally determined character defenses.

Incestuous fantasies are overdeveloped in the neurotic individual, indicative of the extent of the conflict and inadequacy of the solution. Successful therapeutic intervention shifts the balance, so that primal scene fantasies become more in evidence as the process of instinctual integration is facilitated through a benign regression. This distinction between incestuous and primal scene fantasies is an extremely important one to make. It can guide a therapist in the conduct of the treatment, and the manifest dream is a valuable aid in its determination.

When the derivative of a defense transference incestuous fantasy is symbolically represented in the dream, it embodies a visualized, forbidden instinctual object, and is accompanied by the heightening of defensive constellations and superego prohibitions.

This was exemplified in the dream of a 30-year-old woman, reported early in the course of her treatment:

I was in the dental chair and was attacked by a dentist who looked somewhat like my father. It was extremely painful, but at the same time sexually exciting.

The manifest content captured the essence of incestuous fantasies, in representing an explicit forbidden sexual object associated with the painful attack of a prohibitive superego response. The dreamer's immobility was indicative of the defensive opposition accompanying this aspect of an oedipal constellation.

When a therapeutic regression is successful in facilitating the expression of the psychic contents in the deeper layers of the personality, and character defenses no longer interfere with the emergence of the derivatives of unconscious instinctual drives, primal scene transference fantasies gain greater access to representation.

This was displayed in the dream of a 35-year-old man who had initiated therapeutic contact suffering acutely from an inability to achieve intimacy in relationships. His rigidly held, fixed character attitudes were designed to control any expression of sadistic aggression, and reenforced the repression of inordinately conflicted infantile genital wishes. During the height of a therapeutic regression he reported a dream:

A girl was putting on a private golf course. Just as she struck the ball a bolt of lightning hit her and the ball rolled in the hole. A lighthouse on a point of land then spoke, "Next time you'll play on a public course." I woke up laughing hysterically.

The bolt of lightning was symbolic of a primal scene fantasy making its impact upon the self system, embodied in the image of the girl on the golf course. Its effect was to be immensely overstimulating, and at the same time provided the impetus to reach a goal. The delayed prohibitive response, symbolized by the warning words of the lighthouse, was a reflection of the diminishing effectiveness of character defenses in preventing this unconscious instinctual movement. The dreamer's laughter was a multidetermined reaction, but included the experience of being infused with instinctual energy.

Incestuous fantasies appear when a defensive stance is necessary. Their derivatives are readily available in the preconscious and they are utilized to defend against primal scene fantasy derivatives. Incestuous imagery is thereby explicit in the manifest content, whereas primal scene fantasies are implicit as they push for expression.

The following dream of a young woman was presented in two clearly defined segments. It demonstrates the interrelationship of incestuous and primal scene fantasies, and underscores the dangers associated with the emergence of such fantasies.

I was with my boyfriend in an apartment on the second floor. I was nine months pregnant, and the man owning the apartment was not there. He had been with another woman whom I was replacing. People were angry with me for replacing her and were throwing filthy rags up at the window to degrade me. I was tempted to turn off the lights so they would miss the window, but then they would know I was there. If I left the lights on they could not be sure.

Latent dream thoughts are woven into the manifest dream by the dream work, around the day residue of the derivative of an emotionally laden unconscious perception. The resulting dream imagery gives a picture of the structural organization of the personality, and of the particular unconscious conflicts in the ascendancy. The objects in the dream include a current relationship, a man whose apartment she occupies, and a woman rival whose place she is taking. In addition, the dreamer is nine months pregnant, symbolically representing the idea of an instinctual body ego experience that is on the verge of being delivered. This overall portrayal of an oedipal conflict is explicit in the manifest content. The overt incestuous attachment is instigating a humiliating attack, the setting on the second floor hints that the source of the difficulty has not yet been reached, and the effort to remain hidden calls attention to its being defensive in nature.

The dreamer is then tempted to turn out the lights, consonant with the attributes of an implied primal scene fantasy lurking in the background, but ultimately opts for leaving them on, preferring not to be exposed. The day residue appears to be the derivative of an unconscious perception pertaining to the therapeutic relationship. It is symbolized by angry people throwing dirty rags, and hints that the therapist has directed an unempathic interpretation to her. Although the setting of the dream is indicative of a fairly well-contained framework enabling regressive infantile wishes and conflicts to be expressed, there does seem to be an unempathic dimension evoking a defensive humiliating prohibitive response. An empathic interpretation might also elicit a need for defense, but in that case it would emanate from a more internally symbolized source.

This part of the dream is dominated by a variety of defenses against unconscious genital instinctual drives, and there is no direct evidence of the dreamer's movement. The idea of turning off the lights suggests the temptation to give expression to unconscious instinctual wishes, but since it would call attention to her presence and verify her location, it is rejected. The decision to leave the lights on is a refusal to grant open expression to a hidden instinctual wish, and highlights the defensive significance of the incestuous fantasy derivative introduced in this dream segment. The dream then shifted:

> I was trying to take a pregnancy test and had the cup to urinate in. I was looking for a bathroom but couldn't find one. I was with my boyfriend in a car, and then I was in a phone booth with a toilet, in a bad section of town. As I was getting ready to urinate, a black man approached me and I ran to the car. This part of the dream was repeated two more times, each time with the same ending but with more black men.

In the opening section of the dream the incestuous meaning of the pregnancy was explicit, and the unseen dimension of instinctual demand was implicitly moving toward symbolic representation with the idea of turning the lights outs.

A shift was then instigated to a preoccupation with urinary functions, and the absence of a suitable place to discharge bodily products. Movement became more pronounced as the underlying instinctual activity appeared in a more regressive modality. With the change in dream imagery, the pregnancy was no longer at the point of delivery, but was being questioned, reflecting the dreamer's attempt to deny the existence of this symbolic representation of a genitally derived impulse. Nevertheless, the demand for expression was insistent, and she discovered herself in a phone booth with a toilet, located in a dangerous setting. This symbolic representation of a narrow space, where communication can take place at a distance and internal contents can be discharged, seemed to capture the threat accompanying the emergence of unconscious drives in the transference relationship. The dreamer was initiating the release of bodily contents, and was confronted by an ominous black man; this part was repeated with the danger escalating. The nature of the threat was unspecified, although its genital instinctual meanings were only thinly disguised, and the mounting anxiety suggested that defensive opposition was becoming ineffective.

In the first part of the dream, there is a temptation to move that is resisted, and primal scene fantasy derivatives are well defended. In the second part, movement is accentuated, the dreamer's space becomes narrow and dangerous, and the symbolized derivatives of primal scene fantasies in the form of the black figures approach accessibility to representation.

The value of a dream in fostering the growth-promoting properties of a treatment relationship is usually not fully appreciated.

Although a dream emerging in the context of the therapeutic interaction has the same significance as any associative material, it is unique because of the vast amount of information it contains. Accurate diagnostic assessments, validation of constructive interventions, the identification of empathic failures, and the interpretation of unconscious communications are all facilitated by an understanding of the manifest content. The dream itself offers guidelines as to whether engaging in a search for the latent dream thoughts is a useful endeavor, and whether it will shed light on the most helpful way to proceed. The manifest dream may also carry prognostic implications, both in regard to an immediate treatment need and in relation to potential obstacles that could arise later.

Because the dream takes place under the special conditions involved in sleep and is reported under a totally different set of conditions, it provides a rare opportunity to elaborate theoretical considerations that have practical importance. Dream content lends itself to exploring the interdependent interplay between perception and mental representation, the nature and composition of a self and self boundary, the effects of differing modes of perception, the process of symbolization, and the role and significance of the day residue.

Finally, the act of dreaming and retaining the contents in consciousness and reporting them is furthered when the end product elicits a constructive therapeutic response. The material provided by the dream can thereby give impetus to integrative functions and in a progressive manner, make dreaming a spur of continuing growth.

# References

Altman, L. L. (1969). *The Dream in Psychoanalysis*. New York: International Universities Press.

Arlow, J. A. (1969). Unconscious fantasy and disturbances of conscious experience. *Psychoanalytic Quarterly* 38:1–51.

Babcock, C. (1966). Panel report: Manifest content of the dream. *Journal of Psychoanalysis* 14:154–171.

Bergmann, M. S. (1966). The intrapsychic and communicative aspects of the dream. *International Journal of Psycho-Analysis* 47:356–363.

Blitzen, N. L., Eissler, R. S., and Eissler, K. R. (1950). Emergence of hidden ego tendencies during dream analysis. *International Journal of Psycho-Analysis* 31:12–17.

Blum, H. (1976). The changing use of dreams in psychoanalytic practice. *International Journal of Psycho-Analysis* 57:315–323.

Brenner, C. (1976). *Psychoanalytic Technique and Psychic Conflict*. New York: International Universities Press.

de Monchaux, C.(1978). Dreaming and the organizing function of the ego. *International Journal of Psycho-Analysis* 59:443–453.

De Saussure, J. (1982). Dreams and dreaming in relation to trauma in childhood. *International Journal of Psycho-Analysis* 63:167–175.

Dowling, S. (1982). Mental organization in the phenomena of sleep. In *Psychoanalytic Study of the Child* 32:285–302. New Haven CT: Yale University Press.

Fisher, C. (1954). Dreams and perception. *Journal of the American Psychoanalytic Association* 2:389–445.

———(1957). A study of the preliminary stages of the construction of dreams and images. *Journal of the American Psychoanalytic Association* 5:5–60.

———(1966). *Dreaming and Sexuality in Psychoanalysis, A General Psychology*, pp. 537–570. New York: International Universities Press.

Foulkes, D. (1969). *Theories of Dream Formation and Recent Studies of Sleep Consciousness in Altered States of Consciousness.* New York: John Wiley.

———(1978). *A Grammar of Dreams.* New York: Basic Books.

French, T. (1953). *The Interpretive Process in Dreams.* Chicago: University of Chicago Press.

———(1970). *Psychoanalytic Interpretations.* Chicago: Quadrangle Books.

French, T. and Fromm, E. (1964). *Dream Interpretation.* New York: Basic Books.

Freud, S. (1900). The interpretation of dreams. *Standard Edition* 4:338.

———(1901). Dreams. *Standard Edition* 5:629–685.

———(1911). Handling of dream interpretation in psychoanalysis. *Standard Edition* 12:91–96.

———(1913). An evidential dream. *Standard Edition* 12:267–278.

———(1917). A metapsychological supplement to the theory of dreams. *Standard Edition* 14:219–235.

———(1923). Remarks on the theory and practice of dream interpretation. *Standard Edition* 19:109–121.

———(1925). Some additional notes on dream interpretation as a whole. *Standard Edition* 19:127–138.

Gitelson, M. (1952). The emotional position of the analyst in the psychoanalytic situation. *International Journal of Psycho-Analysis* 33:102–112.

Greenberg, R., and Pearlman, C. (1975). A psychoanalytic dream continuum. *International Review of Psycho-Analysis* 2:441–448.

Greenson, R. (1970). The exceptional position of the dream in psychoanalytic practice. *Psychoanalytic Quarterly* 39:519–549.

Grolnick, S. A. (1978). Dreams and dreaming as transitional phenomena. In *Between Reality and Fantasy*, pp. 211–233. New York: Jason Aronson.

Harris, I. D. (1963). Dreams about the analyst. *International Journal of Psycho-Analysis* 43:151–158.

Hartmann, E. (1970). *The Functions of Sleep.* London: Yale University Press.

Hendrick, I. (1958). Dream resistance and schizophrenia. *Journal of the American Psychoanalytic Association* 6:672–690.

Hirschberg, J. C. (1966). Dreaming, drawing, and the dream screen in the psychoanalysis of a 2½-year-old boy. *American Journal of Psychiatry* 122:37–45.

Isakower, O. (1938). A contribution to the psychopathology of phenomena associated with falling asleep. *International Journal of Psycho-Analysis* 19:331–345.

———(1954). Spoken words in dreams. *Psychoanalytic Quarterly* 23:1–6.

Jones, R. M. (1970). *The Psychology of Dreaming*. New York: Grune and Stratton.

Kanzer, M. (1955). The communicative function of the dream. *International Journal of Psycho-Analysis* 36:260–266.

Khan, M. M. R. (1962). Dream psychology and the evolution of the psychoanalytic situation. *International Journal of Psycho-Analysis* 43:21–31.

———(1976). The changing use of dreams in psychoanalytic practice. In search of the dreaming experience. *International Journal of Psycho-Analysis* 57:325–330.

Klauber, J. (1967). On the significance of reporting dreams in psychoanalysis. *International Journal of Psycho-Analysis* 48:424–432.

Knapp, P. H. (1956). Sensory impressions in dreams. *Psychoanalytic Quarterly* 25:325–347.

Kohut, H. (1977). *The Restoration of the Self*. New York: International Universities Press.

Kramer, M. (1969). Manifest dream content in psychopathological states in *Dream Psychology and the New Biology of Dreaming*. Springfield, IL: Charles C Thomas.

Langs, R. (1971). Day residues, recall residues, and dreams. Reality and the psyche. *Journal of the American Psychoanalytic Association* 19:499–523.

Lewin, B. D. (1953). Reconsiderations of the dream screen. *Psychoanalytic Quarterly* 22:174–199.

———(1955). Dream psychology and the analytic situation. *Psychoanalytic Quarterly* 24:169–199.

Mendelsohn, R. M. (1987). *The Principles Guiding the Ideal Therapist*. New York: Plenum.

Pontalis, J. B. (1974). Dream as an object. *International Review of Psychoanalysis* 1:125–133.

Renik, O. (1984). Report on the clinical use of the manifest dream. *Journal of the American Psychoanalytic Association* 32:157–163.

Rosenbaum, M. (1965). Dreams in which the analyst appears undisguised, a clinical and statistical study. *International Journal of Psycho-Analysis* 46:429–437.

Rycroft, C. (1979). *The Innocence of Dreams*. London: Hogarth.

Saul, L. J. (1967). Dream form and strength of impulse in dreams of falling and other dreams of descent. *International Journal of Psycho-Analysis* 48:281–287.

Sharpe, E. (1937). *Dream Analysis*. New York: Norton.

Silber, A. (1983). A significant "dream within a dream." *Journal of the American Psychoanalytic Association* 31:899–916.

Sloane, P. (1979). *Psychoanalytic Understanding of the Dream*. New York: Jason Aronson.

Steiner, M. (1937). The dream symbolism of the analytic situation. *International Journal of Psycho-Analysis* 18:294–305.

Wasserman, M. D. (1984) Psychoanalytic dream theory and recent neurobiological findings about REM sleep. *Journal of the American Psychoanalytic Association* 32:831–846.

Winnicott, D. W. (1965). *The Maturational Processes and the Facilitating Environment*. London: Hogarth.

# Index